ONE
GREEN FIELD

AND OTHER ESSAYS ON
THE APPRECIATION OF NATURE

By

VARIOUS

Rich,

I always recall our conversation on the wonder g nature, the need for "awe" and an appreciation that beauty in nature can be perceived differently depending on the perceiver

Love you x

Read & Co.

Copyright © 2020 A Thousand Fields

This edition is published by A Thousand Fields,
an imprint of Read & Co.

This book is copyright and may not be reproduced or copied in any
way without the express permission of the publisher in writing.

British Library Cataloguing-in-Publication Data
A catalogue record for this book is available
from the British Library.

Read & Co. is part of Read Books Ltd.
For more information visit
www.readandcobooks.co.uk

CONTENTS

3

NATURE

The rounded world is fair to see,
   Nine times folded in mystery:
Though baffled seers cannot impart
   The secret of its laboring heart,
Throb thine with Nature's throbbing breast,
   And all is clear from east to west.
Spirit that lurks each form within
   Beckons to spirit of its kin;
Self-kindled every atom glows,
   And hints the future which it owes.

—Ralph Waldo Emerson

NATURE

By Ralph Waldo Emerson

THERE are days which occur in this climate, at almost any season of the year, wherein the world reaches its perfection; when the air, the heavenly bodies and the earth, make a harmony, as if nature would indulge her offspring; when, in these bleak upper sides of the planet, nothing is to desire that we have heard of the happiest latitudes, and we bask in the shining hours of Florida and Cuba; when everything that has life gives sign of satisfaction, and the cattle that lie on the ground seem to have great and tranquil thoughts. These halcyons may be looked for with a little more assurance in that pure October weather which we distinguish by the name of the Indian summer. The day, immeasurably long, sleeps over the broad hills and warm wide fields. To have lived through all its sunny hours, seems longevity enough. The solitary places do not seem quite lonely. At the gates of the forest, the surprised man of the world is forced to leave his city estimates of great and small, wise and foolish. The knapsack of custom falls off his back with the first step he makes into these precincts. Here is sanctity which shames our religions, and reality which discredits our heroes. Here we find Nature to be the circumstance which dwarfs every other circumstance, and judges like a god all men that come to her. We have crept out of our close and crowded houses into the night and morning, and we see what majestic beauties daily wrap us in their bosom. How willingly we would escape the barriers which render them comparatively impotent, escape the sophistication and second thought, and suffer nature to intrance us. The tempered light of the woods is like a perpetual morning, and is stimulating and heroic. The anciently reported spells of these places creep on us. The stems of pines, hemlocks, and oaks almost gleam like iron on the excited eye. The incommunicable trees begin to persuade us to live with them, and quit our life of solemn trifles. Here no history, or church, or state, is interpolated on the divine sky and the immortal year. How easily we might walk onward into the opening landscape, absorbed by new pictures and by thoughts fast succeeding each other, until by degrees the recollection of home was crowded out of the mind, all memory obliterated by the tyranny of the present, and we were led in triumph by nature.

These enchantments are medicinal, they sober and heal us. These are plain pleasures, kindly and native to us. We come to our own, and make friends with matter, which the ambitious chatter of the schools would persuade us to despise. We never can part with it; the mind loves its old home: as water to our thirst, so is the rock, the ground, to our eyes and hands and feet. It is firm water; it is cold flame; what health, what affinity! Ever an old friend, ever like a dear friend and brother when we chat affectedly with strangers, comes in this honest face, and takes a grave liberty with us, and shames us out of our nonsense. Cities give not the human senses room enough. We go out daily and nightly to feed the eyes on the horizon, and require so much scope, just as we need water for our bath. There are all degrees of natural influence, from these quarantine powers of nature, up to her dearest and gravest ministrations to the imagination and the soul. There is the bucket of cold water from the spring, the wood-fire to which the chilled traveller rushes for safety,—and there is the sublime moral of autumn and of noon. We nestle in nature, and draw our living as parasites from her roots and grains, and we receive glances from the heavenly bodies, which call us to solitude and foretell the remotest future. The blue zenith is the point in which romance and reality meet. I think if we should be rapt away into all that we dream of heaven, and should converse with Gabriel and Uriel, the upper sky would be all that would remain of our furniture.

It seems as if the day was not wholly profane in which we have given heed to some natural object. The fall of snowflakes in a still air, preserving to each crystal its perfect form; the blowing of sleet over a wide sheet of water, and over plains; the waving ryefield; the mimic waving of acres of houstonia, whose innumerable florets whiten and ripple before the eye; the reflections of trees and flowers in glassy lakes; the musical steaming odorous south wind, which converts all trees to windharps; the crackling and spurting of hemlock in the flames, or of pine logs, which yield glory to the walls and faces in the sittingroom,—these are the music and pictures of the most ancient religion. My house stands in low land, with limited outlook, and on the skirt of the village. But I go with my friend to the shore of our little river, and with one stroke of the paddle I leave the village politics and personalities, yes, and the world of villages and personalities behind, and pass into a delicate realm of sunset and moonlight, too bright almost for spotted man to enter without novitiate and probation. We penetrate bodily this incredible beauty; we dip our hands in this painted element; our eyes are bathed in these lights and forms. A holiday, a villeggiatura, a royal revel, the proudest, most heart-rejoicing festival that valor and beauty, power and taste, ever decked and enjoyed, establishes itself on the instant. These sunset clouds, these delicately emerging stars, with their private and ineffable glances, signify it and proffer it. I am taught the poorness of our invention, the ugliness of towns and palaces. Art and luxury have early learned that they must work as enhancement and sequel to this original beauty. I am overinstructed for my return. Henceforth I shall be hard to please. I cannot go back to toys. I am grown expensive and sophisticated. I can no longer live without elegance, but a countryman shall be my master of revels. He who knows the most; he who knows what sweets and virtues are in the ground, the waters, the plants, the heavens, and how to come at these enchantments,—is the rich and royal man. Only as far as the masters of the world have called in nature to their aid, can they reach the height of magnificence. This is the meaning of their hanging-gardens, villas, garden-houses, islands, parks and preserves, to back their faulty personality with these strong accessories. I do not wonder that the landed interest should be invincible in the State with these dangerous auxiliaries. These bribe and invite; not kings, not palaces, not men, not women, but these tender and poetic stars, eloquent of secret promises. We heard what the rich man said, we knew of his villa, his grove, his wine and his company, but the provocation and point of the invitation came out of these beguiling stars. In their soft glances I see what men strove to realize in some Versailles, or Paphos, or Ctesiphon. Indeed, it is the magical lights of the horizon and the blue sky for the background which save all our works of art, which were otherwise bawbles. When the rich tax the poor with servility and obsequiousness, they should consider the effect of men reputed to be the possessors of nature, on imaginative minds. Ah! if the rich were rich as the poor fancy riches! A boy hears a military band play on the field at night, and he has kings and queens and famous chivalry palpably before him. He hears the echoes of a horn in a hill country, in the Notch Mountains, for example, which converts the mountains into an Aeolian harp,—and this supernatural tiralira restores to him the Dorian mythology, Apollo, Diana, and all divine hunters and huntresses. Can a musical note be so lofty, so haughtily beautiful! To the poor young poet, thus fabulous is his picture of society; he is loyal; he respects the rich; they are rich for the sake of his imagination; how poor his fancy would be, if they were not rich! That they have some high-fenced grove which they call a park; that they live in larger and better-garnished saloons than he has visited, and go in coaches, keeping only the society of the elegant, to watering-places and to distant cities,—these make the groundwork from which he has delineated estates of romance, compared with which their actual possessions are shanties and paddocks. The muse herself betrays her son, and enhances the gifts of wealth and well-born beauty by a radiation out of the air, and clouds, and forests that skirt the road,—a certain haughty favor, as if from patrician genii to patricians, a kind of aristocracy in nature, a prince of the power of the air.

The moral sensibility which makes Edens and Tempes so easily, may not be always found, but the material landscape is never far off. We can find these enchantments without visiting the Como Lake, or the Madeira Islands. We exaggerate the praises of local scenery. In every landscape the point of astonishment is the meeting of the sky and the earth, and that is seen from the first hillock as well as from the top of the Alleghanies. The stars at night stoop down over the brownest, homeliest common with all the spiritual magnificence which they shed on the Campagna, or on the marble deserts of Egypt. The uprolled clouds and the colors of morning and evening will transfigure maples and alders. The difference between landscape and landscape is small, but there is great difference in the beholders. There is nothing so wonderful in any particular landscape as the necessity of being beautiful under which every landscape lies. Nature cannot be surprised in undress. Beauty breaks in everywhere.

But it is very easy to outrun the sympathy of readers on this topic, which schoolmen called natura naturata, or nature passive. One can hardly speak directly of it without excess. It is as easy to broach in mixed companies what is called "the subject of religion." A susceptible person does not like to indulge his tastes in this kind without the apology of some trivial necessity: he goes to see a wood-lot, or to look at the crops, or to fetch a plant or a mineral from a remote locality, or he carries a fowling-piece or a fishing-rod. I suppose this shame must have a good reason. A dilettantism in nature is barren and unworthy. The fop of fields is no better than his brother of Broadway. Men are naturally hunters and inquisitive of wood-craft, and I suppose that such a gazetteer as wood-cutters and Indians should furnish facts for, would take place in the most arrives at last at the most complex forms; and yet so poor is nature with all her craft, that from the beginning to the end of the universe she has but one stuff,—but one stuff with its two ends, to serve up all her dream-like variety. Compound it how she will, star, sand, fire, water, tree, man, it is still one stuff, and betrays the same properties.

Nature is always consistent, though she feigns to contravene her own laws. She keeps her laws, and seems to transcend them. She arms and equips an animal to find its place and living in the earth, and at the same time she arms and equips another animal to destroy it. Space exists to divide creatures; but by clothing the sides of a bird with a few feathers she gives him a petty omnipresence. The direction is forever onward, but the artist still goes back for materials and begins again with the first elements on the most advanced stage: otherwise all goes to ruin. If we look at her work, we seem to catch a glance of a system in transition. Plants are the young of the world, vessels of health and vigor; but they grope ever upward towards consciousness; the trees are imperfect men, and seem to bemoan their imprisonment, rooted in the ground. The animal is the novice and probationer of a more advanced order. The men, though young, having tasted the first drop from the cup of thought, are already dissipated: the maples and ferns are still uncorrupt; yet no doubt when they come to consciousness they too will curse and swear. Flowers so strictly belong to youth that we adult men soon come to feel that their beautiful generations concern not us: we have had our day; now let the children have theirs. The flowers jilt us, and we are old bachelors with our ridiculous tenderness.

Things are so strictly related, that according to the skill of the eye, from any one object the parts and properties of any other may be predicted. If we had eyes to see it, a bit of stone from the city wall would certify us of the necessity that man must exist, as readily as the city. That identity makes us all one, and reduces to nothing great intervals on our customary scale. We talk of deviations from natural life, as if artificial life were not also natural. The smoothest curled courtier in the boudoirs of a palace has an animal nature, rude and aboriginal as a white bear, omnipotent to its own ends, and is directly related, there amid essences and billetsdoux, to Himmaleh mountain-chains and the axis of the globe. If we consider how much we are nature's, we need not be superstitious about towns, as if that terrific or benefic force did not find us there also, and fashion cities. Nature, who made the mason, made the house. We may easily hear too much of rural influences. The cool disengaged air of natural objects makes them enviable to us, chafed and irritable creatures with red faces, and we think we shall be as grand as they if we camp out and eat roots; but let us be men instead of woodchucks and the oak and the elm shall gladly serve us, though we sit in chairs of ivory on carpets of silk.

This guiding identity runs through all the surprises and contrasts of the piece, and characterizes every law. Man carries the world in his head, the whole astronomy and chemistry suspended in a thought. Because the history of nature is charactered in his brain, therefore is he the prophet and discoverer of her secrets. Every known fact in natural science was divined by the presentiment of somebody, before it was actually verified. A man does not tie his shoe without recognizing laws which bind the farthest regions of nature: moon, plant, gas, crystal, are concrete geometry and numbers. Common sense knows its own, and recognizes the fact at first sight in chemical experiment. The common sense of Franklin, Dalton, Davy and Black, is the same common sense which made the arrangements which now it discovers.

If the identity expresses organized rest, the counter action runs also into organization. The astronomers said, 'Give us matter and a little motion and we will construct the universe. It is not enough that we should have matter, we must also have a single impulse, one shove to launch the mass and generate the harmony of the centrifugal and centripetal forces. Once heave the ball from the hand, and we can show how all this mighty order grew.'—'A very unreasonable postulate,' said the metaphysicians, 'and a plain begging of the question. Could you not prevail to know the genesis of projection, as well as the continuation of it?' Nature, meanwhile, had not waited for the discussion, but, right or wrong, bestowed the impulse, and the balls rolled. It was no great affair, a mere push, but the astronomers were right in making much of it, for there is no end to the consequences of the act. That famous aboriginal push propagates itself through all the balls of the system, and through every atom of every ball; through all the races of creatures, and through the history and performances of every individual. Exaggeration is in the course of things. Nature sends no creature, no man into the world without adding a small excess of his proper quality. Given the planet, it is still necessary to add the impulse; so to every creature nature added a little violence of direction in its proper path, a shove to put it on its way; in every instance a slight generosity, a drop too much. Without electricity the air would rot, and without this violence of direction which men and women have, without a spice of bigot and fanatic, no excitement, no efficiency. We aim above the mark to hit the mark. Every act hath some falsehood of exaggeration in it. And when now and then comes along some sad, sharp-eyed man, who sees how paltry a game is played, and refuses to play, but blabs the secret;—how then? Is the bird flown? O no, the wary Nature sends a new troop of fairer forms, of lordlier youths, with a little more excess of direction to hold them fast to their several aim; makes them a little wrongheaded in that direction in which they are rightest, and on goes the game again with new whirl, for a generation or two more. The child with his sweet pranks, the fool of his senses, commanded by every sight and sound, without any power to compare and rank his sensations, abandoned to a whistle or a painted chip, to a lead dragoon or a gingerbread-dog, individualizing everything, generalizing nothing, delighted with every new thing, lies down at night overpowered by the fatigue which this day of continual pretty madness has incurred. But Nature has answered her purpose with the curly, dimpled lunatic. She has tasked every faculty, and has secured the symmetrical growth of the bodily frame by all these attitudes and exertions,—an end of the first importance, which could not be trusted to any care less perfect than her own. This glitter, this opaline lustre plays round the top of every toy to his eye to insure his fidelity, and he is deceived to his good. We are made alive and kept alive by the same arts. Let the stoics say what they please, we do not eat for the good of living, but because the meat is savory and the appetite is keen. The vegetable life does not content itself with casting from the flower or the tree a single seed, but it fills the air and earth with a prodigality of seeds, that, if thousands perish, thousands may plant themselves; that hundreds may come up, that tens may live to maturity; that at least one may replace the parent. All things betray the same calculated profusion. The excess of fear with which the animal frame is hedged round, shrinking from cold, starting at sight of a snake, or at a sudden noise, protects us, through a multitude of groundless alarms, from some one real danger at last. The lover seeks in marriage his private felicity and perfection, with no prospective end; and nature hides in his happiness her own end, namely, progeny, or the perpetuity of the race.

But the craft with which the world is made, runs also into the mind and character of men. No man is quite sane; each has a vein of folly in his composition, a slight determination of blood to the head, to make sure of holding him hard to some one point which nature had taken to heart. Great causes are never tried on their merits; but the cause is reduced to particulars to suit the size of the partisans, and the contention is ever hottest on minor matters. Not less remarkable is the overfaith of each man in the importance of what he has to do or say. The poet, the prophet, has a higher value for what he utters than any hearer, and therefore it gets spoken. The strong, self-complacent Luther declares with an emphasis not to be mistaken, that "God himself cannot do without wise men." Jacob Behmen and George Fox betray their egotism in the pertinacity of their controversial tracts, and James Naylor once suffered himself to be worshipped as the Christ. Each prophet comes presently to identify himself with his thought, and to esteem his hat and shoes sacred. However this may discredit such persons with the judicious, it helps them with the people, as it gives heat, pungency, and publicity to their words. A similar experience is not infrequent in private life. Each young and ardent person writes a diary, in which, when the hours of prayer and penitence arrive, he inscribes his soul. The pages thus written are to him burning and fragrant; he reads them on his knees by midnight and by the morning star; he wets them with his tears; they are sacred; too good for the world, and hardly yet to be shown to the dearest friend. This is the man-child that is born to the soul, and her life still circulates in the babe. The umbilical cord has not yet been cut. After some time has elapsed, he begins to wish to admit his friend to this hallowed experience, and with hesitation, yet with firmness, exposes the pages to his eye. Will they not burn his eyes? The friend coldly turns them over, and passes from the writing to conversation, with easy transition, which strikes the other party with astonishment and vexation. He cannot suspect the writing itself. Days and nights of fervid life, of communion with angels of darkness and of light have engraved their shadowy characters on that tear-stained book. He suspects the intelligence or the heart of his friend. Is there then no friend? He cannot yet credit that one may have impressive experience and yet may not know how to put his private fact into literature; and perhaps the discovery that wisdom has other tongues and ministers than we, that though we should hold our peace the truth would not the less be spoken, might check injuriously the flames of our zeal. A man can only speak so long as he does not feel his speech to be partial and inadequate. It is partial, but he does not see it to be so whilst he utters it. As soon as he is released from the instinctive and particular and sees its partiality, he shuts his

18

mouth in disgust. For no man can write anything who does not think that what he writes is for the time the history of the world; or do anything well who does not esteem his work to be of importance. My work may be of none, but I must not think it of none, or I shall not do it with impunity.

In like manner, there is throughout nature something mocking, something that leads us on and on, but arrives nowhere; keeps no faith with us. All promise outruns the performance. We live in a system of approximations. Every end is prospective of some other end, which is also temporary; a round and final success nowhere. We are encamped in nature, not domesticated. Hunger and thirst lead us on to eat and to drink; but bread and wine, mix and cook them how you will, leave us hungry and thirsty, after the stomach is full. It is the same with all our arts and performances. Our music, our poetry, our language itself are not satisfactions, but suggestions. The hunger for wealth, which reduces the planet to a garden, fools the eager pursuer. What is the end sought? Plainly to secure the ends of good sense and beauty, from the intrusion of deformity or vulgarity of any kind. But what an operose method! What a train of means to secure a little conversation! This palace of brick and stone, these servants, this kitchen, these stables, horses and equipage, this bank-stock and file of mortgages; trade to all the world, country-house and cottage by the waterside, all for a little conversation, high, clear, and spiritual! Could it not be had as well by beggars on the highway? No, all these things came from successive efforts of these beggars to remove friction from the wheels of life, and give opportunity. Conversation, character, were the avowed ends; wealth was good as it appeased the animal cravings, cured the smoky chimney, silenced the creaking door, brought friends together in a warm and quiet room, and kept the children and the dinner-table in a different apartment. Thought, virtue, beauty, were the ends; but it was known that men of thought and virtue sometimes had the headache, or wet feet, or could lose good time whilst the room

one condition of nature, namely, Motion. But the drag is never taken from the wheel. Wherever the impulse exceeds, the Rest or Identity insinuates its compensation. All over the wide fields of earth grows the prunella or self-heal. After every foolish day we sleep off the fumes and furies of its hours; and though we are always engaged with particulars, and often enslaved to them, we bring with us to every experiment the innate universal laws. These, while they exist in the mind as ideas, stand around us in nature forever embodied, a present sanity to expose and cure the insanity of men. Our servitude to particulars betrays into a hundred foolish expectations. We anticipate a new era from the invention of a locomotive, or a balloon; the new engine brings with it the old checks. They say that by electro-magnetism your salad shall be grown from the seed whilst your fowl is roasting for dinner; it is a symbol of our modern aims and endeavors, of our condensation and acceleration of objects;—but nothing is gained; nature cannot be cheated; man's life is but seventy salads long, grow they swift or grow they slow. In these checks and impossibilities however we find our advantage, not less than in the impulses. Let the victory fall where it will, we are on that side. And the knowledge that we traverse the whole scale of being, from the centre to the poles of nature, and have some stake in every possibility, lends that sublime lustre to death, which philosophy and religion have too outwardly and literally striven to express in the popular doctrine of the immortality of the soul. The reality is more excellent than the report. Here is no ruin, no discontinuity, no spent ball. The divine circulations never rest nor linger. Nature is the incarnation of a thought, and turns to a thought again, as ice becomes water and gas. The world is mind precipitated, and the volatile essence is forever escaping again into the state of free thought. Hence the virtue and pungency of the influence on the mind of natural objects, whether inorganic or organized. Man imprisoned, man crystallized, man vegetative, speaks to man impersonated. That power which does not respect quantity, which makes the whole and the particle its equal channel, delegates its smile to the morning, and distils its essence into every drop of rain. Every moment instructs, and every object: for wisdom is infused into every form. It has been poured into us as blood; it convulsed us as pain; it slid into us as pleasure; it enveloped us in dull, melancholy days, or in days of cheerful labor; we did not guess its essence until after a long time.

AN ESSAY FROM
Essays, Second Series, 1844

WALKING

by Henry David Thoreau

1861

I wish to speak a word for Nature, for absolute Freedom and Wildness, as contrasted with a freedom and culture merely civil,—to regard man as an inhabitant, or a part and parcel of Nature, rather than a member of society. I wish to make an extreme statement, if so I may make an emphatic one, for there are enough champions of civilization: the minister and the school committee and every one of you will take care of that.

I have met with but one or two persons in the course of my life who understood the art of Walking, that is, of taking walks— who had a genius, so to speak, for *sauntering*, which word is beautifully derived "from idle people who roved about the country, in the Middle Ages, and asked charity, under pretense of going *à la Sainte Terre*," to the Holy Land, till the children exclaimed, "There goes a *Sainte-Terrer*," a Saunterer, a Holy-Lander. They who never go to the Holy Land in their walks, as they pretend, are indeed mere idlers and vagabonds; but they who do go there are saunterers in the good sense, such as I mean. Some, however, would derive the word from *sans terre* without land or a home, which, therefore, in the good sense, will mean, having no particular home, but equally at home everywhere. For this is the secret of successful sauntering. He who sits still in a house all the time may be the greatest vagrant of all; but the saunterer, in the good sense, is no more vagrant than the

25

meandering river, which is all the while sedulously seeking the shortest course to the sea. But I prefer the first, which, indeed, is the most probable derivation. For every walk is a sort of crusade, preached by some Peter the Hermit in us, to go forth and reconquer this Holy Land from the hands of the Infidels.

It is true, we are but faint-hearted crusaders, even the walkers, nowadays, who undertake no persevering, never-ending enterprises. Our expeditions are but tours, and come round again at evening to the old hearth-side from which we set out. Half the walk is but retracing our steps. We should go forth on the shortest walk, perchance, in the spirit of undying adventure, never to return,—prepared to send back our embalmed hearts only as relics to our desolate kingdoms. If you are ready to leave father and mother, and brother and sister, and wife and child and friends, and never see them again,—if you have paid your debts, and made your will, and settled all your affairs, and are a free man; then you are ready for a walk.

To come down to my own experience, my companion and I, for I sometimes have a companion, take pleasure in fancying ourselves knights of a new, or rather an old, order—not Equestrians or Chevaliers, not Ritters or Riders, but Walkers, a still more ancient and honorable class, I trust. The chivalric and heroic spirit which once belonged to the Rider seems now to reside in, or perchance to have subsided into, the Walker— not the Knight, but Walker Errant. He is a sort of fourth estate, outside of Church and State and People.

We have felt that we almost alone hereabouts practiced this noble art; though, to tell the truth, at least if their own assertions are to be received, most of my townsmen would fain walk sometimes, as I do, but they cannot. No wealth can buy the requisite leisure, freedom, and independence which are the capital in this profession. It comes only by the grace of God. It requires a direct dispensation from Heaven to become a walker. You must be born into the family of the Walkers. *Ambulator nascitur, non fit.* Some of my townsmen, it is true, can remember and have described to me some walks which they took ten years ago, in which they were so blessed as to lose themselves for half an hour in the woods; but I know very well that they have confined themselves to the highway ever since, whatever pretensions they may make to belong to this select class. No doubt they were elevated for a moment as by the reminiscence of a previous state of existence, when even they were foresters and outlaws.

> "When he came to grene wode,
>   In a mery mornynge,
> There he herde the notes small
>   Of byrdes mery syngynge.
>
> "It is ferre gone, sayd Robyn,
>   That I was last here;
> Me lyste a lytell for to shote
>   At the donne dere."

I think that I cannot preserve my health and spirits, unless I spend four hours a day at least—and it is commonly more than that—sauntering through the woods and over the hills and fields, absolutely free from all worldly engagements. You may safely say, A penny for your thoughts, or a thousand pounds. When sometimes I am reminded that the mechanics and shopkeepers stay in their shops not only all the forenoon, but all the afternoon too, sitting with crossed legs, so many of them—as if the legs were made to sit upon, and not to stand or walk upon—I think that they deserve some credit for not having all committed suicide long ago.

I, who cannot stay in my chamber for a single day without acquiring some rust, and when sometimes I have stolen forth for a walk at the eleventh hour, or four o'clock in the afternoon, too late to redeem the day, when the shades of night were already beginning to be mingled with the daylight, have felt as if I had committed some sin to be atoned for,—I confess that I am astonished at the power of endurance, to say nothing of the moral insensibility, of my neighbors who confine themselves to shops and offices the whole day for weeks and months, aye, and years almost together. I know not what manner of stuff they are of—sitting there now at three o'clock in the afternoon, as if it were three o'clock in the morning. Bonaparte may talk of the three-o'clock-in-the-morning courage, but it is nothing to the courage which can sit down cheerfully at this hour in the afternoon over against one's self whom you have known all the morning, to starve out a garrison to whom you are bound by such strong ties of sympathy. I wonder that about this time, or say between four and five o'clock in the afternoon, too late for the morning papers and too early for the evening ones, there is not a general explosion heard up and down the street, scattering a legion of antiquated and house-bred notions and whims to the four winds for an airing—and so the evil cure itself.

How womankind, who are confined to the house still more than men, stand it I do not know; but I have ground to suspect that most of them do not *stand* it at all. When, early in a summer afternoon, we have been shaking the dust of the village from the skirts of our garments, making haste past those houses with purely Doric or Gothic fronts, which have such an air of repose about them, my companion whispers that probably about these times their occupants are all gone to bed. Then it is that I appreciate the beauty and the glory of architecture, which itself never turns in, but forever stands out and erect, keeping watch over the slumberers.

No doubt temperament, and, above all, age, have a good deal to do with it. As a man grows older, his ability to sit still and follow indoor occupations increases. He grows vespertinal in his habits as the evening of life approaches, till at last he comes forth only just before sundown, and gets all the walk that he requires in half an hour.

But the walking of which I speak has nothing in it akin to

taking exercise, as it is called, as the sick take medicine at stated hours—as the swinging of dumb-bells or chairs; but is itself the enterprise and adventure of the day. If you would get exercise, go in search of the springs of life. Think of a man's swinging dumb-bells for his health, when those springs are bubbling up in far-off pastures unsought by him!

Moreover, you must walk like a camel, which is said to be the only beast which ruminates when walking. When a traveler asked Wordsworth's servant to show him her master's study, she answered, "Here is his library, but his study is out of doors."

Living much out of doors, in the sun and wind, will no doubt produce a certain roughness of character—will cause a thicker cuticle to grow over some of the finer qualities of our nature, as on the face and hands, or as severe manual labor robs the hands of some of their delicacy of touch. So staying in the house, on the other hand, may produce a softness and smoothness, not to say thinness of skin, accompanied by an increased sensibility to certain impressions. Perhaps we should be more susceptible to some influences important to our intellectual and moral growth, if the sun had shone and the wind blown on us a little less; and no doubt it is a nice matter to proportion rightly the thick and thin skin. But methinks that is a scurf that will fall off fast enough—that the natural remedy is to be found in the proportion which the night bears to the day, the winter to the summer, thought to experience. There will be so much the more air and sunshine in our thoughts. The callous palms of the laborer are conversant with finer tissues of self-respect and heroism, whose touch thrills the heart, than the languid fingers of idleness. That is mere sentimentality that lies abed by day and thinks itself white, far from the tan and callus of experience.

When we walk, we naturally go to the fields and woods: what would become of us, if we walked only in a garden or a mall? Even some sects of philosophers have felt the necessity of importing the woods to themselves, since they did not go to the woods. "They planted groves and walks of Platanes," where they took *subdiales ambulationes* in porticos open to the air. Of course it is of no use to direct our steps to the woods, if they do not carry us thither. I am alarmed when it happens that I have walked a mile into the woods bodily, without getting there in spirit. In my afternoon walk I would fain forget all my morning occupations and my obligations to society. But it sometimes happens that I cannot easily shake off the village. The thought of some work will run in my head and I am not where my body is—I am out of my senses. In my walks I would fain return to my senses. What business have I in the woods, if I am thinking of something out of the woods? I suspect myself, and cannot help a shudder when I find myself so implicated even in what are called good works—for this may sometimes happen.

My vicinity affords many good walks; and though for so many years I have walked almost every day, and sometimes for several days together, I have not yet exhausted them. An absolutely new prospect is a great happiness, and I can still get this any afternoon. Two or three hours' walking will carry me to as strange a country as I expect ever to see. A single farmhouse which I had not seen before is sometimes as good as the dominions of the king of Dahomey. There is in fact a sort of harmony discoverable between the capabilities of the landscape within a circle of ten miles' radius, or the limits of an afternoon walk, and the threescore years and ten of human life. It will never become quite familiar to you.

Nowadays almost all man's improvements, so called, as the building of houses and the cutting down of the forest and of all large trees, simply deform the landscape, and make it more and more tame and cheap. A people who would begin by burning the fences and let the forest stand! I saw the fences half consumed, their ends lost in the middle of the prairie, and some worldly miser with a surveyor looking after his bounds, while heaven had taken place around him, and he did not see the angels going to and fro, but was looking for an old post-hole in the midst of paradise. I looked again, and saw him standing in the middle of a boggy Stygian fen, surrounded by devils, and he had found his bounds without a doubt, three little stones, where a stake had been driven, and looking nearer, I saw that the Prince of Darkness was his surveyor.

I can easily walk ten, fifteen, twenty, any number of miles, commencing at my own door, without going by any house, without crossing a road except where the fox and the mink do: first along by the river, and then the brook, and then the meadow and the wood-side. There are square miles in my vicinity which have no inhabitant. From many a hill I can see civilization and the abodes of man afar. The farmers and their works are scarcely more obvious than woodchucks and their burrows. Man and his affairs, church and state and school, trade and commerce, and manufactures and agriculture even politics, the most alarming of them all,—I am pleased to see how little space they occupy in the landscape. Politics is but a narrow field, and that still narrower highway yonder leads to it. I sometimes direct the traveler thither. If you would go to the political world, follow the great road,—follow that market-man, keep his dust in your eyes, and it will lead you straight to it; for it, too, has its place merely, and does not occupy all space. I pass from it as from a bean field into the forest, and it is forgotten. In one half hour I can walk off to some portion of the earth's surface where a man does not stand from one year's end to another, and there, consequently, politics are not, for they are but as the cigar smoke of a man.

The village is the place to which the roads tend, a sort of expansion of the highway, as a lake of a river. It is the body of which roads are the arms and legs—a trivial or quadrivial place, the thoroughfare and ordinary of travelers. The word is from the Latin *villa* which together with *via*, a way, or more anciently *ved* and *vella*, Varro derives from *veho*, to carry, because the villa is the place to and from which things are carried. They who got their living by teaming were said *vellaturam facere*. Hence, too, the Latin word *vilis* and our *vile*; also *villain*. This suggests what kind of degeneracy villagers are liable to. They are wayworn by the travel that goes by and over them, without traveling themselves.

Some do not walk at all; others walk in the highways; a few walk across lots. Roads are made for horses and men of business. I do not travel in them much, comparatively, because I am not in a hurry to get to any tavern or grocery or livery-stable or depot to which they lead. I am a good horse to travel, but not from choice a roadster. The landscape-painter uses the figures of men to mark a road. He would not make that use of my figure. I walk out into a nature such as the old prophets and poets, Menu, Moses, Homer, Chaucer, walked in. You may name it America, but it is not America: neither Americus Vespucius, nor Columbus, nor the rest were the discoverers of it. There is a truer amount of it in mythology than in any history of America, so called, that I have seen.

However, there are a few old roads that may be trodden with profit, as if they led somewhere now that they are nearly discontinued. There is the Old Marlborough Road, which does not go to Marlborough now, methinks, unless that is Marlborough where it carries me. I am the bolder to speak of it here, because I presume that there are one or two such roads in every town.

THE OLD MARLBOROUGH ROAD

Where they once dug for money,
But never found any;
Where sometimes Martial Miles
Singly files,
And Elijah Wood,
I fear for no good:
No other man,
Save Elisha Dugan—
O man of wild habits,
Partridges and rabbits,

Who hast no cares
Only to set snares,
Who liv'st all alone,
Close to the bone;
And where life is sweetest
Constantly eatest.
When the spring stirs my blood
With the instinct to travel,
I can get enough gravel
On the Old Marlborough Road.
Nobody repairs it,
For nobody wears it;
It is a living way,
As the Christians say.
Not many there be
Who enter therein,
Only the guests of the
Irishman Quin.
What is it, what is it
But a direction out there,
And the bare possibility
Of going somewhere?
Great guide boards of stone,
But travelers none;
Cenotaphs of the towns
Named on their crowns.
It is worth going to see
Where you might be.
What king
Did the thing,
I am still wondering;
Set up how or when,
By what selectmen,
Gourgas or Lee,
Clark or Darby?

They're a great endeavor
To be something forever;
Blank tablets of stone,
Where a traveler might groan,
And in one sentence
Grave all that is known
Which another might read,
In his extreme need.
I know one or two
Lines that would do,
Literature that might stand
All over the land,
Which a man could remember
Till next December,
And read again in the spring,
After the thawing.
If with fancy unfurled
You leave your abode,
You may go round the world
By the Old Marlborough Road.

At present, in this vicinity, the best part of the land is not private property; the landscape is not owned, and the walker enjoys comparative freedom. But possibly the day will come when it will be partitioned off into so-called pleasure grounds, in which a few will take a narrow and exclusive pleasure only,—when fences shall be multiplied, and man traps and other engines invented to confine men to the *public* road, and walking over the surface of God's earth shall be construed to mean trespassing on some gentleman's grounds. To enjoy a thing exclusively is commonly to exclude yourself from the true enjoyment of it. Let us improve our opportunities, then, before the evil days come.

What is it that makes it so hard sometimes to determine whither we will walk? I believe that there is a subtle magnetism in Nature, which, if we unconsciously yield to it, will direct us aright. It is not indifferent to us which way we walk. There is a right way; but we are very liable from heedlessness and stupidity to take the wrong one. We would fain take that walk, never yet taken by us through this actual world, which is perfectly symbolical of the path which we love to travel in the interior and ideal world; and sometimes, no doubt, we find it difficult to choose our direction, because it does not yet exist distinctly in our idea.

When I go out of the house for a walk, uncertain as yet whither I will bend my steps, and submit myself to my instinct to decide for me, I find, strange and whimsical as it may seem, that I finally and inevitably settle southwest, toward some particular wood or meadow or deserted pasture or hill in that direction. My needle is slow to settle—varies a few degrees, and does not always point due southwest, it is true, and it has good authority for this variation, but it always settles between west and south-southwest. The future lies that way to me, and the earth seems more unexhausted and richer on that side. The outline which would bound my walks would be, not a circle, but a parabola, or rather like one of those cometary orbits which have been thought to be non-returning curves, in this case opening westward, in which my house occupies the place of the sun. I turn round and round irresolute sometimes for a quarter of an hour, until I decide, for a thousandth time, that I will walk into the southwest or west. Eastward I go only by force; but westward I go free. Thither no business leads me. It is hard for me to believe that I shall find fair landscapes or sufficient wildness and freedom behind the eastern horizon. I am not excited by the prospect of a walk thither; but I believe that the forest which I see in the western horizon stretches uninterruptedly toward the setting sun, and there are no towns nor cities in it of enough consequence to disturb me. Let me live where I will, on this side is the city, on that the wilderness, and ever I am leaving the city more and more, and withdrawing

35

into the wilderness. I should not lay so much stress on this fact, if I did not believe that something like this is the prevailing tendency of my countrymen. I must walk toward Oregon, and not toward Europe. And that way the nation is moving, and I may say that mankind progress from east to west. Within a few years we have witnessed the phenomenon of a southeastward migration, in the settlement of Australia; but this affects us as a retrograde movement, and, judging from the moral and physical character of the first generation of Australians, has not yet proved a successful experiment. The eastern Tartars think that there is nothing west beyond Thibet. "The world ends there," say they; "beyond there is nothing but a shoreless sea." It is unmitigated East where they live.

We go eastward to realize history and study the works of art and literature, retracing the steps of the race; we go westward as into the future, with a spirit of enterprise and adventure. The Atlantic is a Lethean stream, in our passage over which we have had an opportunity to forget the Old World and its institutions. If we do not succeed this time, there is perhaps one more chance for the race left before it arrives on the banks of the Styx; and that is in the Lethe of the Pacific, which is three times as wide.

I know not how significant it is, or how far it is an evidence of singularity, that an individual should thus consent in his pettiest walk with the general movement of the race; but I know that something akin to the migratory instinct in birds and quadrupeds,—which, in some instances, is known to have affected the squirrel tribe, impelling them to a general and mysterious movement, in which they were seen, say some, crossing the broadest rivers, each on its particular chip, with its tail raised for a sail, and bridging narrower streams with their dead,—that something like the *furor* which affects the domestic cattle in the spring, and which is referred to a worm in their tails,—affects both nations and individuals, either perennially or from time to time. Not a flock of wild geese cackles over our town, but it to some extent unsettles the value of real estate here, and, if I were a broker, I should probably take that disturbance into account.

> "Than longen folk to gon on pilgrimages,
> And palmeres for to seken strange strondes."

Every sunset which I witness inspires me with the desire to go to a West as distant and as fair as that into which the sun goes down. He appears to migrate westward daily, and tempt us to follow him. He is the Great Western Pioneer whom the nations follow. We dream all night of those mountain ridges in the horizon, though they may be of vapor only, which were last gilded by his rays. The island of Atlantis, and the islands and gardens of the Hesperides, a sort of terrestrial paradise, appear to have been the Great West of the ancients, enveloped in mystery and poetry. Who has not seen in imagination, when looking into the sunset sky, the gardens of the Hesperides, and the foundation of all those fables?

Columbus felt the westward tendency more strongly than any before. He obeyed it, and found a New World for Castile and Leon. The herd of men in those days scented fresh pastures from afar.

> "And now the sun had stretched out all the hills,
> And now was dropped into the western bay;
> At last he rose, and twitched his mantle blue;
> To-morrow to fresh woods and pastures new."

Where on the globe can there be found an area of equal extent with that occupied by the bulk of our States, so fertile and so rich and varied in its productions, and at the same time so habitable by the European, as this is? Michaux, who knew but part of them, says that "the species of large trees are much more numerous in North America than in Europe; in the United States there are more than one hundred and forty species that exceed thirty feet in height; in France there are but thirty that attain this size." Later botanists more than confirm his observations. Humboldt came to America to realize his youthful dreams of a tropical vegetation, and he beheld it in its greatest perfection in the primitive forests of the Amazon, the most gigantic wilderness on the earth, which he has so eloquently described. The geographer Guyot, himself a European, goes further—further than I am ready to follow him; yet not when he says: "As the plant is made for the animal, as the vegetable world is made for the animal world, America is made for the man of the Old World.... The man of the Old World sets out upon his way. Leaving the highlands of Asia, he descends from station to station towards Europe. Each of his steps is marked by a new civilization superior to the preceding, by a greater power of development. Arrived at the Atlantic, he pauses on the shore of this unknown ocean, the bounds of which he knows not, and turns upon his footprints for an instant." When he has exhausted the rich soil of Europe, and reinvigorated himself, "then recommences his adventurous career westward as in the earliest ages." So far Guyot.

From this western impulse coming in contact with the barrier of the Atlantic sprang the commerce and enterprise of modern times. The younger Michaux, in his Travels West of the Alleghanies in 1802, says that the common inquiry in the newly settled West was, "'From what part of the world have you come?' As if these vast and fertile regions would naturally be the place of meeting and common country of all the inhabitants of the globe."

To use an obsolete Latin word, I might say, *Ex oriente lux; ex occidente FRUX.* From the East light; from the West fruit.

Sir Francis Head, an English traveler and a Governor-General of Canada, tells us that "in both the northern and southern hemispheres of the New World, Nature has not only outlined her works on a larger scale, but has painted the whole picture with brighter and more costly colors than she used in delineating and in beautifying the Old World.... The heavens of America appear infinitely higher, the sky is bluer, the air is fresher, the cold is intenser, the moon looks larger, the stars are brighter the thunder is louder, the lightning is vivider, the wind is stronger, the rain is heavier, the mountains are higher, the rivers longer, the forests bigger, the plains broader." This statement will do at least to set against Buffon's account of this part of the world and its productions.

Linnæus said long ago, "Nescio quæ facies *læta, glabra* plantis Americanis" (I know not what there is of joyous and smooth in the aspect of American plants); and I think that in this country there are no, or at most very few, *Africanæ bestiæ*, African beasts, as the Romans called them, and that in this respect also it is peculiarly fitted for the habitation of man. We are told that within three miles of the center of the East Indian city of Singapore, some of the inhabitants are annually carried off by tigers; but the traveler can lie down in the woods at night almost anywhere in North America without fear of wild beasts.

These are encouraging testimonies. If the moon looks larger here than in Europe, probably the sun looks larger also. If the heavens of America appear infinitely higher, and the stars brighter, I trust that these facts are symbolical of the height to which the philosophy and poetry and religion of her inhabitants may one day soar. At length, perchance, the immaterial heaven will appear as much higher to the American mind, and the intimations that star it as much brighter. For I believe that climate does thus react on man—as there is something in the mountain air that feeds the spirit and inspires. Will not man grow to greater perfection intellectually as well as physically under these influences? Or is it unimportant how many foggy days there are in his life? I trust that we shall be more imaginative, that our thoughts will be clearer, fresher, and more ethereal, as our sky—our understanding more comprehensive and broader, like our plains—our intellect generally on a grander scale, like our thunder and lightning, our rivers and mountains and forests,—

and our hearts shall even correspond in breadth and depth and grandeur to our inland seas. Perchance there will appear to the traveler something, he knows not what, of *læta* and *glabra*, of joyous and serene, in our very faces. Else to what end does the world go on, and why was America discovered?

To Americans I hardly need to say—

"Westward the star of empire takes its way."

As a true patriot, I should be ashamed to think that Adam in paradise was more favorably situated on the whole than the backwoodsman in this country.

Our sympathies in Massachusetts are not confined to New England; though we may be estranged from the South, we sympathize with the West. There is the home of the younger sons, as among the Scandinavians they took to the sea for their inheritance. It is too late to be studying Hebrew; it is more important to understand even the slang of today.

Some months ago I went to see a panorama of the Rhine. It was like a dream of the Middle Ages. I floated down its historic stream in something more than imagination, under bridges built by the Romans, and repaired by later heroes, past cities and castles whose very names were music to my ears, and each of which was the subject of a legend. There were Ehrenbreitstein and Rolandseck and Coblentz, which I knew only in history. They were ruins that interested me chiefly. There seemed to come up from its waters and its vine-clad hills and valleys a hushed music as of crusaders departing for the Holy Land. I floated along under the spell of enchantment, as if I had been transported to an heroic age, and breathed an atmosphere of chivalry.

Soon after, I went to see a panorama of the Mississippi, and as I worked my way up the river in the light of to-day, and saw the steamboats wooding up, counted the rising cities, gazed on the fresh ruins of Nauvoo, beheld the Indians moving west across the stream, and, as before I had looked up the Moselle, now looked up the Ohio and the Missouri and heard the legends of Dubuque and of Wenona's Cliff—still thinking more of the future than of the past or present—I saw that this was a Rhine stream of a different kind; that the foundations of castles were yet to be laid, and the famous bridges were yet to be thrown over the river; and I felt that *this was the heroic age itself*, though we know it not, for the hero is commonly the simplest and obscurest of men.

The West of which I speak is but another name for the Wild; and what I have been preparing to say is, that in Wildness is the preservation of the World. Every tree sends its fibers forth in search of the Wild. The cities import it at any price. Men plow and sail for it. From the forest and wilderness come the tonics and barks which brace mankind. Our ancestors were savages. The story of Romulus and Remus being suckled by a wolf is not a meaningless fable. The founders of every state which has risen to eminence have drawn their nourishment and vigor from a similar wild source. It was because the children of the Empire were not suckled by the wolf that they were conquered and displaced by the children of the northern forests who were.

I believe in the forest, and in the meadow, and in the night in which the corn grows. We require an infusion of hemlock spruce or arbor vitæ in our tea. There is a difference between eating and drinking for strength and from mere gluttony. The Hottentots eagerly devour the marrow of the koodoo and other antelopes raw, as a matter of course. Some of our northern Indians eat raw the marrow of the Arctic reindeer, as well as various other parts, including the summits of the antlers, as long as they are soft. And herein, perchance, they have stolen a march on the cooks of Paris. They get what usually goes to feed the fire. This is probably better than stall-fed beef and slaughterhouse pork to make a man of. Give me a wildness whose glance no civilization can endure,—as if we lived on the marrow of koodoos devoured raw.

There are some intervals which border the strain of the wood-thrush, to which I would migrate—wild lands where no settler has squatted; to which, methinks, I am already acclimated.

The African hunter Cumming tells us that the skin of the eland, as well as that of most other antelopes just killed, emits the most delicious perfume of trees and grass. I would have every man so much like a wild antelope, so much a part and parcel of Nature, that his very person should thus sweetly advertise our senses of his presence, and remind us of those parts of nature which he most haunts. I feel no disposition to be satirical, when the trapper's coat emits the odor of musquash even; it is a sweeter scent to me than that which commonly exhales from the merchant's or the scholar's garments. When I go into their wardrobes and handle their vestments, I am reminded of no grassy plains and flowery meads which they have frequented, but of dusty merchants' exchanges and libraries rather.

A tanned skin is something more than respectable, and perhaps olive is a fitter color than white for a man—a denizen of the woods. "The pale white man!" I do not wonder that the African pitied him. Darwin the naturalist says, "A white man bathing by the side of a Tahitian was like a plant bleached by the gardener's art, compared with a fine, dark green one, growing vigorously in the open fields."

Ben Jonson exclaims,—

"How near to good is what is fair!"

So I would say,—

"How near to good is what is wild!"

Life consists with wildness. The most alive is the wildest. Not yet subdued to man, its presence refreshes him. One who pressed forward incessantly and never rested from his labors, who grew fast and made infinite demands on life, would always find himself in a new country or wilderness, and surrounded by the raw material of life. He would be climbing over the prostrate stems of primitive forest trees.

Hope and the future for me are not in lawns and cultivated fields, not in towns and cities, but in the impervious and quaking swamps. When, formerly, I have analyzed my partiality for some farm which I had contemplated purchasing, I have frequently found that I was attracted solely by a few square rods of impermeable and unfathomable bog—a natural sink in one corner of it. That was the jewel which dazzled me. I derive more of my subsistence from the swamps which surround my native town than from the cultivated gardens in the village. There are no richer parterres to my eyes than the dense beds of dwarf andromeda (*Cassandra calyculata*) which cover these tender places on the earth's surface. Botany cannot go farther than tell me the names of the shrubs which grow there—the high-blueberry, panicled andromeda, lamb-kill, azalea, and rhodora—all standing in the quaking sphagnum. I often think that I should like to have my house front on this mass of dull red bushes, omitting other flower plots and borders, transplanted spruce and trim box, even graveled walks—to have this fertile spot under my windows, not a few imported barrow-fuls of soil only to cover the sand which was thrown out in digging the cellar. Why not put my house, my parlor, behind this plot, instead of behind that meager assemblage of curiosities, that poor apology for a Nature and art, which I call my front yard? It is an effort to clear up and make a decent appearance when the carpenter and mason have departed, though done as much for the passer-by as the dweller within. The most tasteful front-yard fence was never an agreeable object of study to me; the most elaborate ornaments, acorn tops, or what not, soon wearied and disgusted me. Bring your sills up to the very edge of the swamp, then (though it may not be the best place for a dry cellar,) so that there be no access on that side to citizens. Front yards are not made to walk in, but, at most, through, and you could go in the back way.

Yes, though you may think me perverse, if it were proposed to me to dwell in the neighborhood of the most beautiful garden that ever human art contrived, or else of a dismal swamp, I should certainly decide for the swamp. How vain, then, have been all your labors, citizens, for me!

My spirits infallibly rise in proportion to the outward dreariness. Give me the ocean, the desert, or the wilderness! In the desert, pure air and solitude compensate for want of moisture and fertility. The traveler Burton says of it—"Your *morale* improves; you become frank and cordial, hospitable and single-minded. . . . In the desert, spirituous liquors excite only disgust. There is a keen enjoyment in a mere animal existence." They who have been traveling long on the steppes of Tartary say, "On reentering cultivated lands, the agitation, perplexity, and turmoil of civilization oppressed and suffocated us; the air seemed to fail us, and we felt every moment as if about to die of asphyxia." When I would recreate myself, I seek the darkest wood, the thickest and most interminable and, to the citizen, most dismal, swamp. I enter a swamp as a sacred place,—a *sanctum sanctorum*. There is the strength, the marrow, of Nature. The wild wood covers the virgin mould,—and the same soil is good for men and for trees. A man's health requires as many acres of meadow to his prospect as his farm does loads of muck. There are the strong meats on which he feeds. A town is saved, not more by the righteous men in it than by the woods and swamps that surround it. A township where one primitive forest waves above while another primitive forest rots below— such a town is fitted to raise not only corn and potatoes, but poets and philosophers for the coming ages. In such a soil grew Homer and Confucius and the rest, and out of such a wilderness comes the reformer eating locusts and wild honey.

To preserve wild animals implies generally the creation of a forest for them to dwell in or resort to. So it is with man. A hundred years ago they sold bark in our streets peeled from our own woods. In the very aspect of those primitive and rugged trees there was, methinks, a tanning principle which hardened and consolidated the fibers of men's thoughts. Ah! already I shudder for these comparatively degenerate days of my native village, when you cannot collect a load of bark of good thickness, and we no longer produce tar and turpentine.

The civilized nations—Greece, Rome, England—have been sustained by the primitive forests which anciently rotted where they stand. They survive as long as the soil is not exhausted. Alas for human culture! little is to be expected of a nation, when the vegetable mould is exhausted, and it is compelled to make manure of the bones of its fathers. There the poet sustains himself merely by his own superfluous fat, and the philosopher comes down on his marrow bones.

It is said to be the task of the American "to work the virgin soil," and that "agriculture here already assumes proportions unknown everywhere else." I think that the farmer displaces the Indian even because he redeems the meadow, and so makes himself stronger and in some respects more natural. I was surveying for a man the other day a single straight line one hundred and thirty-two rods long, through a swamp at whose entrance might have been written the words which Dante read over the entrance to the infernal regions,—"Leave all hope, ye that enter"—that is, of ever getting out again; where at one time I saw my employer actually up to his neck and swimming for his life in his property, though it was still winter. He had another similar swamp which I could not survey at all, because it was completely under water, and nevertheless, with regard to a third swamp, which I did *survey* from a distance, he remarked to me, true to his instincts, that he would not part with it for any consideration, on account of the mud which it contained. And that man intends to put a girdling ditch round the whole in the course of forty months, and so redeem it by the magic of his spade. I refer to him only as the type of a class.

The weapons with which we have gained our most important victories, which should be handed down as heirlooms from father to son, are not the sword and the lance, but the bushwhack, the turf-cutter, the spade, and the bog hoe, rusted with the blood of many a meadow, and begrimed with the dust of many a hard-fought field. The very winds blew the Indian's cornfield into the meadow, and pointed out the way which he had not the skill to follow. He had no better implement with which to intrench himself in the land than a clam-shell. But the farmer is armed with plow and spade.

In literature it is only the wild that attracts us. Dullness is but another name for tameness. It is the uncivilized free and wild thinking in Hamlet and the Iliad, in all the scriptures and mythologies, not learned in the schools, that delights us. As the wild duck is more swift and beautiful than the tame, so is the wild—the mallard—thought, which 'mid falling dews wings its way above the fens. A truly good book is something as natural, and as unexpectedly and unaccountably fair and perfect, as a wild flower discovered on the prairies of the west or in the jungles of the east. Genius is a light which makes the darkness visible, like the lightning's flash, which perchance shatters the temple of knowledge itself—and not a taper lighted at the hearthstone of the race, which pales before the light of common day.

English literature, from the days of the minstrels to the Lake Poets—Chaucer and Spenser and Milton, and even Shakespeare included—breathes no quite fresh and in this sense wild strain. It is an essentially tame and civilized literature, reflecting Greece and Rome. Her wilderness is a green wood, her wild man a Robin Hood. There is plenty of genial love of Nature, but not so much of Nature herself. Her chronicles inform us when her wild animals, but not when the wild man in her, became extinct.

The science of Humboldt is one thing, poetry is another thing. The poet today, notwithstanding all the discoveries of science, and the accumulated learning of mankind, enjoys no advantage over Homer.

Where is the literature which gives expression to Nature? He would be a poet who could impress the winds and streams into his service, to speak for him; who nailed words to their primitive senses, as farmers drive down stakes in the spring, which the frost has heaved; who derived his words as often as he used them—transplanted them to his page with earth adhering to their roots; whose words were so true and fresh and natural that they would appear to expand like the buds at the approach of spring, though they lay half smothered between two musty leaves in a library,—aye, to bloom and bear fruit there, after their kind, annually, for the faithful reader, in sympathy with surrounding Nature.

I do not know of any poetry to quote which adequately expresses this yearning for the Wild. Approached from this side, the best poetry is tame. I do not know where to find in any literature, ancient or modern, any account which contents me of that Nature with which even I am acquainted. You will perceive that I demand something which no Augustan nor Elizabethan age, which no *culture*, in short, can give. Mythology comes nearer to it than anything. How much more fertile a Nature, at least, has Grecian mythology its root in than English literature! Mythology is the crop which the Old World bore before its soil was exhausted, before the fancy and imagination were affected with blight; and which it still bears, wherever its pristine vigor is unabated. All other literatures endure only as the elms which overshadow our houses; but this is like the great dragon-tree of the Western Isles, as old as mankind, and, whether that does or not, will endure as long; for the decay of other literatures makes the soil in which it thrives.

The West is preparing to add its fables to those of the East. The valleys of the Ganges, the Nile, and the Rhine, having yielded their crop, it remains to be seen what the valleys of the Amazon, the Plate, the Orinoco, the St. Lawrence, and the Mississippi will produce. Perchance, when, in the course of ages, American liberty has become a fiction of the past,—as it is to some extent a fiction of the present,—the poets of the world will be inspired by American mythology.

The wildest dreams of wild men, even, are not the less true, though they may not recommend themselves to the sense which is most common among Englishmen and Americans to-day. It is not every truth that recommends itself to the common sense. Nature has a place for the wild clematis as well as for the cabbage. Some expressions of truth are reminiscent,—others merely *sensible*, as the phrase is,—others prophetic. Some forms of disease, even, may prophesy forms of health. The geologist has discovered that the figures of serpents, griffins, flying dragons, and other fanciful embellishments of heraldry, have their prototypes in the forms of fossil species which were extinct before man was created, and hence "indicate a faint and shadowy knowledge of a previous state of organic existence." The Hindoos dreamed that the earth rested on an elephant, and the elephant on a tortoise, and the tortoise on a serpent; and though it may be an unimportant coincidence, it will not be out of place here to state, that a fossil tortoise has lately been discovered in Asia large enough to support an elephant. I confess that I am partial to these wild fancies, which transcend the order of time and development. They are the sublimest recreation of the intellect. The partridge loves peas, but not those that go with her into the pot.

In short, all good things are wild and free. There is something in a strain of music, whether produced by an instrument or by the human voice—take the sound of a bugle in a summer night, for instance,—which by its wildness, to speak without satire, reminds me of the cries emitted by wild beasts in their native forests. It is so much of their wildness as I can understand. Give me for my friends and neighbors wild men, not tame ones. The wildness of the savage is but a faint symbol of the awful ferity with which good men and lovers meet.

I love even to see the domestic animals reassert their native rights—any evidence that they have not wholly lost their original wild habits and vigor; as when my neighbor's cow breaks out of her pasture early in the spring and boldly swims the river, a cold, gray tide, twenty-five or thirty rods wide, swollen by the melted snow. It is the buffalo crossing the Mississippi. This exploit confers some dignity on the herd in my eyes—already dignified. The seeds of instinct are preserved under the thick hides of cattle and horses, like seeds in the bowels of the earth, an indefinite period.

Any sportiveness in cattle is unexpected. I saw one day a herd of a dozen bullocks and cows running about and frisking in unwieldy sport, like huge rats, even like kittens. They shook their heads, raised their tails, and rushed up and down a hill, and I perceived by their horns, as well as by their activity, their relation to the deer tribe. But, alas! a sudden loud *Whoa!* would have damped their ardor at once, reduced them from venison to beef, and stiffened their sides and sinews like the locomotive. Who but the Evil One has cried "Whoa!" to mankind? Indeed, the life of cattle, like that of many men, is but a sort of locomotiveness; they move a side at a time, and man, by his machinery, is meeting the horse and the ox half way. Whatever part the whip has touched is thenceforth palsied. Who would ever think of a *side* of any of the supple cat tribe, as we speak of a *side* of beef?

I rejoice that horses and steers have to be broken before they can be made the slaves of men, and that men themselves have some wild oats still left to sow before they become submissive members of society. Undoubtedly, all men are not equally fit subjects for civilization; and because the majority, like dogs and sheep, are tame by inherited disposition, this is no reason why the others should have their natures broken that they may be reduced to the same level. Men are in the main alike, but they were made several in order that they might be various. If a low use is to be served, one man will do nearly or quite as well as another; if a high one, individual excellence is to be regarded. Any man can stop a hole to keep the wind away, but no other man could serve so rare a use as the author of this illustration did. Confucius says,—"The skins of the tiger and the leopard, when they are tanned, are as the skins of the dog and the sheep tanned." But it is not the part of a true culture to tame tigers, any more than it is to make sheep ferocious; and tanning their skins for shoes is not the best use to which they can be put.

When looking over a list of men's names in a foreign language, as of military officers, or of authors who have written on a particular subject, I am reminded once more that there is nothing in a name. The name Menschikoff, for instance, has nothing in it to my ears more human than a whisker, and it may belong to a rat. As the names of the Poles and Russians are to us, so are ours to them. It is as if they had been named by the child's rigmarole—*Iery-wiery ichery van, tittle-tol-tan*. I see in my mind a herd of wild creatures swarming over the earth, and to each the herdsman has affixed some barbarous sound in his own dialect. The names of men are, of course, as cheap and meaningless as *Bose* and *Tray*, the names of dogs.

Methinks it would be some advantage to philosophy if men were named merely in the gross, as they are known. It would be necessary only to know the genus and perhaps the race or variety, to know the individual. We are not prepared to believe that every private soldier in a Roman army had a name of his own—because we have not supposed that he had a character of his own. At present our only true names are nicknames. I knew a boy who, from his peculiar energy, was called "Buster" by his playmates, and this rightly supplanted his Christian name. Some travellers tell us that an Indian had no name given him at first, but earned it, and his name was his fame; and among some tribes he acquired a new name with every new exploit. It is pitiful when a man bears a name for convenience merely, who has earned neither name nor fame.

I will not allow mere names to make distinctions for me, but still see men in herds for all them. A familiar name cannot make a man less strange to me. It may be given to a savage who retains in secret his own wild title earned in the woods. We have a wild savage in us, and a savage name is perchance somewhere recorded as ours. I see that my neighbor, who bears the familiar epithet William or Edwin, takes it off with his jacket. It does not adhere to him when asleep or in anger, or aroused by any passion or inspiration. I seem to hear pronounced by some of his kin at such a time his original wild name in some jaw-breaking or else melodious tongue.

Here is this vast, savage, hovering mother of ours, Nature, lying all around, with such beauty, and such affection for her children, as the leopard; and yet we are so early weaned from her breast to society, to that culture which is exclusively an interaction of man on man,—a sort of breeding in and in, which produces at most a merely English nobility, a civilization destined to have a speedy limit.

In society, in the best institutions of men, it is easy to detect a certain precocity. When we should still be growing children, we are already little men. Give me a culture which imports much muck from the meadows, and deepens the soil—not that which trusts to heating manures, and improved implements and modes of culture only!

Many a poor sore-eyed student that I have heard of would grow faster, both intellectually and physically, if, instead of sitting up so very late, he honestly slumbered a fool's allowance.

There may be an excess even of informing light. Niepce, a Frenchman, discovered "actinism," that power in the sun's rays which produces a chemical effect; that granite rocks, and stone structures, and statues of metal "are all alike destructively acted upon during the hours of sunshine, and, but for provisions of Nature no less wonderful, would soon perish under the delicate touch of the most subtle of the agencies of the universe." But he observed that "those bodies which underwent this change during the daylight possessed the power of restoring themselves to their original conditions during the hours of night, when this excitement was no longer influencing them." Hence it has been inferred that "the hours of darkness are as necessary to the inorganic creation as we know night and sleep are to the organic kingdom." Not even does the moon shine every night, but gives place to darkness.

I would not have every man nor every part of a man cultivated, any more than I would have every acre of earth cultivated: part will be tillage, but the greater part will be meadow and forest, not only serving an immediate use, but preparing a mould against a distant future, by the annual decay of the vegetation which it supports.

There are other letters for the child to learn than those which Cadmus invented. The Spaniards have a good term to express this wild and dusky knowledge—*Gramatica parda*—tawny grammar, a kind of mother-wit derived from that same leopard to which I have referred.

We have heard of a Society for the Diffusion of Useful Knowledge. It is said that knowledge is power, and the like. Methinks there is equal need of a Society for the Diffusion of Useful Ignorance, what we will call Beautiful Knowledge, a knowledge useful in a higher sense: for what is most of our boasted so-called knowledge but a conceit that we know something, which robs us of the advantage of our actual ignorance? What we call knowledge is often our positive ignorance; ignorance our negative knowledge. By long years of patient industry and reading of the newspapers—for what are the libraries of science but files of newspapers—a man accumulates a myriad facts, lays them up in his memory, and then when in some spring of his life he saunters abroad into the Great Fields of thought, he, as it were, goes to grass like a horse and leaves all his harness behind in the stable. I would say to the Society for the Diffusion of Useful Knowledge, sometimes,— Go to grass. You have eaten hay long enough. The spring has come with its green crop. The very cows are driven to their country pastures before the end of May; though I have heard of one unnatural farmer who kept his cow in the barn and fed her on hay all the year round. So, frequently, the Society for the Diffusion of Useful Knowledge treats its cattle.

52

A man's ignorance sometimes is not only useful, but beautiful—while his knowledge, so called, is oftentimes worse than useless, besides being ugly. Which is the best man to deal with—he who knows nothing about a subject, and, what is extremely rare, knows that he knows nothing, or he who really knows something about it, but thinks that he knows all?

My desire for knowledge is intermittent, but my desire to bathe my head in atmospheres unknown to my feet is perennial and constant. The highest that we can attain to is not Knowledge, but Sympathy with Intelligence. I do not know that this higher knowledge amounts to anything more definite than a novel and grand surprise on a sudden revelation of the insufficiency of all that we called Knowledge before—a discovery that there are more things in heaven and earth than are dreamed of in our philosophy. It is the lighting up of the mist by the sun. Man cannot *know* in any higher sense than this, any more than he can look serenely and with impunity in the face of the sun: Ὡς τὶ νοῶν, οὐ κεῖνον νοήσεις,—"You will not perceive that, as perceiving a particular thing," say the Chaldean Oracles.

There is something servile in the habit of seeking after a law which we may obey. We may study the laws of matter at and for our convenience, but a successful life knows no law. It is an unfortunate discovery certainly, that of a law which binds us where we did not know before that we were bound. Live free, child of the mist—and with respect to knowledge we are all children of the mist. The man who takes the liberty to live is superior to all the laws, by virtue of his relation to the law-maker. "That is active duty," says the Vishnu Purana, "which is not for our bondage; that is knowledge which is for our liberation: all other duty is good only unto weariness; all other knowledge is only the cleverness of an artist."

It is remarkable how few events or crises there are in our histories, how little exercised we have been in our minds, how few experiences we have had. I would fain be assured that I am growing apace and rankly, though my very growth disturb this dull equanimity—though it be with struggle through long, dark, muggy nights or seasons of gloom. It would be well if all our lives were a divine tragedy even, instead of this trivial comedy or farce. Dante, Bunyan, and others appear to have been exercised in their minds more than we: they were subjected to a kind of culture such as our district schools and colleges do not contemplate. Even Mahomet, though many may scream at his name, had a good deal more to live for, aye, and to die for, than they have commonly.

When, at rare intervals, some thought visits one, as perchance he is walking on a railroad, then, indeed, the cars go by without his hearing them. But soon, by some inexorable law, our life goes by and the cars return.

> "Gentle breeze, that wanderest unseen,
> And bendest the thistles round Loira of storms,
> Traveler of the windy glens,
> Why hast thou left my ear so soon?"

While almost all men feel an attraction drawing them to society, few are attracted strongly to Nature. In their relation to Nature men appear to me for the most part, notwithstanding their arts, lower than the animals. It is not often a beautiful relation, as in the case of the animals. How little appreciation of the beauty of the landscape there is among us! We have to be told that the Greeks called the world Κόσμος Beauty, or Order, but we do not see clearly why they did so, and we esteem it at best only a curious philological fact.

For my part, I feel that with regard to Nature I live a sort of border life, on the confines of a world into which I make occasional and transient forays only, and my patriotism and allegiance to the state into whose territories I seem to retreat are those of a moss-trooper. Unto a life which I call natural I would gladly follow even a will-o'-the-wisp through bogs and sloughs unimaginable, but no moon nor firefly has shown me the causeway to it. Nature is a personality so vast and universal that we have never seen one of her features. The walker in the familiar fields which stretch around my native town sometimes finds himself in another land than is described in their owners' deeds, as it were in some faraway field on the confines of the actual Concord, where her jurisdiction ceases, and the idea which the word Concord suggests ceases to be suggested. These farms which I have myself surveyed, these bounds which I have set up, appear dimly still as through a mist; but they have no chemistry to fix them; they fade from the surface of the glass, and the picture which the painter painted stands out dimly from beneath. The world with which we are commonly acquainted leaves no trace, and it will have no anniversary.

I took a walk on Spaulding's Farm the other afternoon. I saw the setting sun lighting up the opposite side of a stately pine wood. Its golden rays straggled into the aisles of the wood as into some noble hall. I was impressed as if some ancient and altogether admirable and shining family had settled there in that part of the land called Concord, unknown to me—to whom the sun was servant—who had not gone into society in the village—who had not been called on. I saw their park, their pleasure-ground, beyond through the wood, in Spaulding's cranberry-meadow. The pines furnished them with gables as they grew. Their house was not obvious to vision; the trees grew through it. I do not know whether I heard the sounds of a suppressed hilarity or not. They seemed to recline on the sunbeams. They have sons and daughters. They are quite well. The farmer's cart-path, which leads directly through their hall, does not in the least put them out, as the muddy bottom of a pool is sometimes seen through the reflected skies. They never heard of Spaulding, and do not know that he is their neighbor,—notwithstanding I heard him whistle as he drove his team through the house. Nothing can equal the serenity of their lives. Their coat-of-arms is simply a lichen. I saw it painted on the pines and oaks. Their attics were in the tops of the trees. They are of no politics. There was no noise of labor. I did not perceive that they were weaving or spinning. Yet I did detect, when the wind lulled and hearing was done away, the finest imaginable sweet musical hum,— as of a distant hive in May, which perchance was the sound of their thinking. They had no idle thoughts, and no one without could see their work, for their industry was not as in knots and excrescences embayed.

But I find it difficult to remember them. They fade irrevocably out of my mind even now while I speak and endeavor to recall them, and recollect myself. It is only after a long and serious effort to recollect my best thoughts that I become again aware of their cohabitancy. If it were not for such families as this, I think I should move out of Concord.

We are accustomed to say in New England that few and fewer pigeons visit us every year. Our forests furnish no mast for them. So, it would seem, few and fewer thoughts visit each growing man from year to year, for the grove in our minds is laid waste,— sold to feed unnecessary fires of ambition, or sent to mill, and there is scarcely a twig left for them to perch on. They no longer build nor breed with us. In some more genial season, perchance, a faint shadow flits across the landscape of the mind, cast by the *wings* of some thought in its vernal or autumnal migration, but, looking up, we are unable to detect the substance of the thought itself. Our winged thoughts are turned to poultry. They no longer soar, and they attain only to a Shanghai and Cochin China grandeur. Those *gra-a-ate thoughts*, those *gra-a-ate men* you hear of!

We hug the earth—how rarely we mount! Methinks we might elevate ourselves a little more. We might climb a tree, at least. I found my account in climbing a tree once. It was a tall white pine, on the top of a hill; and though I got well pitched, I was well paid for it, for I discovered new mountains in the horizon which I had never seen before,—so much more of the earth and the heavens. I might have walked about the foot of the tree for threescore years and ten, and yet I certainly should never have seen them. But, above all, I discovered around me,—it was near the end of June,—on the ends of the topmost branches only, a few minute and delicate red conelike blossoms, the fertile flower of the white pine looking heavenward. I carried straightway to the village the topmost spire, and showed it to stranger jurymen who walked the streets,—for it was court week—and to farmers and lumber-dealers and wood-choppers and hunters, and not one had ever seen the like before, but they wondered as at a star dropped down. Tell of ancient architects finishing their works on the tops of columns as perfectly as on the lower and more visible parts! Nature has from the first expanded the minute blossoms of the forest only toward the heavens, above men's heads and unobserved by them. We see only the flowers that are under our feet in the meadows. The pines have developed their delicate blossoms on the highest twigs of the wood every summer for ages, as well over the heads of Nature's red children as of her white ones; yet scarcely a farmer or hunter in the land has ever seen them.

Above all, we cannot afford not to live in the present. He is blessed over all mortals who loses no moment of the passing life in remembering the past. Unless our philosophy hears the cock crow in every barn-yard within our horizon, it is belated. That sound commonly reminds us that we are growing rusty and antique in our employments and habits of thoughts. His philosophy comes down to a more recent time than ours. There is something suggested by it that is a newer testament,—the gospel according to this moment. He has not fallen astern; he has got up early and kept up early, and to be where he is, is to be in season, in the foremost rank of time. It is an expression of the health and soundness of Nature, a brag for all the world,— healthiness as of a spring burst forth, a new fountain of the Muses, to celebrate this last instant of time. Where he lives no fugitive slave laws are passed. Who has not betrayed his master many times since last he heard that note?

The merit of this bird's strain is in its freedom from all

plaintiveness. The singer can easily move us to tears or to laughter, but where is he who can excite in us a pure morning joy? When, in doleful dumps, breaking the awful stillness of our wooden sidewalk on a Sunday, or, perchance, a watcher in the house of mourning, I hear a cockerel crow far or near, I think to myself, "There is one of us well, at any rate,"—and with a sudden gush return to my senses.

We had a remarkable sunset one day last November. I was walking in a meadow, the source of a small brook, when the sun at last, just before setting, after a cold grey day, reached a clear stratum in the horizon, and the softest, brightest morning sunlight fell on the dry grass and on the stems of the trees in the opposite horizon and on the leaves of the shrub-oaks on the hillside, while our shadows stretched long over the meadow eastward, as if we were the only motes in its beams. It was such a light as we could not have imagined a moment before, and the air also was so warm and serene that nothing was wanting to make a paradise of that meadow. When we reflected that this was not a solitary phenomenon, never to happen again, but that it would happen forever and ever, an infinite number of evenings, and cheer and reassure the latest child that walked there, it was more glorious still.

The sun sets on some retired meadow, where no house is visible, with all the glory and splendor that it lavishes on cities, and perchance as it has never set before,—where there is but a solitary marsh hawk to have his wings gilded by it, or only a musquash looks out from his cabin, and there is some little black-veined brook in the midst of the marsh, just beginning to meander, winding slowly round a decaying stump. We walked in so pure and bright a light, gilding the withered grass and leaves, so softly and serenely bright, I thought I had never bathed in such a golden flood, without a ripple or a murmur to it. The west side of every wood and rising ground gleamed like the boundary of Elysium, and the sun on our backs seemed like a gentle herdsman driving us home at evening.

So we saunter toward the Holy Land, till one day the sun shall shine more brightly than ever he has done, shall perchance shine into our minds and hearts, and light up our whole lives with a great awakening light, as warm and serene and golden as on a bank-side in Autumn.

READING THE
BOOK OF NATURE

By John Burroughs

In studying Nature, the important thing is not so much what we see as how we interpret what we see. Do we get at the true meaning of the facts? Do we draw the right inference? The fossils in the rocks were long observed before men drew the right inference from them. So with a hundred other things in nature and life.

During May and a part of June of 1903, a drouth of unusual severity prevailed throughout the land. The pools and marshes nearly all dried up. Late in June the rains came again and filled them up. Then an unusual thing happened: suddenly, for two or three days and nights, the marshes about me were again vocal with the many voices of the hyla, the "peepers" of early spring. That is the fact. Now, what is the interpretation? With me the peepers become silent in early May, and, I suppose, leave the marshes for their life in the woods. Did the drouth destroy all their eggs and young, and did they know this and so come back to try again? How else shall one explain their second appearance in the marshes? But how did they know of the destruction of their young, and how can we account for their concerted action? These are difficulties not easily overcome. A more rational explanation to me is this, namely, that the extreme dryness of the woods—nearly two months without rain—drove the little frogs to seek for moisture in their spring haunts, where in places a little water would be pretty certain to be found. Here they were holding out, probably hibernating again, as such creatures do in the tropics during the dry season, when the rains came, and here again they sent up their spring chorus of voices, and, for aught I know, once more deposited their eggs. This to me is much more like the ways of Nature with her creatures than is the theory of the frogs' voluntary return to the swamps and pools to start the season over again.

The birds at least show little or no wit when a new problem is presented to them. They have no power of initiative. Instinct runs in a groove, and cannot take a step outside of it. One May day we started a meadowlark from her nest. There were three just hatched young in the nest, and one egg lying on the ground about two inches from the nest. I suspected that this egg was infertile and that the bird had had the sense to throw it out, but on examination it was found to contain a nearly grown bird. The inference was, then, that the egg had been accidentally carried out of the nest some time when the sitting bird had taken a sudden flight, and that she did not have the sense to roll or carry it back to its place.

There is another view of the case which no doubt the sentimental "School of Nature Study" would eagerly adopt: A very severe drouth reigned throughout the land; food was probably scarce, and was becoming scarcer; the bird foresaw her inability to care for four young ones, and so reduced the possible number by ejecting one of the eggs from the nest. This sounds pretty and plausible, and so credits the bird with the wisdom that the public is so fond of believing it possesses. Something like this wisdom often occurs among the hive bees in seasons of scarcity; they will destroy the unhatched queens. But birds have no such foresight, and make no such calculations. In cold, backward seasons, I think, birds lay fewer eggs than when the season is early and warm, but that is not a matter of calculation on their part; it is the result of outward conditions.

A great many observers and nature students at the present time are possessed of the notion that the birds and beasts instruct their young, train them and tutor them, much after the human manner. In the familiar sight of a pair of crows foraging with their young about a field in summer, one of our nature writers sees the old birds giving their young a lesson in flying. She says that the most important thing that the elders had to do was to teach the youngsters how to fly. This they did by circling about the pasture, giving a peculiar call while they were followed by their flock—all but one. This was a bobtailed crow, and he did not obey the word of command. His mother took note of his disobedience and proceeded to discipline him. He stood upon a big stone, and she came down upon him and knocked him off his perch. "He squawked and fluttered his wings to keep from falling, but the blow came so suddenly that he had not time to save himself, and he fell flat on the ground. In a minute he clambered back upon his stone, and I watched him closely. The next time the call came to fly he did not linger, but went with the rest, and so long as I could watch him he never disobeyed again." I should interpret this fact of the old and young crows flying about a field in summer quite differently. The young are fully fledged, and are already strong flyers, when this occurs. They do not leave the nest until they can fly well and need no tutoring. What the writer really saw was what any one may see on the farm in June and July: she saw the parent crows foraging with their young in a field The old birds flew about, followed by their brood, clamorous for the food which their parents found. The bobtailed bird, which had probably met with some accident, did not follow, and the mother returned to feed it; the young crow lifted its wings and flapped them, and in its eagerness probably fell off its perch; then when its parent flew away, it followed.

I think it highly probable that the sense or faculty by which animals find their way home over long stretches of country, and which keeps them from ever being lost as man so often is, is a faculty entirely unlike anything man now possesses. The same may be said of the faculty that guides the birds back a thousand miles or more to their old breeding-haunts. In caged or housed animals I fancy this faculty soon becomes blunted.

President Roosevelt tells in his "Ranch Life" of a horse he owned that ran away two hundred miles across the plains, swimming rivers on the way to its old home. It is very certain, I think, that this homing feat is not accomplished by the aid of either sight or scent, for usually the returning animal seems to follow a comparatively straight line. It is, or seems to be, a consciousness of direction that is as unerring as the magnetic needle. Reason, calculation, and judgment err, but these primary instincts of the animal seem almost infallible.

In Bronx Park in New York a grebe and a loon lived together in an inclosure in which was a large pool of water. The two birds became much attached to each other and were never long separated. One winter day on which the pool was frozen over, except a small opening in one end of it, the grebe dived under the ice and made its way to the far end of the pool, where it remained swimming about aimlessly for some moments. Presently the loon missed its companion, and with an apparent look of concern dived under the ice and joined it at the closed end of the pool. The grebe seemed to be in distress for want of air. Then the loon settled upon the bottom, and with lifted beak sprang up with much force against the ice, piercing it with its dagger-like bill, but not breaking it. Down to the bottom it went again, and again hurled itself up against the ice, this time shattering it and rising to the surface, where the grebe was quick to follow. Now it looked as if the loon had gone under the ice to rescue its friend from a dangerous situation, for had not the grebe soon found the air, it must have perished, and persons who witnessed the incident interpreted it in this way. It is in such cases that we are so apt to read our human motives and emotions into the acts of the lower animals. I do not suppose the loon realized the danger of its companion, nor went under the ice to rescue it. It followed the grebe because it wanted to be with it, or to share in any food that might be detaining it there, and then, finding no air-hole, it proceeded to make one, as it and its ancestors must often have done before. All our northern

64

divers must be more or less acquainted with ice, and must know how to break it. The grebe itself could doubtless have broken the ice had it desired to. The birds and the beasts often show much intelligence, or what looks like intelligence, but, as Hamerton says, "the moment we think of them as *human*, we are lost."

A farmer had a yearling that sucked the cows. To prevent this, he put on the yearling a muzzle set full of sharpened nails. These of course pricked the cows, and they would not stand to be drained of their milk. The next day the farmer saw the yearling rubbing the nails against a rock in order, as he thought, to dull them so they would not prick the cows! How much easier to believe that the beast was simply trying to get rid of the awkward incumbrance upon its nose. What can a calf or a cow know about sharpened nails, and the use of a rock to dull them? This is a kind of outside knowledge—outside of their needs and experiences—that they could not possess.

An Arizona friend of mine lately told me this interesting incident about the gophers that infested his cabin when he was a miner. The gophers ate up his bread. He could not hide it from them or put it beyond their reach. Finally, he bethought him to stick his loaf on the end of a long iron poker that he had, and then stand up the poker in the middle of his floor. Still, when he came back to his cabin, he would find his loaf eaten full of holes. One day, having nothing to do, he concluded to watch and see how the gophers reached the bread, and this was what he saw: The animals climbed up the side of his log cabin, ran along one of the logs to a point opposite the bread, and then sprang out sidewise toward the loaf, which each one struck, but upon which only one seemed able to effect a lodgment. Then this one would cling to the loaf and act as a stop to his fellows when they tried a second time, his body affording them the barrier they required. My friend felt sure that this leader deliberately and consciously aided the others in securing a footing on the loaf. But I read the incident differently. This successful jumper aided his fellows without designing it. The exigencies of the situation compelled him to the course he pursued. Having effected a lodgment upon the impaled loaf, he would of course cling to it when the others jumped so as not to be dislodged, thereby, willy nilly, helping them to secure a foothold. The coöperation was inevitable, and not the result of design.

The power to see straight is the rarest of gifts; to see no more and no less than is actually before you; to be able to detach yourself and see the thing as it actually is, uncolored or unmodified by your own sentiments or prepossessions. In short, to see with your reason as well as with your perceptions, that is to be an observer and to read the book of nature aright.

AN ESSAY FROM
Ways of Nature, 1905

A GEOLOGIST'S WINTER WALK

By John Muir

After reaching Turlock, I sped afoot over the stubble fields and through miles of brown hemizonia and purple erigeron, to Hopeton, conscious of little more than that the town was behind and beneath me, and the mountains above and before me; on through the oaks and chaparral of the foothills to Coulterville; and then ascended the first great mountain step upon which grows the sugar pine. Here I slackened pace, for I drank the spicy, resiny wind, and beneath the arms of this noble tree I felt that I was safely home. Never did pine trees seem so dear. How sweet was their breath and their song, and how grandly they winnowed the sky! I tingled my fingers among their tassels, and rustled my feet among their brown needles and burrs, and was exhilarated and joyful beyond all I can write.

When I reached Yosemite, all the rocks seemed talkative, and more telling and lovable than ever. They are dear friends, and seemed to have warm blood gushing through their granite flesh; and I love them with a love intensified by long and close companionship. After I had bathed in the bright river, sauntered over the meadows, conversed with the domes, and played with the pines, I still felt blurred and weary, as if tainted in some way with the sky of your streets. I determined, therefore, to run out for a while to say my prayers in the higher mountain temples. "The days are sunful," I said, "and, though now winter, no great danger need be encountered, and no sudden storm will block my return, if I am watchful."

67

The morning after this decision, I started up the cañon of Tenaya, caring little about the quantity of bread I carried; for, I thought, a fast and a storm and a difficult cañon were just the medicine I needed. When I passed Mirror Lake, I scarcely noticed it, for I was absorbed in the great Tissiack—her crown a mile away in the hushed azure; her purple granite drapery flowing in soft and graceful folds down to my feet, embroidered gloriously around with deep, shadowy forest. I have gazed on Tissiack a thousand times—in days of solemn storms, and when her form shone divine with the jewelry of winter, or was veiled in living clouds; and I have heard her voice of winds, and snowy, tuneful waters when floods were falling; yet never did her soul reveal itself more impressively than now. I hung about her skirts, lingering timidly, until the higher mountains and glaciers compelled me to push up the cañon.

This cañon is accessible only to mountaineers, and I was anxious to carry my barometer and clinometer through it, to obtain sections and altitudes, so I chose it as the most attractive highway. After I had passed the tall groves that stretch a mile above Mirror Lake, and scrambled around the Tenaya Fall, which is just at the head of the lake groves, I crept through the dense and spiny chaparral that plushes the roots of the mountains here for miles in warm green, and was ascending a precipitous rock front, smoothed by glacial action, when I suddenly fell—for the first time since I touched foot to Sierra rocks. After several somersaults, I became insensible from the shock, and when consciousness returned I found myself wedged among short, stiff bushes, trembling as if cold, not injured in the slightest.

Judging by the sun, I could not have been insensible very long; probably not a minute, possibly an hour; and I could not remember what made me fall, or where I had fallen from; but I saw that if I had rolled a little further, my mountain climbing would have been finished, for just beyond the bushes the cañon wall steepened and I might have fallen to the bottom. "There," said I, addressing my feet, to whose separate skill I had learned to trust night and day on any mountain, "that is what you get by intercourse with stupid town stairs, and dead pavements." I felt degraded and worthless. I had not yet reached the most difficult portion of the cañon, but I determined to guide my humbled body over the most nerve-trying places I could find; for I was now awake, and felt confident that the last of the town fog had been shaken from both head and feet.

I camped at the mouth of a narrow gorge which is cut into the bottom of the main cañon, determined to take earnest exercise next day. No plushy boughs did my ill-behaved bones enjoy that night, nor did my bumped head get a spicy cedar plume pillow mixed with flowers. I slept on a naked boulder, and when I awoke all my nervous trembling was gone.

The gorged portion of the cañon, in which I spent all the next day, is about a mile and a half in length; and I passed the time in tracing the action of the forces that determined this peculiar bottom gorge, which is an abrupt, ragged-walled, narrow-throated cañon, formed in the bottom of the wide-mouthed, smooth, and beveled main cañon. I will not stop now to tell you more; some day you may see it, like a shadowy line, from Cloud's Rest. In high water, the stream occupies all the bottom of the gorge, surging and chafing in glorious power from wall to wall. But the sound of the grinding was low as I entered the gorge, scarcely hoping to be able to pass through its entire length. By cool efforts, along glassy, ice-worn slopes, I reached the upper end in a little over a day, but was compelled to pass the second night in the gorge, and in the moonlight I wrote you this short pencil-letter in my notebook:—

The moon is looking down into the cañon, and how marvelously the great rocks kindle to her light! Every dome, and brow, and swelling boss touched by her white rays, glows as if lighted with snow. I am now only a mile from last night's camp; and have been climbing and sketching all day in this difficult but instructive gorge. It is formed in the bottom of the main cañon, among the roots of Cloud's Rest. It begins at the filled-up lake basin where I camped last night, and ends a few hundred yards above, in another basin of the same kind. The walls everywhere are craggy and vertical, and in some places they overlean. It is only from twenty to sixty feet wide, and not, though black and broken enough, the thin, crooked mouth of some mysterious abyss; but it was eroded, for in many places I saw its solid, seamless floor.

I am sitting on a big stone, against which the stream divides, and goes brawling by in rapids on both sides; half of my rock is white in the light, half in shadow. As I look from the opening jaws of this shadowy gorge, South Dome is immediately in front—high in the stars, her face turned from the moon, with the rest of her body gloriously muffled in waved folds of granite. On the left, sculptured from the main Cloud's Rest ridge, are three magnificent rocks, sisters of the great South Dome. On the right is the massive, moonlit front of Mount Watkins, and between, low down in the furthest distance, is Sentinel Dome, girdled and darkened with forest. In the near foreground Tenaya Creek is singing against boulders that are white with snow and moonbeams. Now look back twenty yards, and you will see a waterfall fair as a spirit; the moonlight just touches it, bringing it into relief against a dark background of shadow. A little to the left, and a dozen steps this side of the fall, a flickering light marks my camp—and a precious camp it is. A huge, glacier-polished slab, falling from the smooth, glossy flank of Cloud's Rest, happened to settle on edge against the wall of the gorge. I did not know that this slab was glacier-polished until I lighted my fire. Judge of my delight. I think it was sent here by an earthquake. It is about twelve feet square. I wish I could take it home for a hearthstone. Beneath this slab is the only place in this torrent-swept gorge where I could find sand sufficient for a bed.

I expected to sleep on the boulders, for I spent most of the afternoon on the slippery wall of the cañon, endeavoring to get around this difficult part of the gorge, and was compelled to hasten down here for water before dark. I shall sleep soundly on this sand; half of it is mica. Here, wonderful to behold, are a few green stems of prickly rubus, and a tiny grass. They are here to meet us. Ay, even here in this darksome gorge, "frightened and tormented" with raging torrents and choking avalanches of snow. Can it be? As if rubus and the grass leaf were not enough of God's tender prattle words of love, which we so much need in these mighty temples of power, yonder in the "benmost bore" are two blessed adiantums. Listen to them! How wholly infused with God is this one big word of love that we call the world! Good-night. Do you see the fire-glow on my ice-smoothed slab, and on my two ferns and the rubus and grass panicles? And do you hear how sweet a sleep- song the fall and cascades are singing?

The water-ground chips and knots that I found fastened between the rocks kept my fire alive all through the night. Next morning I rose nerved and ready for another day of sketching and noting, and any form of climbing. I escaped from the gorge about noon, after accomplishing some of the most delicate feats of mountaineering I ever attempted; and here the cañon is all broadly open again—the floor luxuriantly forested with pine, and spruce, and silver fir, and brown-trunked libocedrus. The walls rise in Yosemite forms, and Tenaya Creek comes down seven hundred feet in a white brush of foam. This is a little Yosemite valley. It is about two thousand feet above the level of the main Yosemite, and about twenty-four hundred below Lake Tenaya.

I found the lake frozen, and the ice was so clear and unruffled that the surrounding mountains and the groves that look down upon it were reflected almost as perfectly as I ever beheld them in the calm evening mirrors of summer. At a little distance, it was difficult to believe the lake frozen at all; and when I walked out on it, cautiously stamping at short intervals to test the strength of the ice, I seemed to walk mysteriously, without adequate faith, on the surface of the water. The ice was so transparent that I could see through it the beautifully wave-rippled, sandy bottom, and the scales of mica glinting back the down-pouring light. When I knelt down with my face close to the ice, through which the sunbeams were pouring, I was delighted to discover myriads of Tyndall's six-rayed water flowers, magnificently colored.

A grand old mountain mansion is this Tenaya region! In the glacier period it was a *mer de glace*, far grander than the *mer de glace* of Switzerland, which is only about half a mile broad. The Tenaya *mer de glace* was not less than two miles broad, late in the glacier epoch, when all the principal dividing crests were bare; and its depth was not less than fifteen hundred feet. Ice streams from Mounts Lyell and Dana, and all the mountains between, and from the nearer Cathedral Peak, flowed hither, welded into one, and worked together. After eroding this Tanaya Lake basin, and all the splendidly sculptured rocks and mountains that surround and adorn it, and the great Tenaya Cañon, with its wealth of all that makes mountains sublime, they were welded with the vast South, Lyell, and Illilouette glaciers on one side, and with those of Hoffman on the other—thus forming a portion of a yet grander *mer de glace* in Yosemite Valley.

I reached the Tenaya Cañon, on my way home, by coming in from the northeast, rambling down over the shoulders of Mount Watkins, touching bottom a mile above Mirror Lake. From thence home was but a saunter in the moonlight.

After resting one day, and the weather continuing calm, I ran up over the left shoulder of South Dome and down in front of its grand split face to make some measurements, completed my work, climbed to the right shoulder, struck off along the ridge for Cloud's Rest, and reached the topmost heave of her sunny wave in ample time to see the sunset.

Cloud's Rest is a thousand feet higher than Tissiack. It is a wavelike crest upon a ridge, which begins at Yosemite with Tissiack, and runs continuously eastward to the thicket of peaks and crests around Lake Tenaya. This lofty granite wall is bent this way and that by the restless and weariless action of glaciers just as if it had been made of dough. But the grand circumference of mountains and forests are coming from far and near, densing into one close assemblage; for the sun, their god and father, with love ineffable, is glowing a sunset farewell. Not one of all the assembled rocks or trees seemed remote. How impressively their faces shone with responsive love!

I ran home in the moonlight with firm strides; for the sun-love made me strong. Down through the junipers; down through the firs; now in jet shadows, now in white light; over sandy moraines and bare, clanking rocks; past the huge ghost of South Dome rising weird through the firs; past the glorious fall of Nevada, the groves of Illilouette; through the pines of the valley; beneath the bright crystal sky blazing with stars. All of this mountain wealth in one day!—one of the rich ripe days that enlarge one's life; so much of the sun upon one side of it, so much of the moon and stars on the other.

A Chapter from
Steep Trails, 1918

ON THE
INDIFFERENCE OF NATURE

By Alfred George Gardiner

There has never, I suppose, been a time when the moon had such a vogue as during the past ten days. For centuries, for thousands of years, for I know not what uncounted ages, she has been sailing the sky, "clustered around with all her starry fays." She has seen this tragi-comedy of man since the beginning, and I daresay will outlive its end. What she thinks of it all we shall never know. Perhaps she laughs at it, perhaps she weeps over it, perhaps she does both in turns, as you and I do. Perhaps she is only indifferent. Yes, I suppose she is indifferent, for she holds up her lamp for the just and the unjust and lights the assassin's way as readily as the lover's and the shepherd's.

But in all her timeless journeyings around this flying ball to which we cling with our feet she has never been a subject of such painful concern as now. Love-sick poets have sung of her, and learned men have studied her countenance and made maps of her hills and her valleys, and children have been lulled to sleep with legends of the old man in the moon and the old woman eternally gathering her eternal sticks. But for most of us she had no more serious import than a Chinese lantern hung on a Christmas tree to please the children.

And suddenly she has become the most sensational fact of our lives. From the King in his palace to the pauper in his workhouse we have all been talking of the moon, and watching the moon and studying the phases of the moon. There are seven millions of Londoners who know more about the moon to-day than they ever dreamed there was to be known, or than they ever dreamed that they would want to know. John Bright once said that the only virtue of war was that it taught people geography, but even he did not think of the geography of the moon and of the firmament. But in the intense school of these days we are learning about everything in heaven above and in the earth beneath and in the waters under the earth. Count Zeppelin taught us about the stars, and now Herr von Gotha is giving us a lesson on the moon. We are not so grateful as we might be.

But the main lesson we are all learning, I think, is that Nature does not take sides in our affairs. We all like to think that she does take sides—that is, our side—that a special providence watches over us, and that invisible powers will see us through. It is a common weakness. The preposterous Kaiser exhibits it in its most grotesque assumption. He does really believe—or did, for dreadful doubts must be invading the armour-plated vanity of this jerry-built Cæsar—that God and Nature are his Imperial agents.

And in a less degree most of us, in times of stress, pin our faith to some special providence. We are so important to ourselves that we cannot conceive that we are unimportant to whatever powers there be. Others may fall, but we have charmed lives. Our cause must prevail because, being ours, it is beyond mortal challenge. A distinguished General was telling me not long ago of an incident in the second battle of Ypres. He stood with another General, since killed, watching the battle at its most critical phase. They saw the British line yield, and the Germans advance, and all seemed over. My friend put up his glasses with the gesture of one who knew the worst had come. His companion turned to him and said, "God will never allow those — to win." It was an odd expression of faith, but it represents the conviction latent in most of us that we can count on invisible allies who, like the goddess in Homer, will intervene if we are in straits, and fling a cloud between us and the foe.

This reliance on the supernatural is one of the sources of

power in men of primitive and intense faith. Cromwell was a practical mystic and never forgot to keep his powder dry, but he saw the hand of the Lord visibly at work for his cause on the winds and the tempest, and that conviction added a fervour to his terrible sword. In his letter to Speaker Lenthall on the battle of Dunbar he tells how in marching from Musselburgh to Haddington the enemy fell upon "the rear-forlorn of our horse" and "had like to have engaged our rear brigade of horse with their whole army—*had not the Lord by His Providence put a cloud over the moon*, hereby giving us opportunity to draw off those horse to the rest of our army."

In the same way Elizabethan England witnessed God Himself in the tempest that scattered the Armada, and a hundred years later the people saw the same Divine sanction in the winds that brought William Prince of Orange to our shores and drove his pursuers away. "The weather had indeed served the Protestant cause so well," says Macaulay, "that some men of more piety than judgment fully believed the ordinary laws of nature to have been suspended for the preservation of the liberty and religion of England. Exactly a hundred years before, they said, the Armada, invincible by man, had been scattered by the wrath of God. Civil freedom and divine truth were again in jeopardy; and again the obedient elements had fought for the good cause. The wind had blown strong from the east while the Prince wished to sail down the Channel, had turned to the south when he wished to enter Torbay, had sunk to a calm during the disembarkation, and, as soon as the disembarkation was completed, had risen to a storm and had met the pursuers in the face."

If we saw such a sequence of winds blowing for our cause, we should, in spite of Macaulay, allow our piety to have the better of our judgment. Indeed, there have been those who in the absence of more solid evidence have accepted the Angels of Mons with as touching and unquestioning a faith as they accepted the legend of the Army of Russians from Archangel. Perhaps it is not "piety" so much as anxiety that accounts for this credulity. In its more degraded form it is responsible for such phenomena as the revival of fortune-telling and the emergence of the Prophet Bottomley. In its more reputable expression it springs from the conviction of the justice of our cause, of the dominion of the spiritual over the material and of the witness of that dominion in the operations of Nature.

Then comes this wonderful harvest moon with its clear sky and its still air to light our enemies to their villainous work and to remind us that, however virtuous our cause, Nature is not concerned about us. She is indifferent whether we win or lose. She is not against us, but she is not for us. Sometimes she helps the enemy, and sometimes she helps us. She blew a snowstorm in the face of the Germans on the most critical day of Verdun, and helped to defeat that great adventure. In August last she came out on the side of the enemy. She rained and blew ceaselessly, and disarranged our plans in Flanders, so that the attack on which so much depended was driven perilously late into the year. And even the brilliant moon and the cloudless nights that have been so disturbing to us in London speak the same language of Nature's impartiality. They serve the enemy here, but they are serving us far more just across the sea, where every bright day and moonlit night snatched from the mud and rain of the coming winter is of priceless value to our Army. That consideration should enable us to bear our affliction with fortitude as we crowd the "tubes" or listen to the roar of the guns from under the domestic table.

But we must admit, on the evidence, that Nature does not care twopence who wins, and is as unconcerned about our affairs as we are about the affairs of a nest of ants that we tread on without knowing that we have trodden on it. She is beyond good and evil. She has no morals and is indifferent about justice and what men call right and wrong. She blasts the wise and leaves the foolish to flourish.

Nature, with equal mind
Sees all her sons at play;
Sees man control the wind,
The wind sweep man away;
Allows the proudly riding and the found'ring barque.

It is a chill, but a chastening thought. It leaves us with a sense of loneliness, but it brings with it, also, a sense of power, the power of the unconquerable human spirit, self-dependent and self-reliant, reaching out to ideals beyond itself, beyond its highest hope of attainment, broken on the wheel of intractable things, but still stumbling forward by its half-lights in search of some Land of Promise that always skips just beyond the horizon.

Happily the moon is skipping beyond the horizon too. Frankly, we have seen enough of her face to last us for a long time. When she comes out again let her clothe herself in good fat clouds and bring the winds in her train. We do not like to think of her as a mere flunkey of the Kaiser and the torch-bearer of his assassins.

An Essay from
Leaves in the Wind, 1919

HOW TO OBSERVE NATURE

By Elizabeth Brightwen

THERE is all the difference between taking a walk simply for exercise, for some special errand, or to enjoy conversation with one's friends, and the sort of quiet observant stroll I am going to ask my kind readers to take with me to-day.

This beautiful world is full of wonders of every kind, full of evidences of the Great Creator's wisdom and skill in adapting each created thing to its special purpose. The whole realm of nature is meant, I believe, to *speak to us*, to teach us lessons in parables—to lead our hearts upward to God who made us and fitted us also for our special place in creation.

In the nineteenth Psalm David speaks of the two great books God has given us for our instruction. In the first six verses he speaks of the teachings of the book of nature and the rest of the Psalm deals with the written Word of God.

We acknowledge and read the Scriptures as the book which reveals the will of God and His wondrous works for the welfare of mankind, but how many fail to give any time or thought to reading the book of nature! Thousands may travel and admire beautiful scenery, and derive a certain amount of pleasure from nature, just glancing at each object, but really observing nothing, and thus failing to learn any of the lessons this world's beauty is intended to teach, they might almost as well have stayed at home save for the benefit of fresh air and change of scene. The habit of minute and careful observation is seldom taught in childhood, and is not very likely to be gained in later life when the mind is filled with other things. Yet if natural objects are presented attractively to the young, how quickly they are interested! Question after question is asked, and unconsciously a vast amount of information may be conveyed to an intelligent child's mind by a simple, happy little chat about some bird or insect. This is *admirably* shown in a chapter on Education in the Life of Mrs. Sewell. I would strongly urge every mother to read and follow the advice there given.

We will now start for our garden walk. We have not taken many steps before we are led to pause and inquire why there should be little patches of grey-looking mud in the small angles of the brickwork of the house. Opening one of the patches with a penknife we find a hollow cell, and in it some green caterpillars just alive but not able to crawl. Now I see that the cell is the work of one of the solitary mason wasps; she brings the material, forms the cell, and when nearly finished lays her egg at the bottom and provides these half-killed caterpillars as food for the young grub when it is hatched, and by the time they are eaten the grub becomes a pupa and then hatches into a young wasp to begin life on its own account. One day I saw a bee go into a hole in the brickwork of the house, and getting my net I waited to capture it; after about five minutes the bee came out and flew into the net. It proved to be a solitary mason bee, and was doubtless forming a place to lay its egg, only, unlike the wasp, she would give the young grub pollen from the stamens of flowers to feed upon instead of green caterpillars. I remember seeing a mass of clay which had been formed into a wasp's nest by one of the solitary species, under the flap of a pembroke table in an unused room. A maid in dusting lifted up the flap, and down fell a quantity of fine, dry mud with young grubs in it which would soon have hatched into wasps, and revealed their rather strange nesting-place. I have in my collection a very interesting hornet's nest, which was being constructed in the hollow of an old tree. I happened to notice a hornet fly into the opening, and, looking in, there was a small beginning of a nest. It hung from a kind of stalk and consisted of only eight cells, each having an egg at the bottom. I captured the two hornets, and though I watched for a long time no others ever came, so I imagine they were the founders of what would have been a colony in due time.

But we have been kept a long time engaged with these mason wasps. Let us start for our walk. As we take our way through the garden we cannot help noticing the happy songs of the different birds, all in full activity preparing their nests, carolling to their mates or seeking food for the little ones. There is a loud tapping noise as we pass an old fir-tree, but no bird is to be seen, so we go round to the other side and trace the noise to a small hole near which a quantity of congealed turpentine shows that the bark has been pierced by a woodpecker and the sap is oozing out. I rap outside the hole and in a minute the grey head of a nuthatch appears. He is evidently chiselling out a "highly desirable residence" for his summer quarters in this cosy nook, and the hole being so small he will not need to get clay to reduce the size of the opening and plaster in his mate, which is said to be the curious habit of this bird. Do you see that hole about forty feet up the stem of the beech opposite? A nuthatch built there six years ago; I often watched him going in and out, and heard his peculiar cry as he brought food for his mate and her young ones. Next year that lodging was taken by a starling, who reared a brood there. The year after the nuthatch had it, and then a jackdaw built there; and each year I always feel interested to see who the lodgers are going to be.

When I was rearing the wild ducks already described, a weasel used often to be prowling near the coop, and when frightened retreated in this direction. It happened one day I was walking softly on the grass and saw the weasel playing and frisking at the root of that young tree; one seldom has such an opportunity of seeing it, for it is very shy and has wonderfully quick hearing. It was seeking about in the grass, leaping here and there, snuffing the wind, with its snake-like, wicked-looking head raised to see over the grass stems, and thus at last it caught sight of me, and in a second it darted into the hole you see there, and I thus learnt where he lived, but I have not been able to trace his history any further at present.

Did you see that snake? We have many of them on the common, and they often cross my path in the garden. Happily there are not many of the venomous kind: they are smaller than this one, and have a V-shaped mark on the head. One day in August I was sitting by the open French window in the drawing-room when one of these harmless snakes came close to me, looked up at me, putting its quivering little tongue in and out. I suppose it decided that I could be trusted, for it glided in and coiled itself round upon my dress skirt and seemed to go to sleep. I let it stay a good while, but fearing some one might be frightened at seeing it there, I reached my parasol and with the hooked handle softly took up the snake and laid it on the grass-plat outside thinking it would go away—but no, it only turned round and came back and coiled itself up in the same place. I found it did not mind being touched, so I stroked it and made it creep all its length through my hand—not a very pleasant sensation, but a curious experience rarely to be met with. When the cold, clammy creature had passed out of my hand it threw out a most disgusting odour, of which I had often read. I imagine it was offended at my touching it and did this in self-defence. I had at last to carry it a long distance to ensure it should not return to the room again.

Some years ago I was witness to the mode in which a snake pursues its victim. A large frog leaped upon the gravel walk before the windows, crying piteously like a child and taking rapid leaps; a moment after a large snake appeared swiftly pursuing the frog. At last it reached it, and gave it a bite which broke its back, and then, being alarmed, it darted away amongst some rock-work, leaving the frog in a dying state.

This bank we are passing is a favourite winter retreat for female humble bees. Early in the autumn they begin to scoop out a little tunnel in this grassy slope, and when it is deep enough to protect them from the frost they retire into it, and pushing up the earth behind them close up the entrance of the hole, and there lie dormant until the warmth of spring tempts them to come out. Then they may be found in great numbers on the early sallow, and other tree-blossoms, recruiting their strength, while they seek a place in some hedge-bank wherein to found a new colony.

The Carder bee forms its nest on the ground and makes a roof of interwoven moss, from which it takes its name. I once gathered the moss from such a nest by chance and saw the little mass of cells with honey in them. I went away, meaning to examine it more closely on my return, but a crow in the apple-tree overhead chanced to spy the nest and made off with it in his beak before I could rescue the honey store of the poor little bees I had so unwittingly injured.

That old tree-stump is being gradually carried away by wasps. The wood is just sufficiently decayed to afford the material of which they make their nests. You see there are several wasps busily rasping pieces of the rotten wood into convenient-sized morsels, which they can carry to the nest, there to be masticated into the papery layers of which the outer walls of the nest are formed. This walk used to have a row of grand old silver firs of great height, but each winter some of them have been blown down till only a few are left.

Some years since I noticed at the root of one of them a pile of fine sawdust more than a foot high, and found that some wood wasps were busily engaged in excavating the interior of the tree and forming tunnels in which to lay their eggs. I watched them for half an hour and found that every half-minute a wasp went in at the aperture carrying a blue-bottle or some kind of fly in its mandibles. Next day I took a friend to see the wasps, and while watching them the wind caused the immense tree-stem to sway to and fro from its base as if in the act of falling, and on examination we found it was only held in its place by a small portion of root, and though the branches were green, it must have been hollow and dead inside, which appears to be the way in which silver firs decay, and the wasps had found it out and made a delightful home in the rotten wood. With some difficulty the great tree was safely taken down, and then it was a most curious sight to see the endless chambers and galleries made in the stem, all tenanted by young wasp-grubs and half-dead flies; and all the summer they were being hatched in countless numbers. The view over our common is lovely from this point; it is golden with rich yellow gorse, giving cover to innumerable rabbits, which find their way into our garden in spite of wire fences and all that the gardener can do to keep them out. One clever little mother rabbit made her burrow deep down in a heap of sawdust close to the stable. My coachman put his arm down to the bottom of the hole and brought out a little grey furred creature, kicking and screaming with wonderful vigour in spite of its tender years. The nest was allowed to remain, and in a few days the mother removed her brood to a hole at the root of a bushy stone-pine, where the little ones frisked in and out and looked so pretty that I was won over to allow them to stay, and, by netting round the tree, we formed a miniature warren for the young family; but I fear that in course of time we may bitterly repent this step, and the numbers may increase to such an extent that pinks and lobelia may become things of the past and the rabbit warren may have to be abolished.

A fox is sometimes seen and hunted in these parts. One surprised me by leaping upon the window-sill and looking into the drawing-room. At first I could not think what it was. It had been dug out of its hole; its fur was muddy and torn, its eyes piteous in their expression, and when it ran slowly on I saw it was very lame. I ran to the window to let it in, but though it leaped up to each window in succession, they all happened to be shut, and I was quite grieved to think the poor, weary creature could find no shelter. I am no admirer of field-sports. I think they give rise to the utmost cruelty to the creatures hunted and shot, to the horses and dogs employed; and to witness torture inflicted on unoffending animals cannot but have a debasing effect on the human mind. When once any one has seen the anguish of a deer, a fox, or hare, at the end of the race, there can be no question about the cruelty of the proceeding, and to one who loves every created thing as I do, it gives the keenest pain to know how much suffering of this kind goes on during the hunting season.[1]

There goes a cuckoo, with quite a flight of small birds pursuing him wherever he goes.

Small birds seem to have an intense hatred of jays and cuckoos, and will often fly at them in the nesting season, giving them no peace till they drive them out of the garden, knowing full well that their own broods are often devoured by the jay, and that the cuckoo has designs upon the nests.

Although we are some distance from home, I can show you one of my own bees on this furze blossom. I have a hive of Swiss, or Ligurian bees, which are said to be in some respects superior to the English species. The honey is of excellent flavour, and the first year I had far more honey from the Ligurian hive. I do not think any other hives of Ligurians are kept within five miles, and, as you see, they have a band of bright yellow on the abdomen. I can always tell my own bees when I meet with

---

1   I cannot resist quoting and strongly endorsing the following lament by Mr. H. Stacy Marks, R.A., as to the way in which birds are too frequently treated by the public at large: "Many people regarding birds in but three aspects—as things to be either eaten, shot, or worn. . . . No natural history of a bird is complete without recording where the last specimen was shot; and should a rare bird visit our shores, the hospitality which we accord to the foreign refugee is denied, and it is bound to be the victim of powder and shot. The fashion of wearing birds or their plumage as part of ladies' attire, threatens to exterminate many beautiful species, such as the humming-birds of South America, the glossy starlings of Africa, and the glorious Impeyan pheasant of the Himalayas, with many other species."

them in my walks on the common or in the lanes. I had a rather trying adventure with these bees last May. One Sunday evening we were just starting for church, about half-past six, when my little niece ran in exclaiming that there was a great bunch of bees hanging on a branch near the hives. I knew what had happened—my very irreverent bees had swarmed on this quiet Sunday evening, and they must be hived if possible.

My bonnet was soon off and the bee-dress put on, and in five minutes the bees were secured and settled into a hive. We went to church and were not even late, but—during the first prayer I heard ominous sounds of a furious bee under my dress; it was, fortunately, a partly transparent material, and glancing furtively about I saw my little friend under the skirt going up and down with an angry biz-z-z. Only the pocket-hole could release him, so I held that safely in my hand all through the service, lest the congregation might suffer the wrath of a furious bee, which in truth is no light matter, for in blind fury it will rush at the first person it meets and leave its sting in the face or hand. Happily I succeeded in bringing the bee home again, and resolved to avoid hiving swarms before church-time in future.

You see under the drooping boughs of the fir-tree yonder an old stone basin, well known to all the birds in the neighbourhood, for there they always find a supply of fresh water and food of various kinds to suit all tastes. As it is opposite the dining-room window, it is very interesting to see a tame jay and sundry squirrels enjoying the acorns which were collected for them last autumn and stored up so as to keep the basin well supplied all through the winter and spring, until other food should be plentiful. Finches, robins, and sparrows find wheat and crumbs to their taste, and take their daily bath not without some squabbling as to who shall have it first—a difficulty which is sometimes settled by a portly blackbird appearing on the scene and scattering the smaller folk, whilst he takes his early tubbing and sends up showers of spray in the process. Very pretty are the scenes on that same stone basin when in early summer a mother bird brings her little tribe of downy, chirping babes, and feeds each little gaping mouth with some suitable morsels from the store she finds there.

A sheaf of corn in winter is also a great boon to the starved-out birdies, when snow has long deprived them of their natural food, and the water supply has to be often renewed on freezing days, for many a bird dies in winter from lack of water, all its usual supplies being frozen. The tameness of birds in severe weather is a touching sign of their distress, and a mute appeal to us to help them.

> "The fowls of heaven
> Tam'd by the cruel season, crowd around
> The winnowing store, and claim the little boon
> Which Providence assigns them."

It is pleasant to think that they seldom appeal in vain. "Crumbs for the birds" are scattered by kindly little hands everywhere in winter, and in many a house a pet sonsie little robin is a cherished visitor, always welcome to his small share of the good things of this life.

Our ramble might be indefinitely prolonged and still be full of interest and instruction, but in these simple remarks enough has been shown, I trust, to lead many to *think* and *observe* closely every, even the minutest, thing that catches their attention whilst out for a ramble in lanes and fields, even a microscopic moss upon an old wall has been suggestive of many lovely thoughts, with which I will conclude our ramble and this chapter.

AN CHAPTER FROM
*Wild Nature Won by Kindness.*1890

BLOODY-NOSE
OF SUNSHINE HILL:
HEMARIS THYSBE

By Gene Stratton-Porter

John Brown lives a mile north of our village, in the little hamlet of Ceylon. Like his illustrious predecessor of the same name he is willing to do something for other people. Mr. Brown owns a large farm, that for a long distance borders the Wabash River where it is at its best, and always the cameras and I have the freedom of his premises.

On the east side of the village, about half its length, swings a big gate, that opens into a long country lane. It leads between fields of wheat and corn to a stretch of woods pasture, lying on a hillside, that ends at the river. This covers many acres, most of the trees have been cut; the land rises gradually to a crest, that is crowned by a straggling old snake fence, velvety black in places, grey with lint in others, and liberally decorated its entire length with lichens, in every shade of grey and green. Its corners are filled with wild flowers, ferns, gooseberries, raspberries, black and red haw, papaw, wild grapevines, and trees of all varieties. Across the fence a sumac covered embankment falls precipitately to the Wabash, where it sweeps around a great curve at Horseshoe Bend. The bed is stone and gravel, the water flows shallow and pure in the sunlight, and mallows and willows fringe the banks.

Beside this stretch of river most of one summer was spent, because there were two broods of cardinals, whose acquaintance I was cultivating, raised in those sumacs. The place was very secluded, as the water was not deep enough for fishing or swimming. On days when the cardinals were contrary, or to do the birds justice, when they had experiences with an owl the previous night, or with a hawk in the morning, and were restless or unduly excited, much grist for my camera could be found on the river banks.

These were the most beautiful anywhere in my locality. The hum of busy life was incessant. From the top twig of the giant sycamore in Rainbow Bottom, the father of the cardinal flock hourly challenged all creation to contest his right to one particular sumac. The cardinals were the attraction there; across the fence where the hill sloped the length of the pasture to the lane, lures were many and imperative. Despite a few large trees, compelling right to life by their majesty, that hillside was open pasture, where the sunshine streamed all day long. Wild roses clambered over stumps of fallen monarchs, and scrub oak sheltered resting sheep. As it swept to the crest, the hillside was thickly dotted with mullein, its pale yellow-green leaves spreading over the grass, and its spiral of canary-coloured bloom stiffly upstanding. There were thistles, the big, rank, richly growing, kind, that browsing cattle and sheep circled widely.

Very beautiful were these frosted thistles, with their large, widespreading base leaves, each spine needle-tipped, their uplifted heads of delicate purple bloom, and their floating globes of silken down, with a seed in their hearts. No wonder artists have painted them, decorators conventionalized them; even potters could not pass by their artistic merit, for I remembered that in a china closet at home there were Belleck cups moulded in the shape of a thistle head.

Experience had taught me how the appreciate this plant. There was a chewink in the Stanley woods, that brought off a brood of four, under the safe shelter of a rank thistle leaf, in the midst of trampling herds of cattle driven wild by flies. There was a ground sparrow near the Hale sand pit, covered by a base leaf of another thistle, and beneath a third on Bob's lease, I had made a study of an exquisite nest. Protection from the rank leaves was not all the birds sought of these plants, for goldfinches were darting around inviting all creation to "See me?" as they gathered the silken down for nest lining. Over the sweetly perfumed purple heads, the humming-birds held high carnival on Sunshine Hillside all the day. The honey and bumble bees fled at the birds' approach, but what were these others, numerous everywhere, that clung to the blooms, greedily thrusting their red noses between the petals, and giving place to nothing else?

For days as I passed among them, I thought them huge bees. The bright colouring of their golden olive-green, and red-wine striped bodies had attracted me in passing. Then one of them approached a thistle head opposite me in such a way its antennae and the long tongue it thrust into the bloom could be seen. That proved it was not a bee, and punishment did not await any one who touched it.

There were so many that with one sweep of the net two were captured. They were examined to my satisfaction and astonishment. They were moths! Truly moths, feeding in the brilliant sunshine all the day; bearing a degree of light and heat I never had known any other moth to endure. Talk about exquisite creatures! These little day moths, not much larger than the largest bumble bees, had some of their gaudiest competitors of moonlight and darkness outdone.

The head was small and pointed, with big eyes, a long tongue, clubbed antennae, and a blood-red nose. The thorax above was covered with long, silky, olive-green hair; the top of the abdomen had half an inch band of warm tan colour, then a quarter of an inch band of velvety red wine, then a band nearer the olive of the shoulders. The males had claspers covered with small red-wine feathers tan tipped. The thorax was cream-coloured below and the under side of the abdomen red wine crossed with cream-coloured lines at each segment.

The front wings had the usual long, silky hairs. They were of olive-green shading into red, at the base, the costa was red, and an escalloped band of red bordered them. The intervening space was transparent like thinnest isinglass, and crossed with fine red veins. The back wings were the same, only the hairs at the base were lighter red, and the band at the edge deeper in colour.

The head of the male seemed sharper, the shoulders stronger olive, the wings more pointed at the apex, where the female's were a little rounded. The top of the abdomen had the middle band of such strong red that it threw the same colour over the bands above and below it; giving to the whole moth a strong red appearance when on wing. They, were so fascinating the birds were forgotten, and the hillside hunted for them until a pair were secured to carry home for identification, before the whistle of the cardinal from Rainbow Bottom rang so sharply that I remembered this was the day I had hoped to secure his likeness; and here I was allowing a little red-nosed moth so to thrust itself upon my attention, that my cameras were not even set up and focused on the sumac.

This tiny sunshine moth, Hemaris Thysbe, was easy of identification, and its whole life history before me on the hillside. I was too busy with the birds to raise many caterpillars, so reference to several books taught me that they all agreed on the main points of Hemaris history.

Hemaris means 'bloody nose.' 'Bloody nose' on account of the red first noticed on the face, though some writers called them 'Clear wings,' because of the transparent spaces on the wings. Certainly 'clear wings' is a most appropriate and poetic name for this moth. Fastidious people will undoubtedly prefer it for common usage. For myself, I always think of the delicate, gaudy little creature, greedily thrusting its blood-red nose into the purple thistle blooms; so to my thought it returns as 'bloody nose.'

The pairs mate early after emerging, and lay about two hundred small eggs to the female, from which the caterpillars soon hatch, and begin their succession of moults. One writer gave black haw and snowball as their favourite foods, and the length of the caterpillar when full grown nearly two inches. They are either a light brown with yellow markings, or green with yellow; all of them have white granules on the body, and a blue-black horn with a yellow base. They spin among the leaves on the ground, and the pupa, while small, is shaped like Regalis, except that it has a sharper point at each end, and more prominent wing shields. It has no raised tongue case, although it belongs to the family of 'long tongues.'

On learning all I could acquire by experience with these moths, and what the books had to teach, I became their warm admirer. One sunny morning climbing the hill on the way to the cardinals, with fresh plates in my cameras, and high hopes in my heart, I passed an unsually large fine thistle, with half a dozen Thysbe moths fluttering over it as if nearly crazed with fragrance, or honey they were sipping.

"Come here! Come here! Come here!" intoned the cardinal, from the sycamore of Rainbow Bottom.

"Just you wait a second, old fellow!" I heard myself answering. Scarcely realizing what I was doing, the tripod was set up, the best camera taken out, and focused on that thistle head. The moths paid no attention to bees, butterflies, or humming-birds visiting the thistle, but this was too formidable, and by the time the choicest heads were in focus, all the little red fellows had darted to another plant. If the camera was moved there, they would change again, so I sat in the shade of a clump of papaws to wait and see if they would not grow accustomed to it.

They kept me longer than I had expected, and the chances are I would have answered the cardinal's call, and gone to the river, had it not been for the interest found in watching a beautiful grey squirrel that homed in an ivy-covered stump in the pasture. He seemed to have much business on the fence at the hilltop, and raced back and forth to it repeatedly. He carried something, I could not always tell what, but at times it was green haws. Once he came with no food, and at such a headlong run that he almost turned somersaults as he scampered up the tree.

For a long time he was quiet, then he cautiously peeped out. After a while he ventured to the ground, raced to a dead stump, and sitting on it, barked and scolded with all his might. Then he darted home again. When he had repeated this performance several times, the idea became apparent. There was some danger to be defied in Rainbow Bottom, but not a sound must be made from his home. The bark of a dog hurried me to the fence in time to see some hunters passing in the bottom, but I thanked mercy they were on the opposite side of the river and it was not probable they would wade, so my birds would not be disturbed. When the squirrel felt that he must bark and chatter, or burst with tense emotions, he discreetly left his mate and nest. I did some serious thinking on the 'instinct' question. He might choose a hollow log for his home by instinct, or eat certain foods because hunger urged him, but could instinct teach him not to make a sound where his young family lay? Without a doubt, for this same reason, the cardinal sang from every tree and bush around Horseshoe Bend, save the sumac where his mate hovered their young.

The matter presented itself in this way. The squirrel has feet, and he runs with them. He has teeth, and he eats with them. He has lungs, and he breathes with them. Every organ of his interior has its purpose, and is used to fulfil it. His big, prominent eyes come from long residence in dark hollows. His bushy tail helps him in long jumps from tree to tree. Every part of his anatomy is created, designed and used to serve some purpose, save only his brain, the most complex and complicated part of him. Its only use and purpose is to form one small 'tidbit' for the palate of the epicure! Like Sir Francis, who preached a sermon to the birds, I found me delivering myself of a lecture to the squirrels, birds, and moths of Sunshine Hill. The final summing up was, that the squirrel used his feet, teeth, eyes and tail; that could be seen easily, and by his actions it could be seen just as clearly that he used his brain also.

There was not a Thysbe in front of the lens, so picking up a long cudgel I always carry afield, and going quietly to surrounding thistles, I jarred them lightly with it, and began rounding up the Hemaris family in the direction of the camera. The trick was a complete success. Soon I had an exposure on two. After they had faced the camera once, and experienced no injury, like the birds, they accepted it as part of the landscape. The work was so fascinating, and the pictures on the ground glass so worth while, that before I realized what I was doing, half a dozen large plates were gone, and for this reason, work with the cardinals that day ended at noon. This is why I feel that at times in bird work the moths literally 'thrust themselves' upon me.

A CHAPTER FROM
Moths of the Limberlost,
A book about Limberlost Cabin, 1912

ON GOING A JOURNEY

By William Hazlitt

One of the pleasantest things in the world is going a journey; but I like to go by myself. I can enjoy society in a room; but out of doors nature is company enough for me. I am then never less alone than when alone.

"The fields his study, nature was his book."

I cannot see the wit of walking and talking at the same time. When I am in the country, I wish to vegetate like the country. I am not for criticising hedgerows and black cattle. I go out of the town in order to forget the town and all that is in it. There are those who for this purpose go to watering-places, and carry the metropolis with them. I like more elbow-room, and fewer encumbrances. I like solitude, when I give myself up to it, for the sake of solitude; nor do I ask for

"A friend in my retreat,
Whom I may whisper solitude is sweet."

The soul of a journey is liberty, perfect liberty, to think, feel, do, just as one pleases. We go a journey chiefly to be free of all impediments and of all inconveniences; to leave ourselves behind, much more to get rid of others. It is because I want a little breathing-space to muse on indifferent matters, where Contemplation

"May plume her feathers, and let grow her wings
That in the various bustle of resort
Were all too ruffled, and sometimes impair'd,"

that I absent myself from the town for a while without feeling at a loss the moment I am left by myself. Instead of a friend in a post-chaise or in a Tilbury, to exchange good things with and vary the same stale topics over again, for once let me have a truce with impertinence. Give me the clear blue sky over my head and the green turf beneath my feet, a winding road before me, and a three hours' march to dinner—and then to thinking! It is hard if I cannot start some game on these lone heaths. I laugh, I run, I leap, I sing for joy. From the point of yonder rolling cloud, I plunge into my past being, and revel there, as the sunburnt Indian plunges headlong into the wave that wafts him to his native shore. Then long-forgotten things, like "sunken wrack and sumless treasuries," burst upon my eager sight, and I begin to feel, think, and be myself again. Instead of an awkward silence, broken by attempts at wit or dull commonplaces, mine is that undisturbed silence of the heart which alone is perfect eloquence.

No one likes puns, alliterations, antitheses, argument, and analysis better than I do; but I sometimes had rather be without them. "Leave, oh, leave me to my repose!" I have just now other business in hand, which would seem idle to you; but is with me "very stuff o' the conscience." Is not this wild rose sweet without a comment? Does not this daisy leap to my heart set in its coat of emerald? Yet if I were to explain to you the circumstance that has so endeared it to me, you would only smile. Had I not better, then, keep it to myself, and let it serve me to brood over, from here to yonder craggy point, and from thence onward to the far-distant horizon? I should be but bad company all that way, and therefore prefer being alone.

I have heard it said that you may, when the moody fit comes on, walk or ride on by yourself, and indulge your reveries. But this looks like a breach of manners, a neglect of others, and you are thinking all the time that you ought to rejoin your party. "Out upon such half-faced fellowship!" say I. I like to be either entirely to myself, or entirely at the disposal of others; to talk or be silent, to walk or sit still, to be sociable or solitary. I was pleased with an observation of Mr Cobbett's, that "he thought it a bad French custom to drink our wine with our meals, and that an Englishman ought to do only one thing at a time." So I cannot talk and think, or indulge in melancholy musing and lively conversation, by fits and starts. "Let me have a companion of my way," says Sterne, "were it but to remark how the shadows lengthen as the sun declines." It is beautifully said; but, in my opinion, this continual comparing of notes interferes with the involuntary impression of things upon the mind, and hurts the sentiment.

If you only hint what you feel in a kind of dumb show, it is insipid; if you have to explain it, it is making a toil of a pleasure. You cannot read the book of nature without being perpetually put to the trouble of translating it for the benefit of others. I am for this synthetical method on a journey in preference to the analytical. I am content to lay in a stock of ideas then, and to examine and anatomise them afterwards. I want to see my vague notions float like the down of the thistle before the breeze, and not to have them entangled in the briars and thorns of controversy. For once, I like to have it all my own way; and this is impossible unless you are alone, or in such company as I do not covet. I have no objection to argue a point with anyone for twenty miles of measured road, but not for pleasure. If you remark the scent of a beanfield crossing the road, perhaps your fellow-traveller has no smell. If you point to a distant object, perhaps he is short-sighted, and has to take out his glass to look at it. There is a feeling in the air, a tone in the colour of a cloud, which hits your fancy, but the effect of which you are unable to account for. There is then no sympathy, but an uneasy craving after it, and a dissatisfaction which pursues you on the way, and in the end probably produces ill-humour.

Now, I never quarrel with myself, and take all my own conclusions for granted till I find it necessary to defend them against objections. It is not merely that you may not be of accord on the objects and circumstances that present themselves before you—these may recall a number of objects, and lead to associations too delicate and refined to be possibly communicated to others. Yet these I love to cherish, and sometimes still fondly clutch them, when I can escape from the throng to do so. To give way to our feelings before company seems extravagance or affectation; and, on the other hand, to have to unravel this mystery of our being at every turn, and to make others take an equal interest in it (otherwise the end is not answered), is a task to which few are competent. We must "give it an understanding, but no tongue." My old friend Coleridge, however, could do both. He could go on in the most delightful explanatory way over hill and dale a summer's day, and convert a landscape into a didactic poem or a Pindaric ode. "He talked far above singing." If I could so clothe my ideas in sounding and flowing words, I might perhaps wish to have some one with me to admire the swelling theme; or I could be more content, were it possible for me still to hear his echoing voice in the woods of All-Foxden. They had "that fine madness in them which our first poets had"; and if they could have been caught by some rare instrument, would have breathed such strains as the following:—

"Here be woods as green
As any, air likewise as fresh and sweet
As when smooth Zephyrus plays on the fleet
Face of the curled stream, with flow'rs as many
As the young spring gives, and as choice as any;
Here be all new delights, cool streams and wells,
Arbours o'ergrown with woodbines, caves and dells;
Choose where thou wilt, whilst I sit by and sing,

Or gather rushes to make many a ring
For thy long fingers; tell thee tales of love,
How the pale Phœbe, hunting in a grove,
First saw the boy Endymion, from whose eyes
She took eternal fire that never dies;
How she conveyed him softly in a sleep,
His temples bound with poppy, to the steep
Head of old Latmos, where she stoops each night,
Gilding the mountain with her brother's light,
To kiss her sweetest."

—FLETCHER
Faithful Shepherdess

Had I words and images at command like these, I would attempt to wake the thoughts that lie slumbering on golden ridges in the evening clouds; but at the sight of nature my fancy, poor as it is, droops and closes up its leaves, like flowers at sunset. I can make nothing out on the spot: I must have time to collect myself.

In general, a good thing spoils out-of-door prospects; it should be reserved for Table-Talk. Lamb is, for this reason, I take it, the worst company in the world out of doors; because he is the best within. I grant there is one subject on which it is pleasant to talk on a journey, and that is, what we shall have for supper when we get to our inn at night. The open air improves this sort of conversation or friendly altercation, by setting a keener edge on appetite. Every mile of the road heightens the flavour of the viands we expect at the end of it. How fine it is to enter some old town, walled and turreted, just at the approach of nightfall; or to come to some straggling village, with the lights streaming through the surrounding gloom; and then after inquiring for the best entertainment that the place affords, to "take one's ease at one's inn!"

These eventful moments in our lives' history are too precious, too full of solid, heartfelt happiness, to be frittered and dribbled away in imperfect sympathy. I would have them all to myself, and drain them to the last drop; they will do to talk of or to write about afterwards. What a delicate speculation it is, after drinking whole goblets of tea,

"The cups that cheer, but not inebriate,"

and letting the fumes ascend into the brain, to sit considering what we shall have for supper—eggs and a rasher, a rabbit smothered in onions, or an excellent veal-cutlet! Sancho in such a situation once fixed on cow-heel; and his choice, though he could not help it, is not to be disparaged. Then, in the intervals of pictured scenery and Shandean contemplation, to catch the preparation and the stir in the kitchen (getting ready for the gentleman in the parlour). *Procul, o procul este profani!* These hours are sacred to silence and to musing, to be treasured up in the memory, and to feed the source of smiling thoughts hereafter. I would not waste them in idle talk; or if I must have the integrity of fancy broken in upon, I would rather it were by a stranger than a friend.

A stranger takes his hue and character from the time and place; he is a part of the furniture and costume of an inn. If he is a Quaker, or from the West Riding of Yorkshire, so much the better. I do not even try to sympathise with him, and he breaks no squares. How I love to see the camps of the gypsies, and to sigh my soul into that sort of life! If I express this feeling to another, he may qualify and spoil it with some objection. I associate nothing with my travelling companion but present objects and passing events. In his ignorance of me and my affairs, I in a manner forget myself. But a friend reminds me of other things, rips up old grievances, and destroys the abstraction of the scene. He comes in ungraciously between us and our imaginary character. Something is dropped in the course of conversation that gives a hint of your profession and pursuits; or from having some one with you that knows the less sublime portions of your history, it seems that other people do. You are no longer a citizen of the world; but your "unhoused free condition is put into circumspection and confine."

The *incognito* of an inn is one of its striking privileges— "lord of one's self, uncumbered with a name." Oh, it is great to shake off the trammels of the world and of public opinion; to lose our importunate, tormenting, everlasting personal identity in the elements of nature, and become the creature of the moment, clear of all ties; to hold to the universe only by a dish of sweetbreads, and to owe nothing but the score of the evening; and no longer seeking for applause and meeting with contempt, to be known by no other title than *the gentleman in the parlour*!

One may take one's choice of all characters in this romantic state of uncertainty as to one's real pretensions, and become indefinitely respectable and negatively right-worshipful. We baffle prejudice and disappoint conjecture; and from being so to others, begin to be objects of curiosity and wonder even to ourselves. We are no more those hackneyed commonplaces that we appear in the world; an inn restores us to the level of nature, and quits scores with society! I have certainly spent some enviable hours at inns—sometimes when I have been left entirely to myself, and have tried to solve some metaphysical problem, as once at Witham Common, where I found out the proof that likeness is not a case of the association of ideas—at other times, when there have been pictures in the room, as at St Neot's (I think it was), where I first met with Gribelins' engravings of the Cartoons, into which I entered at once, and at a little inn on the borders of Wales, where there happened to be hanging some of Westall's drawings, which I compared triumphantly (for a theory that I had, not for the admired artist) with the figure of a girl who had ferried me over the Severn standing up in a boat between me and the twilight. At other times I might mention luxuriating in books, with a peculiar interest in this way, as I remember sitting up half the night to read *Paul and Virginia*, which I picked up at an inn at Bridgewater, after being drenched in the rain all day; and at the same place I got through two volumes of Madame D'Arblay's *Camilla.*

It was on the 10th of April 1798, that I sat down to a volume of the *New Heloïse*, at the inn at Llangollen, over a bottle of sherry and a cold chicken. The letter I chose was that in which St Preux describes his feelings as he first caught a glimpse from the heights of the Jura of the Pays de Vaud, which I had brought with me as a *bon bouche* to crown the evening with. It was my birthday, and I had for the first time come from a place in the neighbourhood to visit this delightful spot. The road to Llangollen turns off between Chirk and Wrexham; and on passing a certain point you come all at once upon the valley, which opens like an amphitheatre, broad, barren hills rising in majestic state on either side, with "green upland swells that echo to the bleat of flocks" below, and the river Dee babbling over its stony bed in the midst of them. The valley at this time "glittered green with sunny showers," and a budding ash-tree dipped its tender branches in the chiding stream.

How proud, how glad I was to walk along the highroad that overlooks the delicious prospect, repeating the lines which I have just quoted from Mr Coleridge's poems! But besides the prospect which opened beneath my feet, another also opened to my inward sight, a heavenly vision on which were written in letters large as Hope could make them, these four words, Liberty, Genius, Love, Virtue, which have since faded into the light of the common day, or mock my idle gaze.

"The beautiful is vanished, and returns not."

Still, I would return some time or other to this enchanted spot; but I would return to it alone. What other self could I find to share that influx of thoughts, of regret, and delight, the fragments of which I could hardly conjure up to myself, so much have they been broken and defaced? I could stand on some tall rock, and overlook the precipice of years that separates me from what I then was. I was at that time going shortly to visit the poet whom I have above named. Where is he now? Not only I myself have changed; the world, which was then new to me, has become old and incorrigible. Yet will I turn to thee in thought, O sylvan Dee, in joy, in youth and gladness, as thou then wert; and thou shalt always be to me the river of Paradise, where I will drink of the waters of life freely!

There is hardly anything that shows the short-sightedness or capriciousness of the imagination more than travelling does. With change of place we change our ideas; nay, our opinions and feelings. We can by an effort, indeed, transport ourselves to old and long-forgotten scenes, and then the picture of the mind revives again; but we forget those that we have just left. It seems that we can think but of one place at a time. The canvas of the fancy is but of a certain extent, and if we paint one set of objects upon it, they immediately efface every other. We cannot enlarge our conceptions, we only shift our point of view. The landscape bares its bosom to the enraptured eye; we take our fill of it, and seem as if we could form no other image of beauty or grandeur. We pass on, and think no more of it: the horizon that shuts it from our sight also blots it from our memory like a dream. In travelling through a wild, barren country, I can form no idea of a woody and cultivated one. It appears to me that all the world must be barren, like what I see of it. In the country we forget the town, and in town we despise the country. "Beyond Hyde Park," says Sir Fopling Flutter, "all is a desert." All that part of the map that we do not see before us is blank. The world in our conceit of it is not much bigger than a nutshell. It is not one prospect expanded into another, county joined to county, kingdom to kingdom, land to seas, making an image voluminous and vast; the mind can form no larger idea of space than the eye can take in at a single glance. The rest is a name written in a map, a calculation of arithmetic.

For instance, what is the true signification of that immense mass of territory and population known by the name of China to us? An inch of pasteboard on a wooden globe, of no more account than a china orange! Things near us are seen of the size of life; things at a distance are diminished to the size of the understanding. We measure the universe by ourselves, and even comprehend the texture of our own being only piecemeal. In this way, however, we remember an infinity of things and places. The mind is like a mechanical instrument that plays a great variety of tunes, but it must play them in succession. One idea recalls another, but at the same time excludes all others. In trying to renew old recollections, we cannot as it were unfold the whole web of our existence; we must pick out the single threads. So in coming to a place where we have formerly lived, and with which we have intimate associations, every one must have found that the feeling grows more vivid the nearer we approach the spot, from the mere anticipation of the actual impression: we remember circumstances, feelings, persons, faces, names that we had not thought of for years; but for the time all the rest of the world is forgotten! To return to the question I have quitted above:

I have no objection to go to see ruins, aqueducts, pictures, in company with a friend or a party, but rather the contrary, for the former reason reversed. They are intelligible matters, and will bear talking about. The sentiment here is not tacit, but communicable and overt. Salisbury Plain is barren of criticism, but Stonehenge will bear a discussion antiquarian, picturesque, and philosophical. In setting out on a party of pleasure, the first consideration always is where we shall go to: in taking a solitary ramble, the question is what we shall meet with by the way. "The mind is its own place"; nor are we anxious to arrive at the end of our journey. I can myself do the honours indifferently well to the works of art and curiosity. I once took a party to Oxford, with no mean *éclat*—showed them that seat of the Muses at a distance,

"With glistering spires and pinnacles adorn'd,"

108

descanted on the learned air that breathes from the grassy quadrangles and stone walls of halls and colleges; was at home in the Bodleian; and at Blenheim quite superseded the powdered cicerone that attended us, and that pointed in vain with his wand to commonplace beauties in matchless pictures.

As another exception to the above reasoning, I should not feel confident in venturing on a journey in a foreign country without a companion. I should want at intervals to hear the sound of my own language. There is an involuntary antipathy in the mind of an Englishman to foreign manners and notions that requires the assistance of social sympathy to carry it off. As the distance from home increases, this relief, which was at first a luxury, becomes a passion and an appetite. A person would almost feel stifled to find himself in the deserts of Arabia without friends and countrymen: there must be allowed to be something in the view of Athens or old Rome that claims the utterance of speech; and I own that the Pyramids are too mighty for any single contemplation. In such situations, so opposite to all one's ordinary train of ideas, one seems a species by one's self, a limb torn off from society, unless one can meet with instant fellowship and support.

Yet I did not feel this want or craving very pressing once, when I first set my foot on the laughing shores of France. Calais was peopled with novelty and delight. The confused, busy murmur of the place was like oil and wine poured into my ears; nor did the mariners' hymn, which was sung from the top of an old crazy vessel in the harbour, as the sun went down, send an alien sound into my soul. I only breathed the air of general humanity. I walked over "the vine-covered hills and gay regions of France," erect and satisfied; for the image of man was not cast down and chained to the foot of arbitrary thrones: I was at no loss for language, for that of all the great schools of painting was open to me. The whole is vanished like a shade. Pictures, heroes, glory, freedom, all are fled; nothing remains but the Bourbons and the French people!

There is undoubtedly a sensation in travelling into foreign parts that is to be had nowhere else; but it is more pleasing at the time than lasting. It is too remote from our habitual associations to be a common topic of discourse or reference, and, like a dream or another state of existence, does not piece into our daily modes of life. It is an animated but a momentary hallucination. It demands an effort to exchange our actual for our ideal identity; and to feel the pulse of our old transports revive very keenly, we must "jump" all our present comforts and connections. Our romantic and itinerant character is not to be domesticated. Dr Johnson remarked how little foreign travel added to the facilities of conversation in those who had been abroad. In fact, the time we have spent there is both delightful and, in one sense, instructive; but it appears to be cut out of our substantial downright existence, and never to join kindly on to it. We are not the same, but another, and perhaps more enviable individual all the time we are out of our own country. We are lost to ourselves as well as to our friends. So the poet somewhat quaintly sings:

"Out of my country and myself I go."

Those who wish to forget painful thoughts do well to absent themselves for a while from the ties and objects that recall them: but we can be said only to fulfil our destiny in the place that gave us birth. I should on this account like well enough to spend the whole of my life in travelling abroad, if I could anywhere borrow another life to spend afterwards at home!

AN ESSAY FROM
Table-Talk, Essays on
Men and Manners, Vol. II, 1821

LAKE SCENERY

By William Wordsworth

The morning was clear and cheerful after a night of sharp frost. At ten o'clock we took our way on foot towards Pooley Bridge on the same side of the lake we had coasted in a boat the day before.—Looked backwards to the south from our favourite station above Blowick. The dazzling sunbeams striking upon the church and village, while the earth was steaming with exhalations not traceable in other quarters, rendered their forms even more indistinct than the partial and flitting veil of unillumined vapour had done two days before. The grass on which we trod, and the trees in every thicket, were dripping with melted hoar-frost. We observed the lemon-coloured leaves of the birches, as the breeze turned them to the sun, sparkle, or rather *flash*, like diamonds, and the leafless purple twigs were tipped with globes of shining crystal.

The day continued delightful, and unclouded to the end. I will not describe the country which we slowly travelled through nor relate our adventures; and will only add, that on the afternoon of the thirteenth we returned along the banks of Ulswater by the usual road. The lake lay in deep repose after the agitations of a wet and stormy morning. The trees in Gowbarrow park were in that state when what is gained by the exposure of their bark and branches compensates, almost, for the loss of foliage, exhibiting the variety which characterises the point of time between autumn and winter. The hawthorns were leafless; their round heads covered with rich scarlet berries, and adorned with arches of green brambles, and eglantines hung

111

with glossy hips; and the grey trunks of some of the ancient oak, which in the summer season might have been regarded only for their venerable majesty, now attracted notice by a pretty embellishment of green mosses and fern intermixed with russet leaves retained by those slender outstarting twigs which the veteran tree would not have tolerated in his strength.

The smooth silver branches of the ashes were bare; most of the alders as green as the Devonshire cottage-myrtle that weathers the snows of Christmas.—Will you accept it as some apology for my having dwelt so long on the woodland ornaments of these scenes—that artists speak of the trees on the banks of Ulswater, and especially along the bays of Stybarrow crags, as having a peculiar character of picturesque intricacy in their stems and branches, which their rocky stations and the mountain winds have combined to give them?

At the end of Gowbarrow park a large herd of deer were either moving slowly or standing still among the fern.

I was sorry when a chance-companion, who had joined us by the way, startled them with a whistle, disturbing an image of grave simplicity and thoughtful enjoyment; for I could have fancied that those natives of this wild and beautiful region were partaking with us a sensation of the solemnity of the closing day. The sun had been set some time; and we could perceive that the light was fading away from the coves of Helvellyn, but the lake under a luminous sky, was more brilliant than before. After tea at Patterdale, set out again:—a fine evening; the seven stars close to the mountain-top; all the stars seemed brighter than usual.

The steeps were reflected in Brotherswater, and, above the lake appeared like enormous black perpendicular walls. The Kirkstone torrents had been swoln by the rain, and now filled the mountain pass with their roaring, which added greatly to the solemnity of our walk.

Behind us, when we had climbed to a great height, we saw one light very distant in the vale, like a large red star—a solitary one in the gloomy region. The cheerfulness of the scene was in the sky above us. Reached home a little before midnight.

A CHAPTER FROM
The Footpath Way, An Anthology for Walkers, 1911

WALKING TOURS

By Robert Louis Stevenson

It must not be imagined that a walking tour, as some would have us fancy, is merely a better or worse way of seeing the country. There are many ways of seeing landscape quite as good; and none more vivid, in spite of canting dilettantes, than from a railway train. But landscape on a walking tour is quite accessory. He who is indeed of the brotherhood does not voyage in quest of the picturesque, but of certain jolly humours—of the hope and spirit with which the march begins at morning, and the peace and spiritual repletion of the evening's rest. He cannot tell whether he puts his knapsack on, or takes it off, with more delight. The excitement of the departure puts him in key for that of the arrival. Whatever he does is not only a reward in itself, but will be further rewarded in the sequel; and so pleasure leads on to pleasure in an endless chain. It is this that so few can understand; they will either be always lounging or always at five miles an hour; they do not play off the one against the other, prepare all day for the evening, and all evening for the next day. And, above all, it is here that your overwalker fails of comprehension. His heart rises against those who drink their curaçoa in liqueur glasses, when he himself can swill it in a brown john. He will not believe that the flavour is more delicate in the smaller dose. He will not believe that to walk this unconscionable distance is merely to stupefy and brutalise himself, and come to his inn, at night, with a sort of frost on his five wits, and a starless night of darkness in his spirit. Not for him the mild luminous evening of the temperate walker! He has nothing left of man but a physical need for bedtime and a double nightcap; and even his pipe, if he be a smoker, will be savourless and disenchanted. It is the fate of such an one to take twice as much trouble as is needed to obtain happiness, and miss the happiness in the end; he is the man of the proverb, in short, who goes further and fares worse.

Now, to be properly enjoyed, a walking tour should be gone upon alone. If you go in a company, or even in pairs, it is no longer a walking tour in anything but name; it is something else and more in the nature of a picnic. A walking tour should be gone upon alone, because freedom is of the essence; because you should be able to stop and go on, and follow this way or that, as the freak takes you; and because you must have your own pace, and neither trot alongside a champion walker, nor mince in time with a girl. And then you must be open to all impressions and let your thoughts take colour from what you see. You should be as a pipe for any wind to play upon. "I cannot see the wit," says Hazlitt, "of walking and talking at the same time. When I am in the country, I wish to vegetate like the country," which is the gist of all that can be said upon the matter. There should be no cackle of voices at your elbow, to jar on the meditative silence of the morning. And so long as a man is reasoning he cannot surrender himself to that fine intoxication that comes of much motion in the open air, that begins in a sort of dazzle and sluggishness of the brain, and ends in a peace that passes comprehension.

During the first day or so of any tour there are moments of bitterness, when the traveller feels more than coldly towards his knapsack, when he is half in a mind to throw it bodily over the hedge and, like Christian on a similar occasion, "give three leaps and go on singing." And yet it soon acquires a property of easiness. It becomes magnetic; the spirit of the journey enters into it. And no sooner have you passed the straps over your shoulder than the lees of sleep are cleared from you, you pull yourself together with a shake, and fall at once into your stride.

And surely, of all possible moods, this, in which a man takes the road, is the best. Of course, if he *will* keep thinking of his anxieties, if he *will* open the merchant Abudah's chest and walk arm in arm with the hag—why, wherever he is, and whether he walk fast or slow, the chances are that he will not be happy. And so much the more shame to himself! There are perhaps thirty men setting forth at that same hour, and I would lay a large wager there is not another dull face among the thirty. It would be a fine thing to follow, in a coat of darkness, one after another of these wayfarers, some summer morning, for the first few miles upon the road. This one, who walks fast, with a keen look in his eyes, is all concentrated in his own mind; he is up at his loom, weaving and weaving, to set the landscape to words. This one peers about, as he goes, among the grasses; he waits by the canal to watch the dragon-flies; he leans on the gate of the pasture, and cannot look enough upon the complacent kine. And here comes another talking, laughing, and gesticulating to himself. His face changes from time to time, as indignation flashes from his eyes or anger clouds his forehead. He is composing articles, delivering orations, and conducting the most impassioned interviews, by the way. A little farther on, and it is as like as not he will begin to sing. And well for him, supposing him to be no great master in that art, if he stumble across no stolid peasant at a corner; for on such an occasion, I scarcely know which is the more troubled, or whether it is worse to suffer the confusion of your troubadour or the unfeigned alarm of your clown. A sedentary population, accustomed, besides, to the strange mechanical bearing of the common tramp, can in no wise explain to itself the gaiety of these passers-by. I knew one man who was arrested as a runaway lunatic, because, although a full-grown person with a red beard, he skipped as he went like a child. And you would be astonished if I were to tell you all the grave and learned heads who have confessed to me that, when on walking tours, they sang—and sang very ill—and had a pair of red ears when, as described above, the inauspicious peasant plumped into their arms from round a corner. And here, lest you think I am exaggerating, is Hazlitt's own confession, from his essay "On going a Journey," which is so good that there should be a tax levied on all who have not read it:—

"Give me the clear blue sky over my head," says he, "and the green turf beneath my feet, a winding road before me, and a three hours' march to dinner—and then to thinking! It is hard if I cannot start some game on these lone heaths. I laugh, I run, I leap, I sing for joy."

Bravo! After that adventure of my friend with the policeman, you would not have cared, would you, to publish that in the first person? But we have no bravery nowadays, and, even in books, must all pretend to be as dull and foolish as our neighbours. It was not so with Hazlitt. And notice how learned he is (as, indeed, throughout the essay) in the theory of walking tours. He is none of your athletic men in purple stockings, who walk their fifty miles a day: three hours' march is his ideal. And then he must have a winding road, the epicure!

Yet there is one thing I object to in these words of his, one thing in the great master's practice that seems to me not wholly wise. I do not approve of that leaping and running. Both of these hurry the respiration; they both shake up the brain out of its glorious open-air confusion; and they both break the pace. Uneven walking is not so agreeable to the body, and it distracts and irritates the mind. Whereas, when once you have fallen into an equable stride, it requires no conscious thought from you to keep it up, and yet it prevents you from thinking earnestly of anything else. Like knitting, like the work of a copying clerk, it gradually neutralises and sets to sleep the serious activity of the mind. We can think of this or that, lightly and laughingly, as a child thinks, or as we think in a morning doze; we can make puns or puzzle out acrostics, and trifle in a thousand ways with words or rhymes; but when it comes to honest work, when we come to gather ourselves together for an effort, we may sound the trumpet as loud and long as we please; the great barons of the mind will not rally to the standard, but sit, each one, at home, warming his hands over his own fire and brooding on his own private thought!

In the course of a day's walk, you see, there is much variance in the mood. From the exhilaration of the start, to the happy phlegm of the arrival, the change is certainly great. As the day goes on, the traveller moves from the one extreme towards the other. He becomes more and more incorporated with the material landscape, and the open-air drunkenness grows upon him with great strides, until he posts along the road, and sees everything about him, as in a cheerful dream. The first is certainly brighter, but the second stage is the more peaceful. A man does not make so many articles towards the end, nor does he laugh aloud; but the purely animal pleasures, the sense of physical well-being, the delight of every inhalation, of every time the muscles tighten down the thigh, console him for the absence of the others, and bring him to his destination still content.

Nor must I forget to say a word on bivouacs. You come to a milestone on a hill, or some place where deep ways meet under trees; and off goes the knapsack, and down you sit to smoke a pipe in the shade. You sink into yourself, and the birds come round and look at you, and your smoke dissipates upon the afternoon under the blue dome of heaven; and the sun lies warm upon your feet, and the cool air visits your neck and turns aside your open shirt. If you are not happy, you must have an evil conscience. You may dally as long as you like by the roadside. It is almost as if the millennium were arrived, when we shall throw our clocks and watches over the housetop, and remember time and seasons no more. Not to keep hours for a lifetime is, I was going to say, to live for ever. You have no idea, unless you have tried it, how endlessly long is a summer's day, that you measure out only by hunger, and bring to an end only when you are drowsy. I know a village where there are hardly any clocks, where no one knows more of the days of the week than by a sort of instinct for the *fête* on Sundays, and where only one person can tell you the day of the month, and she is generally wrong; and if people were aware how slow Time journeyed in that village, and what armfuls of spare hours he gives, over and above the bargain, to its wise inhabitants, I believe there would be a stampede out of London, Liverpool, Paris, and a variety of large towns, where the clocks lose their heads, and shake the hours out each one faster than the other, as though they were all in a wager. And all these foolish pilgrims would each bring his own misery along with him, in a watch-pocket! It is to be noticed, there were no clocks and watches in the much-vaunted days before the flood. It follows, of course, there were no appointments, and punctuality was not yet thought upon. "Though ye take from a covetous man all his treasure," says Milton, "he has yet one jewel left; ye cannot deprive him of his covetousness." And so I would say of a modern man of business, you may do what you will for him, put him in Eden, give him the elixir of life—he has still a flaw at heart, he still has his business habits. Now, there is no time when business habits are more mitigated than on a walking tour. And so during these halts, as I say, you will feel almost free.

But it is at night, and after dinner, that the best hour comes. There are no such pipes to be smoked as those that follow a good day's march; the flavour of the tobacco is a thing to be remembered, it is so dry and aromatic, so full and so fine. If you wind up the evening with grog, you will own there was never such grog; at every sip a jocund tranquillity spreads about your limbs, and sits easily in your heart. If you read a book—and you will never do so save by fits and starts—you find the language strangely racy and harmonious; words take a new meaning; single sentences possess the ear for half an hour together; and the writer endears himself to you, at every page, by the nicest coincidence of sentiment. It seems as if it were a book you had written yourself in a dream. To all we have read on such occasions we look back with special favour. "It was on the 10th of April 1798," says Hazlitt, with amorous precision, "that I sat down to a volume of the new *Heloïse*, at the Inn at Llangollen,

120

over a bottle of sherry and a cold chicken." I should wish to quote more, for though we are mighty fine fellows nowadays, we cannot write like Hazlitt. And, talking of that, a volume of Hazlitt's essays would be a capital pocket-book on such a journey; so would a volume of Heine's songs; and for *Tristram Shandy* I can pledge a fair experience.

If the evening be fine and warm, there is nothing better in life than to lounge before the inn door in the sunset, or lean over the parapet of the bridge, to watch the weeds and the quick fishes. It is then, if ever, that you taste joviality to the full significance of that audacious word. Your muscles are so agreeably slack, you feel so clean and so strong and so idle, that whether you move or sit still, whatever you do is done with pride and a kingly sort of pleasure. You fall in talk with any one, wise or foolish, drunk or sober. And it seems as if a hot walk purged you, more than of anything else, of all narrowness and pride, and left curiosity to play its part freely, as in a child or a man of science. You lay aside all your own hobbies, to watch provincial humours develop themselves before you, now as a laughable farce, and now grave and beautiful like an old tale.

Or perhaps you are left to your own company for the night, and surly weather imprisons you by the fire. You may remember how Burns, numbering past pleasures, dwells upon the hours when he has been "happy thinking." It is a phrase that may well perplex a poor modern girt about on every side by clocks and chimes, and haunted, even at night, by flaming dial-plates. For we are all so busy, and have so many far-off projects to realise, and castles in the fire to turn into solid, habitable mansions on a gravel soil, that we can find no time for pleasure trips into the Land of Thought and among the Hills of Vanity. Changed times, indeed, when we must sit all night, beside the fire, with folded hands; and a changed world for most of us, when we find we can pass the hours without discontent, and be happy thinking. We are in such haste to be doing, to be writing, to be gathering gear, to make our voice audible a moment in the derisive silence of eternity, that we forget that one thing, of which these are but the parts—namely, to live. We fall in love, we drink hard, we run to and fro upon the earth like frightened sheep. And now you are to ask yourself if, when all is done, you would not have been better to sit by the fire at home, and be happy thinking. To sit still and contemplate,—to remember the faces of women without desire, to be pleased by the great deeds of men without envy, to be everything and everywhere in sympathy, and yet content to remain where and what you are—is not this to know both wisdom and virtue, and to dwell with happiness? After all, it is not they who carry flags, but they who look upon it from a private chamber, who have the fun of the procession. And once you are at that, you are in the very humour of all social heresy. It is no time for shuffling, or for big empty words. If you ask yourself what you mean by fame, riches, or learning, the answer is far to seek; and you go back into that kingdom of light imaginations, which seem so vain in the eyes of Philistines perspiring after wealth, and so momentous to those who are stricken with the disproportions of the world, and, in the face of the gigantic stars, cannot stop to split differences between two degrees of the infinitesimally small, such as a tobacco pipe or the Roman Empire, a million of money or a fiddlestick's end.

You lean from the window, your last pipe reeking whitely into the darkness, your body full of delicious pains, your mind enthroned in the seventh circle of content; when suddenly the mood changes, the weathercock goes about, and you ask yourself one question more: whether, for the interval, you have been the wisest philosopher or the most egregious of donkeys? Human experience is not yet able to reply; but at least you have had a fine moment, and looked down upon all the kingdoms of the earth. And whether it was wise or foolish, to-morrow's travel will carry you, body and mind, into some different parish of the infinite.

AN ESSAY FROM
Virginibus Puerisque and Other Papers, 1881

122

IN PRAISE OF WALKING

By Leslie Stephen

As a man grows old, he is told by some moralists that he may find consolation for increasing infirmities in looking back upon a well-spent life. No doubt such a retrospect must be very agreeable, but the question must occur to many of us whether our life offers the necessary materials for self-complacency. What part of it, if any, has been well spent? To that I find it convenient to reply, for my own purposes, any part in which I thoroughly enjoyed myself. If it be proposed to add "innocently," I will not quarrel with the amendment. Perhaps, indeed, I may have a momentary regret for some pleasures which do not quite deserve that epithet, but the pleasure of which I am about to speak is obtrusively and pre-eminently innocent. Walking is among recreations what ploughing and fishing are among industrial labours: it is primitive and simple; it brings us into contact with mother earth and unsophisticated nature; it requires no elaborate apparatus and no extraneous excitement. It is fit even for poets and philosophers, and he who can thoroughly enjoy it must have at least some capacity for worshipping the "cherub Contemplation." He must be able to enjoy his own society without the factitious stimulants of the more violent physical recreations. I have always been a humble admirer of athletic excellence. I retain, in spite of much head-shaking from wise educationalists, my early veneration for the heroes of the river and the cricket-field. To me they have still the halo which surrounded them in the days when "muscular Christianity" was first preached and the whole duty of man said

123

to consist in fearing God and walking a thousand miles in a thousand hours. I rejoice unselfishly in these later days to see the stream of bicyclists restoring animation to deserted highroads or to watch even respected contemporaries renewing their youth in the absorbing delights of golf. While honouring all genuine delight in manly exercises, I regret only the occasional admixture of lower motives which may lead to its degeneration. Now it is one merit of walking that its real devotees are little exposed to such temptations. Of course there are such things as professional pedestrians making "records" and seeking the applause of the mob. When I read of the immortal Captain Barclay performing his marvellous feats, I admire respectfully, but I fear that his motives included a greater admixture of vanity than of the emotions congenial to the higher intellect. The true walker is one to whom the pursuit is in itself delightful; who is not indeed priggish enough to be above a certain complacency in the physical prowess required for his pursuit, but to whom the muscular effort of the legs is subsidiary to the "cerebration" stimulated by the effort; to the quiet musings and imaginings which arise most spontaneously as he walks, and generate the intellectual harmony which is the natural accompaniment to the monotonous tramp of his feet. The cyclist or the golf-player, I am told, can hold such intercourse with himself in the intervals of striking the ball or working his machine. But the true pedestrian loves walking because, so far from distracting his mind, it is favourable to the equable and abundant flow of tranquil and half-conscious meditation. Therefore I should be sorry if the pleasures of cycling or any other recreation tended to put out of fashion the habit of the good old walking tour.

For my part, when I try to summon up remembrance of "well-spent" moments, I find myself taking a kind of inverted view of the past; inverted, that is, so far as the accidental becomes the essential. If I turn over the intellectual album which memory is always compiling, I find that the most distinct pictures which it contains are those of old walks. Other memories of incomparably greater intrinsic value coalesce into wholes. They are more massive but less distinct. The memory of a friendship that has brightened one's whole life survives not as a series of incidents but as a general impression of the friend's characteristic qualities due to the superposition of innumerable forgotten pictures. I remember him, not the specific conversations by which he revealed himself. The memories of walks, on the other hand, are all localised and dated; they are hitched on to particular times and places; they spontaneously form a kind of calendar or connecting thread upon which other memories may be strung. As I look back, a long series of little vignettes presents itself, each representing a definite stage of my earthly pilgrimage summed up and embodied in a walk. Their background of scenery recalls places once familiar, and the thoughts associated with the places revive thoughts of the contemporary occupations. The labour of scribbling books happily leaves no distinct impression, and I would forget that it had ever been undergone; but the picture of some delightful ramble includes incidentally a reference to the nightmare of literary toil from which it relieved me. The author is but the accidental appendage of the tramp. My days are bound each to each not by "natural piety" (or not, let me say, by natural piety alone) but by pedestrian enthusiasm. The memory of school days, if one may trust to the usual reminiscences, generally clusters round a flogging, or some solemn words from the spiritual teacher instilling the seed of a guiding principle of life. I remember a sermon or two rather ruefully; and I confess to memories of a flogging so unjust that I am even now stung by the thought of it. But what comes most spontaneously to my mind is the memory of certain strolls, "out of bounds," when I could forget the Latin grammar, and enjoy such a sense of the beauties of nature as is embodied for a child in a pond haunted by water-rats, or a field made romantic by threats of "mantraps and spring-guns." Then, after a crude fashion, one was becoming more or less of a reflecting and individual being, not a mere automaton set in movement by pedagogic machinery.

The day on which I was fully initiated into the mysteries is marked by a white stone. It was when I put on a knapsack and started from Heidelberg for a march through the Odenwald. Then I first knew the delightful sensation of independence and detachment enjoyed during a walking tour. Free from all bothers of railway time-tables and extraneous machinery, you trust to your own legs, stop when you please, diverge into any track that takes your fancy, and drop in upon some quaint variety of human life at every inn where you put up for the night. You share for the time the mood in which Borrow settled down in the dingle after escaping from his bondage in the publishers' London slums. You have no dignity to support, and the dress-coat of conventional life has dropped into oblivion, like the bundle from Christian's shoulders. You are in the world of Lavengro, and would be prepared to take tea with Miss Isopel Berners or with the Welsh preacher who thought that he had committed the unpardonable sin. Borrow, of course, took the life more seriously than the literary gentleman who is only escaping on ticket-of-leave from the prison-house of respectability, and is quite unequal to a personal conflict with "blazing Bosville"— the flaming tinman. He is only dipping in the element where his model was thoroughly at home. I remember, indeed, one figure in that first walk which I associate with Benedict Moll, the strange treasure-seeker whom Borrow encountered in his Spanish rambles. My acquaintance was a mild German innkeeper, who sat beside me on a bench while I was trying to assimilate certain pancakes, the only dinner he could provide, still fearful in memory, but just attackable after a thirty-miles' tramp. He confided to me that, poor as he was, he had discovered the secret of perpetual motion. He kept his machine upstairs, where it discharged the humble duty of supplying the place of a shoe-black; but he was about to go to London to offer it to a British capitalist. He looked wistfully at me as possibly a capitalist in (very deep) disguise, and I thought it wise to evade a full explanation. I have not been worthy to encounter many of such quaint incidents and characters as seem to have been normal in Borrow's experience; but the first walk, commonplace enough, remains distinct in my memory. I kept no journal, but I could still give the narrative day by day—the sights which I dutifully admired and the very state of my bootlaces. Walking tours thus rescue a bit of one's life from oblivion. They play in one's personal recollections the part of those historical passages in which Carlyle is an unequalled master; the little islands of light in the midst of the darkening gloom of the past, on which you distinguish the actors in some old drama actually alive and moving. The devotee of other athletic sports remembers special incidents: the occasion on which he hit a cricket-ball over the pavilion at Lord's, or the crab which he caught as his boat was shooting Barnes Bridge. But those are memories of exceptional moments of glory or the reverse, and apt to be tainted by vanity or the spirit of competition. The walks are the unobtrusive connecting thread of other memories, and yet each walk is a little drama in itself, with a definite plot with episodes and catastrophes, according to the requirements of Aristotle; and it is naturally interwoven with all the thoughts, the friendships, and the interests that form the staple of ordinary life.

Walking is the natural recreation for a man who desires not absolutely to suppress his intellect but to turn it out to play for a season. All great men of letters have, therefore, been enthusiastic walkers (exceptions, of course, excepted). Shakespeare, besides being a sportsman, a lawyer, a divine, and so forth, conscientiously observed his own maxim, "Jog on, jog on, the footpath way"; though a full proof of this could only be given in an octavo volume. Anyhow, he divined the connection between walking and a "merry heart"; that is, of course, a cheerful acceptance of our position in the universe founded upon the deepest moral and philosophical principles. His friend, Ben Jonson, walked from London to Scotland. Another gentleman of the period (I forget his name) danced from London to Norwich. Tom Coryate hung up in his parish church the shoes in which he walked from Venice and then started to walk (with occasional lifts) to India. Contemporary walkers of more serious character might be quoted, such as the admirable Barclay, the famous Quaker apologist, from whom the great Captain Barclay inherited his prowess. Every one, too, must remember the incident in Walton's *Life of Hooker*. Walking from Oxford to Exeter, Hooker went to see his godfather, Bishop Jewel, at Salisbury. The Bishop said that he would lend him "a horse which hath carried me many a mile, and, I thank God, with much ease," and "presently delivered into his hands a walking staff with which he professed he had travelled through many parts of Germany." He added ten groats and munificently promised ten groats more when Hooker should restore the "horse." When, in later days, Hooker once rode to London, he expressed more passion than that mild divine was ever known to show upon any other occasion against a friend who had dissuaded him from "footing it." The hack, it seems, "trotted when he did not," and discomposed the thoughts which had been soothed by the walking staff. His biographer must be counted, I fear, among those who do not enjoy walking without the incidental stimulus of sport. Yet the *Compleat Angler* and his friends start by a walk of twenty good miles before they take their "morning draught." Swift, perhaps, was the first person to show a full appreciation of the moral and physical advantages of walking. He preached constantly upon this text to Stella, and practised his own advice. It is true that his notions of a journey were somewhat limited. Ten miles a day was his regular allowance when he went from London to Holyhead, but then he spent time in lounging at wayside inns to enjoy the talk of the tramps and ostlers. The fact, though his biographers are rather scandalised, shows that he really appreciated one of the true charms of pedestrian expeditions. Wesley is generally credited with certain moral reforms, but one secret of his power is not always noticed. In his early expeditions he went on foot to save horse hire, and made the great discovery that twenty or thirty miles a day was a wholesome allowance for a healthy man. The fresh air and exercise put "spirit into his sermons," which could not be rivalled by the ordinary parson of the period, who too often passed his leisure lounging by his fireside. Fielding points the contrast. Trulliber, embodying the clerical somnolence of the day, never gets beyond his pig-sties, but the model Parson Adams steps out so vigorously that he distances the stagecoach, and disappears in the distance rapt in the congenial pleasures of walking and composing a sermon. Fielding, no doubt, shared his hero's taste, and that explains the contrast between his vigorous naturalism and the sentimentalism of Richardson, who was to be seen, as he tells us, "stealing along from Hammersmith to Kensington with his eyes on the ground, propping his unsteady limbs with a stick." Even the ponderous Johnson used to dissipate his early hypochondria by walking from Lichfield to Birmingham and back (thirty-two miles), and his later melancholy would have changed to a more cheerful view of life could he have kept up the practice in his beloved London streets. The literary movement at the end of the eighteenth century was obviously due in great part, if not mainly, to the renewed practice of walking. Wordsworth's poetical autobiography shows how every stage in his early mental development was connected with some walk in the Lakes. The sunrise which startled him on a walk after a night spent in dancing first set him apart as a "dedicated spirit." His walking tour in the Alps—then a novel performance—roused him to his first considerable poem. His chief performance is the record of an excursion on foot. He kept up the practice, and De Quincey calculates somewhere what multiple of the earth's circumference he had measured on his legs, assuming, it appears, that he averaged ten miles a day. De Quincey himself, we are told, slight and fragile as he was, was a good walker, and would run up a hill "like a squirrel." Opium-eating is not congenial to walking, yet even Coleridge, after beginning the habit, speaks of walking forty miles a day in Scotland, and, as we all know, the great manifesto of the new school of poetry, the Lyrical

Ballads, was suggested by the famous walk with Wordsworth, when the first stanzas of the *Ancient Mariner* were composed. A remarkable illustration of the wholesome influence might be given from the cases of Scott and Byron. Scott, in spite of his lameness, delighted in walks of twenty and thirty miles a day, and in climbing crags, trusting to the strength of his arms to remedy the stumblings of his foot. The early strolls enabled him to saturate his mind with local traditions, and the passion for walking under difficulties showed the manly nature which has endeared him to three generations. Byron's lameness was too severe to admit of walking, and therefore all the unwholesome humours which would have been walked off in a good cross-country march accumulated in his brain and caused the defects, the morbid affectation and perverse misanthropy, which half ruined the achievement of the most masculine intellect of his time.

It is needless to accumulate examples of a doctrine which will no doubt be accepted as soon as it is announced. Walking is the best of panaceas for the morbid tendencies of authors. It is, I need only observe, as good for reasoners as for poets. The name of "peripatetic" suggests the connection. Hobbes walked steadily up and down the hills in his patron's park when he was in his venerable old age. To the same practice may be justly ascribed the utilitarian philosophy. Old Jeremy Bentham kept himself up to his work for eighty years by his regular "post-jentacular circumgyrations." His chief disciple, James Mill, walked incessantly and preached as he walked. John Stuart Mill imbibed at once psychology, political economy, and a love of walks from his father. Walking was his one recreation; it saved him from becoming a mere smoke-dried pedant; and though he put forward the pretext of botanical researches, it helped him to perceive that man is something besides a mere logic machine. Mill's great rival as a spiritual guide, Carlyle, was a vigorous walker, and even in his latest years was a striking figure when performing his regular constitutionals in London.

One of the vivid passages in the *Reminiscences* describes his walk with Irving from Glasgow to Drumclog. Here they sat on the "brow of a peat hag, while far, far away to the westward, over our brown horizon, towered up white and visible at the many miles of distance a high irregular pyramid. Ailsa Craig we at once guessed, and thought of the seas and oceans over yonder." The vision naturally led to a solemn conversation, which was an event in both lives. Neither Irving nor Carlyle himself feared any amount of walking in those days, it is added, and next day Carlyle took his longest walk, fifty-four miles. Carlyle is unsurpassable in his descriptions of scenery: from the pictures of mountains in *Sartor Resartus* to the battle-pieces in *Frederick*. Ruskin, himself a good walker, is more rhetorical but not so graphic; and it is self-evident that nothing educates an eye for the features of a landscape so well as the practice of measuring it by your own legs.

The great men, it is true, have not always acknowledged their debt to the genius, whoever he may be, who presides over pedestrian exercise. Indeed, they have inclined to ignore the true source of their impulse. Even when they speak of the beauties of nature, they would give us to understand that they might have been disembodied spirits, taking aerial flights among mountain solitudes, and independent of the physical machinery of legs and stomachs. When long ago the Alps cast their spell upon me, it was woven in a great degree by the eloquence of *Modern Painters*. I hoped to share Ruskin's ecstasies in a reverent worship of Mont Blanc and the Matterhorn. The influence of any cult, however, depends upon the character of the worshipper, and I fear that in this case the charm operated rather perversely. I stimulated a passion for climbing which absorbed my energies and distracted me from the prophet's loftier teaching. I might have followed him from the mountains to picture-galleries, and spent among the stones of Venice hours which I devoted to attacking hitherto unascended peaks and so losing my last chance of becoming an art critic. I became a fair judge of an Alpine guide, but I do not even know how to make a judicious allusion to Botticelli or Tintoretto. I can't say that I feel the smallest remorse. I had a good time, and at least escaped one temptation to talking nonsense. It follows, however, that my passion for the mountains had something earthly in its composition. It is associated with memories of eating and drinking. It meant delightful comradeship with some of the best of friends; but our end, I admit, was not always of the most exalted or æsthetic strain. A certain difficulty results. I feel an uncomfortable diffidence. I hold that Alpine walks are the poetry of the pursuit; I could try to justify the opinion by relating some of the emotions suggested by the great scenic effects: the sunrise on the snow fields; the storm-clouds gathering under the great peaks; the high pasturages knee-deep in flowers; the torrents plunging through the "cloven ravines," and so forth. But the thing has been done before, better than I could hope to do it; and when I look back at those old passages in *Modern Painters*, and think of the enthusiasm which prompted to exuberant sentences of three or four hundred words, I am not only abashed by the thought of their unapproachable eloquence, but feel as though they conveyed a tacit reproach. You, they seem to say, are, after all, a poor prosaic creature, affecting a love of sublime scenery as a cloak for more grovelling motives. I could protest against this judgment, but it is better at present to omit the topic, even though it would give the strongest groundwork for my argument.

Perhaps, therefore, it is better to trust the case for walking to where the external stimulus of splendours and sublimities is not so overpowering. A philosophic historian divides the world into the regions where man is stronger than nature and the regions where nature is stronger than man. The true charm of walking is most unequivocally shown when it is obviously dependent upon the walker himself. I became an enthusiast in the Alps, but I have found almost equal pleasure in walks such as one described by Cowper, where the view from a summit is bounded, not by Alps or Apennines, but by "a lofty quickset hedge." Walking gives a charm to the most commonplace British scenery. A love of walking not only makes any English county tolerable but seems to make the charm inexhaustible. I know only two or three districts minutely, but the more familiar I have become with any of them the more I have wished to return, to invent some new combination of old strolls or to inspect some hitherto unexplored nook. I love the English Lakes, and certainly not on account of associations. I cannot "associate." Much as I respect Wordsworth, I don't care to see the cottage in which he lived: it only suggests to me that anybody else might have lived there. There is an intrinsic charm about the Lake Country, and to me at least a music in the very names of Helvellyn and Skiddaw and Scawfell. But this may be due to the suggestion that it is a miniature of the Alps. I appeal, therefore, to the Fen Country, the country of which Alton Locke's farmer boasted that it had none of your "darned ups and downs" and "was as flat as his barn-door for forty miles on end." I used to climb the range of the Gogmagogs, to see the tower of Ely, some sixteen miles across the dead level, and I boasted that every term I devised a new route for walking to the cathedral from Cambridge. Many of these routes led by the little public-house called "Five Miles from Anywhere": which in my day was the Mecca to which a remarkable club, called—from the name of the village—the "Upware Republic," made periodic pilgrimages. What its members specifically did when they got there beyond consuming beer is unknown to me; but the charm was in the distance "from anywhere"—a sense of solitude under the great canopy of the heavens, where, like emblems of infinity,

"The trenched waters run from sky to sky."

I have always loved walks in the Fens. In a steady march along one of the great dykes by the monotonous canal with the exuberant vegetation dozing in its stagnant waters, we were imbibing the spirit of the scenery. Our talk might be of senior wranglers or the University crew, but we felt the curious charm of the great flats. The absence, perhaps, of definite barriers makes you realise that you are on the surface of a planet rolling through free and boundless space. One queer figure comes back to me—a kind of scholar-gipsy of the fens. Certain peculiarities made it undesirable to trust him with cash, and his family used to support him by periodically paying his score at riverside publics. They allowed him to print certain poems, moreover, which he would impart when one met him on the towpath. In my boyhood, I remember, I used to fancy that the most delightful of all lives must be that of a bargee—enjoying a perpetual picnic. This gentleman seemed to have carried out the idea; and in the intervals of lectures, I could fancy that he had chosen the better part. His poems, alas! have long vanished from my memory, and I therefore cannot quote what would doubtless have given the essence of the local sentiment and invested such names as Wicken Fen or Swaffham Lode with associations equal to those of Arnold's Hincksey ridge and Fyfield elm.

Another set of walks may, perhaps, appeal to more general sympathy. The voice of the sea, we know, is as powerful as the voice of the mountain; and, to my taste, it is difficult to say whether the Land's End is not in itself a more impressive station than the top of Mont Blanc. The solitude of the frozen peaks suggests tombstones and death. The sea is always alive and at work. The hovering gulls and plunging gannets and the rollicking porpoises are animating symbols of a gallant struggle with wind and wave. Even the unassociative mind has a vague sense of the Armada and Hakluyt's heroes in the background. America and Australia are just over the way. "Is not this a dull place?" asked some one of an old woman whose cottage was near to the Lizard lighthouse. "No," she replied, "it is so 'cosmopolitan.'" That was a simple-minded way of expressing the charm suggested in Milton's wonderful phrase:

"Where the great Vision of the guarded Mount
Looks towards Namancos and Bayona's hold."

She could mentally follow the great ships coming and going, and shake hands with people at the ends of the earth. The very sight of a fishing-boat, as painters seem to have found out, is a poem in itself. But is it not all written in *Westward Ho!* and in the *Prose Idylls*, in which Kingsley put his most genuine power? Of all walks that I have made, I can remember none more delightful than those round the south-western promontory. I have followed the coast at different times from the mouth of the Bristol Avon by the Land's End to the Isle of Wight, and I am only puzzled to decide which bay or cape is the most delightful. I only know that the most delightful was the more enjoyable when placed in its proper setting by a long walk. When you have made an early start, followed the coastguard track on the slopes above the cliffs, struggled through the gold and purple carpeting of gorse and heather on the moors, dipped down into quaint little coves with a primitive fishing village, followed the blinding whiteness of the sands round a lonely bay, and at last emerged upon a headland where you can settle into a nook of the rocks, look down upon the glorious blue of the Atlantic waves breaking into foam on the granite, and see the distant sea-levels glimmering away till they blend imperceptibly into cloudland; then you can consume your modest sandwiches, light your pipe, and feel more virtuous and thoroughly at peace with the universe than it is easy even to conceive yourself elsewhere. I have fancied myself on such occasions to be a felicitous blend of poet and saint—which is an agreeable sensation. What I wish to point out, however, is that the sensation is confined to the walker. I respect the cyclist, as I have said; but he is enslaved by his machine: he has to follow the highroad, and can only come upon what points of view open to the commonplace tourist. He can see nothing of the retired scenery which may be close to him, and cannot have his mind brought into due harmony by the solitude and by the long succession of lovely bits of scenery which stand so coyly aside from public notice.

The cockney cyclist who wisely seeks to escape at intervals from the region "where houses thick and sewers annoy the air," suffers the same disadvantages. To me, for many years, it was a necessity of life to interpolate gulps of fresh air between the periods of inhaling London fogs. When once beyond the "town" I looked out for notices that trespassers would be prosecuted. That gave a strong presumption that the trespass must have some attraction. The cyclist could only reflect that trespassing for him was not only forbidden but impossible. To me it was a reminder of the many delicious bits of walking which, even in the neighbourhood of London, await the man who has no superstitious reverence for legal rights. It is indeed surprising how many charming walks can be contrived by a judicious combination of a little trespassing with the rights of way happily preserved over so many commons and footpaths. London, it is true, goes on stretching its vast octopus arms farther into the country. Unlike the devouring dragon of Wantley, to whom "houses and churches" were like "geese and turkies," it spreads houses and churches over the fields of our childhood. And yet, between the great lines of railway there are still fields not yet desecrated by advertisements of liver pills. It is a fact that within twenty miles of London two travellers recently asked their way at a lonely farmhouse; and that the mistress of the house, seeing that they were far from an inn, not only gave them a seat and luncheon, but positively refused to accept payment. That suggested an idyllic state of society which, it is true, one must not count upon discovering. Yet hospitality, the virtue of primitive regions, has not quite vanished, it would appear, even from this over-civilised region. The travellers, perhaps, had something specially attractive in their manners. In that or some not distant ramble they made time run back for a couple of centuries. They visited the quiet grave where Penn lies under the shadow of the old Friends' meeting-house, and came to the cottage where the seat on which Milton talked to Ellwood about *Paradise Regained* seems to be still waiting for his return; and climbed the hill to the queer monument which records how Captain Cook demonstrated the goodness of Providence by disproving the existence of a continent in the South Sea— (the argument is too obvious to require exposition); and then gazed reverently upon the obelisk, not far off, which marks the point at which George III. concluded a famous stag hunt. A little valley in the quiet chalk country of Buckinghamshire leads past these and other memorials, and the lover of historical associations, with the help of Thorne's *Environs of London*, may add indefinitely to the list. I don't object to an association when it presents itself spontaneously and unobtrusively. It should not be the avowed goal but the accidental addition to the interest of a walk; and it is then pleasant to think of one's ancestors as sharers in the pleasures. The region enclosed within a radius of thirty miles from Charing Cross has charms enough even for the least historical of minds. You can't hold a fire in your hand, according to a high authority, by thinking on the frosty Caucasus; but I can comfort myself now and then, when the fellow-passengers who tread on my heels in London have put me out of temper, by thinking of Leith Hill. It only rises to the height of a thousand feet by help of the "Folly" on the top, but you can see, says my authority, twelve counties from the tower; and, if certain legendary ordnance surveyors spoke the truth, distinguish the English Channel to the south, and Dunstable Hill, far beyond London, to the north. The Crystal Palace, too, as we are assured, "sparkles like a diamond." That is gratifying; but to me the panorama suggests a whole network of paths, which have been the scene of personally conducted expeditions, in which I displayed the skill on which I most pride myself—skill, I mean, in devising judicious geographical combinations, and especially of contriving admirable short cuts. The persistence of some companions in asserting that my short cuts might be the longest way round shows that the best of men are not free from jealousy. Mine, at any rate, led me and my friends through pleasant places innumerable. My favourite passage in *Pilgrim's Progress*—an allegory which could have occurred, by the way, to no one who was not both a good man and a good walker—was always that in which Christian and Hopeful leave the highroad to cross a stile into "Bypath Meadow." I should certainly have approved the plan. The path led them, it is true, into the castle of Giant Despair; but the law of trespass has become milder; and the incident really added that spice of adventure which is delightful to the genuine pilgrim. We defied Giant Despair; and if our walks were not quite so edifying as those of Christian and his friends, they add a pleasant strand to the thread of memory which joins the past years. Conversation, we are often told, like letter-writing, is a lost art. We live too much in crowds. But if ever men can converse pleasantly, it is when they are invigorated by a good march: when the reserve is lowered by the long familiarity of a common pursuit, or when, if bored, you can quietly drop behind, or perhaps increase the pace sufficiently to check the breath of the persistent argufier.

Nowhere, at least, have I found talk flow so freely and pleasantly as in a march through pleasant country. And yet there is also a peculiar charm in the solitary expedition when your interlocutor must be yourself. That may be enjoyed, perhaps even best enjoyed, in London streets themselves. I have read somewhere of a distinguished person who composed his writings during such perambulations, and the statement was supposed to prove his remarkable power of intellectual concentration. My own experience would tend to diminish the wonder. I hopelessly envy men who can think consecutively under conditions distracting to others—in a crowded meeting or in the midst of their children—for I am as sensitive as most people to distraction; but if I can think at all, I am not sure that the roar of the Strand is not a more favourable environment than the quiet of my own study. The mind—one must only judge from one's own—seems to me to be a singularly ill-constructed apparatus. Thoughts are slippery things. It is terribly hard to keep them in the track presented by logic. They jostle each other, and suddenly skip aside to make room for irrelevant and accidental neighbours; till the stream of thought, of which people talk, resembles rather such a railway journey as one makes in dreams, where at every few yards you are shunted on to the wrong line. Now, though a London street is full of distractions, they become so multitudinous that they neutralise each other. The whirl of conflicting impulses becomes a continuous current because it is so chaotic and determines a mood of sentiment if not a particular vein of reflection. Wordsworth describes the influence upon himself in a curious passage of his *Prelude*. He wandered through London as a raw country lad, seeing all the sights from Bartholomew Fair to St Stephen's, and became a unit of the "monstrous ant-hill in a too busy world." Of course, according to his custom, he drew a moral, and a most excellent moral, from the bewildering complexity of his new surroundings. He learnt, it seems, to recognise the unity of man and to feel that the spirit of nature was upon him "in London's vast domain" as well as on the mountains. That comes of being a philosophical poet with a turn for optimism. I will not try to interpret or to comment, for I am afraid that I have not shared the emotions which he expresses. A cockney, born and bred, takes surroundings for granted. The hubbub has ceased to distract him; he is like the people who were said to become deaf because they always lived within the roar of a waterfall: he realises the common saying that the deepest solitude is solitude in a crowd; he derives a certain stimulus from a vague sympathy with the active life around him, but each particular stimulus remains, as the phrase goes, "below the threshold of consciousness." To some such effect, till psychologists will give me a better theory, I attribute the fact that what I please to call my "mind" seems to work more continuously and coherently in a street walk than elsewhere. This, indeed, may sound like a confession of cynicism. The man who should open his mind to the impressions naturally suggested by the "monstrous ant-hill" would be in danger of becoming a philanthropist or a pessimist, of being overpowered by thoughts of gigantic problems, or of the impotence of the individual to solve them. Carlyle, if I remember rightly, took Emerson round London in order to convince his optimistic friend that the devil was still in full activity. The gates of hell might be found in every street. I remember how, when coming home from a country walk on a sweltering summer night, and seeing the squalid population turning out for a gasp of air in their only playground, the vast labyrinth of hideous lanes, I seemed to be in Thomson's *City of Dreadful Night*. Even the vanishing of quaint old nooks is painful when one's attention is aroused. There is a certain churchyard wall, which I pass sometimes, with an inscription to commemorate the benefactor who erected it "to keep out the pigs." I regret the pigs and the village green which they presumably imply. The heart, it may be urged, must be hardened not to be moved by many such texts for melancholy reflection. I will not argue the point. None of us can be always thinking over the riddle of the universe, and I confess that my mind is generally employed on much humbler topics. I do not defend my insensibility nor argue that London walks are the best. I only maintain that even in London, walking has a peculiar fascination. The top of an omnibus is an excellent place for meditation; but it has not, for me at least, that peculiar hypnotic influence which seems to be favourable to thinking, and to pleasant daydreaming when locomotion is carried on by one's own muscles. The charm, however, is that even a walk in London often vaguely recalls better places and nobler forms of the exercise. Wordsworth's Susan hears a thrush at the corner of Wood Street, and straightway sees

> "A mountain ascending, a vision of trees,
> Bright volumes of vapour through Lothbury glide,
> And a river flows on through the vale of Cheapside."

The gulls which seem lately to have found out the merits of London give to occasional Susans, I hope, a whiff of fresh sea-breezes. But, even without gulls or wood-pigeons, I can often find occasions in the heart of London for recalling the old memories, without any definable pretext; little pictures of scenery, sometimes assignable to no definable place, start up invested with a faint aroma of old friendly walks and solitary meditations and strenuous exercise, and I feel convinced that, if I am not a thorough scoundrel, I owe that relative excellence to the harmless monomania which so often took me, to appropriate Bunyan's phrase, from the amusements of *Vanity Fair* to the *Delectable Mountains* of pedestrianism.

AN ESSAY FROM
Studies of a Biographer, 1898

MINCHMOOR

By Dr John Brown

Now that everybody is out of town, and every place in the guide-books is as well known as Princes Street or Pall-Mall, it is something to discover a hill everybody has not been to the top of, and which is not in *Black*. Such a hill is *Minchmoor*, nearly three times as high as Arthur's Seat, and lying between Tweed and Yarrow.

The best way to ascend it is from Traquair. You go up the wild old Selkirk road, which passes almost right over the summit, and by which Montrose and his cavaliers fled from Philiphaugh, where Sir Walter's mother remembered crossing, when a girl, in a coach-and-six, on her way to a ball at Peebles, several footmen marching on either side of the carriage to prop it up or drag it out of the moss *haggs*; and where, to our amazement, we learned that the Duchess of Buccleuch had lately driven her ponies. Before this we had passed the grey, old-world entrance to Traquair House, and looked down its grassy and untrod avenue to the pallid, forlorn mansion, stricken all o'er with eld, and noticed the wrought-iron gate embedded in a foot deep and more of soil, never having opened since the '45. There are the huge Bradwardine bears on each side—most grotesque supporters—with a superfluity of ferocity and canine teeth. The whole place, like the family whose it has been, seems dying out—everything subdued to settled desolation. The old race, the old religion, the gaunt old house, with its small, deep, comfortless windows, the decaying trees, the stillness about the doors, the grass overrunning everything, nature reinstating herself in her

143

quiet way—all this makes the place look as strange and pitiful among its fellows in the vale as would the Earl who built it three hundred years ago if we met him tottering along our way in the faded dress of his youth; but it looks the Earl's house still, and has a dignity of its own.

We soon found the Minchmoor road, and took at once to the hill, the ascent being, as often is with other ascents in this world, steepest at first. Nothing could be more beautiful than the view as we ascended, and got a look of the "eye-sweet" Tweed hills, and their "silver stream." It was one of the five or six good days of this summer—in early morning, "soft" and doubtful; but the mists drawing up, and now the noble, tawny hills were dappled with gleams and shadows—

"Sunbeams upon distant hills gliding apace"—

the best sort of day for mountain scenery—that ripple of light and shadow brings out the forms and the depths of the hills far better than a cloudless sky; and the horizon is generally wider.

Before us and far away was the round flat head of Minchmoor, with a dark, rich bloom on it from the thick, short heather— the hills around being green. Near the top, on the Tweed side, its waters trotting away cheerily to the glen at Bold, is the famous *Cheese Well*—always full, never overflowing. Here every traveler—Duchess, shepherd, or houseless *mugger*—stops, rests, and is thankful; doubtless so did Montrose, poor fellow, and his young nobles and their jaded steeds, on their scurry from Lesly and his Dragoons. It is called the Cheese Well from those who rest there dropping in bits of their provisions, as votive offerings to the fairies whose especial haunt this mountain was. After our rest and drink, we left the road and made for the top. When there we were well rewarded. The great round-backed, kindly, solemn hills of Tweed, Yarrow, and Ettrick lay all about like sleeping mastiffs—too plain to be grand, too ample and beautiful to be commonplace.

There, to the north-east, is the place—*Williamhope* ridge—where Sir Walter Scott bade farewell to his heroic friend Mungo Park. They had come up from *Ashestiel*, where Scott then lived, and where *Marmion* was written and its delightful epistles inspired—where he passed the happiest part of his life—leaving it, as Hogg said, "for gude an' a'"; for his fatal "dreams about his cottage" were now begun. He was to have "a hundred acres, two spare bed-rooms, with dressing rooms, each of which will on a pinch have a couch-bed." We all know what the dream, and the cottage, and the hundred acres came to—the ugly Abbotsford; the over-burdened, shattered brain driven wild, and the end, death, and madness. Well, it was on the ridge that the two friends—each romantic, but in such different ways—parted never to meet again. There is the ditch Park's horse stumbled over and all but fell. "I am afraid, Mungo, that's a bad omen," said the Sheriff; to which he answered, with a bright smile on his handsome, fearless face—"*Freits* (omens) follow those who look to them." With this expression, he struck the spurs into his horse, and Scott never saw him again. He had not long been married to a lovely and much-loved woman, and had been speaking to Scott about his new African scheme, and how he meant to tell his family he had some business in Edinburgh—send them his blessing, and be off—alas! never to return! Scott used to say, when speaking of this parting, "I stood and looked back, but he did not." A more memorable place for two such men to part in would not easily be found.

Where we are standing is the spot Scott speaks of when writing to Joanna Baillie about her new tragedies—"Were it possible for me to hasten the treat I expect in such a composition with you, I would promise to read the volume *at the silence of noonday upon the top of Minchmoor*. The hour is allowed, by those skilful in demonology, *to be as full of witching* as midnight itself; and I assure you I have felt really oppressed with a sort of fearful loneliness when looking around the naked towering ridges of desolate barrenness, which is all the eye takes in from the top of such a mountain, the patches of cultivation being hidden in the little glens, or only appearing to make one feel how feeble and ineffectual man has been to contend with the genius of the soil. It is in such a scene that the unknown and gifted author of *Albania* places the superstition which consists in hearing the noise of a chase, the baying of the hounds, the throttling sobs of the deer, the wild hollos of the huntsmen, and the 'hoof thick beating on the hollow hill.' I have often repeated his verses with some sensations of awe, in this place." The lines—and they are noble, and must have sounded wonderful with his voice and look—are as follows.

Can no one tell us anything more of their author?—

> "There oft is heard, at midnight, or at noon,
> Beginning faint, but rising still more loud,
> And nearer, voice of hunters, and of hounds;
> And horns, hoarse-winded, blowing far and keen!
> Forthwith the hubbub multiplies; the gale
> Labours with wilder shrieks, and rifer din
> Of hot pursuit; the broken cry of deer
> Mangled by throttling dogs; the shouts of men,
> And hoofs thick beating on the hollow hill.
> Sudden the grazing heifer in the vale
> Starts at the noise, and both the herdman's ears
> Tingle with inward dread—aghast he eyes
> The mountain's height, and all the ridges round,
> Yet not one trace of living wight discerns,
> Nor knows, o'erawed and trembling as he stands,
> To what or whom he owes his idle fear—
> To ghost, to witch, to fairy, or to fiend;
> But wonders, and no end of wondering finds."

We listened for the hunt, but could only hear the wind sobbing from the blind "*Hopes*."[2]

The view from the top reaches from the huge *Harestane Broadlaw*—nearly as high as Ben Lomond—whose top is as flat as a table, and would make a race-course of two miles, and where the clouds are still brooding, to the *Cheviot*; and from the *Maiden Paps* in Liddesdale, and that wild huddle of hills at *Moss Paul*, to *Dunse Law*, and the weird *Lammermoors*. There is *Ruberslaw*, always surly and dark. The *Dunion*, beyond which lies Jedburgh. There are the *Eildons*, with their triple heights; and you can get a glimpse of the upper woods of Abbotsford, and the top of the hill above Cauldshiels Loch, that very spot where the "wondrous potentate,"—when suffering from languor and pain, and beginning to break down under his prodigious fertility,—composed those touching lines:—

"The sun upon the Weirdlaw Hill
In Ettrick's vale is sinking sweet;
The westland wind is hushed and still;
The lake lies sleeping at my feet.
Yet not the landscape to mine eye
Bears those bright hues that once it bore,
Though evening, with her richest dye,
Flames o'er the hills of Ettrick's shore.
With listless look along the plain
I see Tweed's silver current glide,
And coldly mark the holy fane
Of Melrose rise in ruined pride.
The quiet lake, and balmy air,
The hill, the stream, the tower, the tree,
Are they still such as once they were,
Or is the dreary change in me?

2   The native word for hollows in the hills: thus, Dryhope, Gameshope, Chapelhope, &c.

Alas! the warped and broken board,
How can it bear the painter's dye!
The harp of strained and tuneless chord,
How to the minstrel's skill reply!
To aching eyes each landscape lowers,
To feverish pulse each gale blows chill;
And Araby or Eden's bowers
Were barren as this moorland hill."

There, too, is *Minto Hill*, as modest and shapely and smooth as Clytie's shoulders, and *Earlston Black Hill*, with Cowdenknowes at its foot; and there, standing stark and upright as a warder, is the stout old *Smailholme Tower*, seen and seeing all around. It is quite curious how unmistakable and important it looks at what must be twenty and more miles. It is now ninety years since that "lonely infant," who has sung its awful joys, was found in a thunderstorm, as we all know, lying on the soft grass at the foot of the grey old Strength, clapping his hands at each flash, and shouting, "Bonny! bonny!"

We now descended into Yarrow, and forgathered with a shepherd who was taking his lambs over to the great Melrose fair. He was a fine specimen of a border herd—young, tall, sagacious, self-contained, and free in speech and air. We got his heart by praising his dog *Jed*, a very fine collie, black and comely, gentle and keen—"Ay, she's a fell yin; she can do a' but speak." On asking him if the sheep dogs needed much teaching—"Whyles ay and whyles no; her kind (Jed's) needs nane. She sooks't in wi' her mither's milk." On asking him if the dogs were ever sold, he said—"Never, but at an orra time. Naebody wad sell a gude dowg, and naebody wad buy an ill ane." He told us with great feeling, of the death of one of his best dogs by poison. It was plainly still a grief to him. "What was he poisoned with?" "Strychnia," he said, as decidedly as might Dr Christison. "How do you know?" "I opened him, puir fallow, and got him analeezed!"

Now we are on Birkindale Brae, and are looking down on the same scene as did

"James Boyd (the Earle of Arran, his brother was he),"

when he crossed Minchmoor on his way to deliver James the Fifth's message to

"Yon outlaw Murray,
Surely whaur bauldly bideth he."
"Down Birkindale Brae when that he cam
He saw the feir Foreste wi' his ee."

How James Boyd fared, and what the outlaw said, and what James and his nobles said and did, and how the outlaw at last made peace with his King, and rose up "Sheriffe of Ettricke Foreste," and how the bold ruffian boasted,

"Fair Philiphaugh is mine by right,
And Lewinshope still mine shall be;
Newark, Foulshiels, and Tinnies baith
My bow and arrow purchased me.
And I have native steads to me
The Newark Lee o' Hangingshaw.
I have many steads in the Forest schaw,
But them by name I dinna knaw."
And how King James snubbed

"The kene Laird of Buckscleuth,
A stalwart man and stern was he."
When the Laird hinted that,

"For a king to gang an outlaw till
Is beneath his state and dignitie.
The man that wins yon forest intill

149

He lives by reif and felony."
"Then out and spak the nobil King,
And round him cast a wilie ee.
'Now haud thy tongue, Sir Walter Scott,
Nor speak o' reif or felonie—
For, had every honest man his awin kye,
A richt puir clan thy name wud be!'"

(by-the-bye, why did Professor Aytoun leave out this excellent hit in his edition?)—all this and much more may you see if you take up *The Border Minstrelsy*, and read "The Song of the Outlaw Murray," with the incomparable notes of Scott. But we are now well down the hill. There to the left, in the hollow, is *Permanscore*, where the King and the outlaw met:—

"Bid him mete me at Permanscore,
And bring four in his companie;
Five Erles sall cum wi' mysel',
Gude reason I sud honoured be."

And there goes our Shepherd with his long swinging stride. As different from his dark, wily companion, the Badenoch drover, as was Harry Wakefield from Robin Oig; or as the big, sunny Cheviot is from the lowering Ruberslaw; and there is *Jed* trotting meekly behind him—may she escape strychnia, and, dying at the fireside among the children, be laid like

"Paddy Tims—whose soul at aise is—
With the point of his nose
And the tips of his toes
Turn'd up to the roots of the daisies"—

unanaleezed, save by the slow cunning of the grave. And may her master get the top price for his lambs!

Do you see to the left that little plantation on the brow of

Foulshiels Hill, with the sunlight lying on its upper corner? If you were there you might find among the brackens and foxglove a little headstone with "I. T." rudely carved on it. That is *Tibbie Tamson's grave*, known and feared all the country round.

This poor outcast was a Selkirk woman, who, under the stress of spiritual despair—that sense of perdition, which, as in Cowper's case, often haunts and overmasters the deepest and gentlest natures, making them think themselves

"Damn'd below Judas, more abhorred than he was,"—

committed suicide; and being, with the gloomy, cruel superstition of the time, looked on by her neighbours as accursed of God, she was hurried into a rough white deal coffin, and carted out of the town, the people stoning it all the way till it crossed the Ettrick. Here, on this wild hillside, it found its rest, being buried where three lairds' lands meet. May we trust that the light of God's reconciled countenance has for all these long years been resting on that once forlorn soul, as His blessed sunshine now lies on her moorland grave! For "the mountains shall depart, and the hills be removed; but my kindness shall not depart from thee, neither shall the covenant of my peace be removed, saith the Lord that hath mercy on thee."

Now, we see down into the Yarrow—there is the famous stream twinkling in the sun. What stream and valley was ever so be-sung! You wonder at first why this has been, but the longer you look the less you wonder. There is a charm about it— it is not easy to say what. The huge sunny hills in which it is embosomed give it a look at once gentle and serious. They are great, and their gentleness makes them greater. Wordsworth has the right words, "pastoral melancholy"; and besides, the region is "not uninformed with phantasy and looks that threaten the profane"—the Flowers of Yarrow, the Douglas Tragedy, the Dowie Dens, Wordsworth's Yarrow Unvisited, Visited, and Re-Visited, and, above all, the glamour of Sir Walter, and Park's

151

fatal and heroic story. Where can you find eight more exquisite lines anywhere than Logan's, which we all know by heart:—

> "His mother from the window looked,
> With all the longing of a mother;
> His little sister, weeping, walked
> The greenwood path to meet her brother.
> They sought him east, they sought him west,
> They sought him all the forest thorough—
> They only saw the cloud of night,
> They only heard the roar of Yarrow."

And there is *Newark Tower* among the rich woods; and *Harehead*, that cosiest, loveliest, and hospitablest of nests. Methinks I hear certain young voices among the hazels; out they come on the little haugh by the side of the deep, swirling stream, *fabulosus* as was ever Hydaspes. There they go "running races in their mirth," and is not that—*an me ludit amabilis insania?*—the voice of *ma pauvre petite—animosa infans*—the wilful, rich-eyed, delicious Eppie?

> "Oh blessed vision, happy child,
> Thou art so exquisitely wild!"

And there is *Black Andro and Glowr owr'em* and *Foulshiels*, where Park was born and bred; and there is the deep pool in the Yarrow where Scott found him plunging one stone after another into the water, and watching anxiously the bubbles as they rose to the surface. "This," said Scott to him, "appears but an idle amusement for one who has seen so much adventure." "Not so idle, perhaps, as you suppose," answered Mungo, "this was the way I used to ascertain the depth of a river in Africa." He was then meditating his second journey, but had said so to no one.

We go down by *Broadmeadows*, now held by that Yair "Hoppringle"—who so well governed Scinde—and into the grounds of Bowhill, and passing *Philiphaugh*, see where stout David Lesly crossed in the mist at daybreak with his heavy dragoons, many of them old soldiers of Gustavus, and routed the gallant Graeme; and there is *Slainmens Lee*, where the royalists lie; and there is *Carterhaugh*, the scene of the strange wild story of *Tamlane* and Lady Janet, when

> "She prinked hersell and prinned hersell
> By the ae light of the moon,
> And she's awa' to Carterhaugh
> To speak wi' young Tamlane."

Noel Paton might paint that night, when

> "'Twixt the hours of twelve and yin
> A north wind *tore the bent*";

when "fair Janet" in her green mantle

> "heard strange elritch sounds
> Upon the wind that went."

And straightway

> "About the dead hour o' the night
> She heard the bridles ring;
> Their oaten pipes blew wondrous shrill,
> The hemlock small blew clear;
> And louder notes from hemlock large
> And bog reed, struck the ear,"

and then the fairy cavalcade swept past, while Janet, filled with love and fear, looked out for the milk-white steed, and "gruppit it fast," and "pu'd the rider doon," the young Tamlane, whom, after dipping "in a stand of milk and then in a stand of water,"

"She wrappit ticht in her green mantle,
And sae her true love won!"

This ended our walk. We found the carriage at the Philiphaugh home-farm, and we drove home by *Yair* and *Fernilee, Ashestiel* and *Elibank*, and passed the bears as ferocious as ever, "the orange sky of evening" glowing through their wild tusks, the old house looking even older in the fading light. And is not this a walk worth making? One of our number had been at the Land's End and Johnnie Groat's, and now on Minchmoor; and we wondered how many other men had been at all the three, and how many had enjoyed Minchmoor more than he.

AN ESSAY FROM
The Footpath Way,
An Anthology for Walkers, 1911

THE LAND
OF LITTLE RAIN

By Mary Hunter Austin

East away from the Sierras, south from Panamint and Amargosa, east and south many an uncounted mile, is the Country of Lost Borders.

Ute, Paiute, Mojave, and Shoshone inhabit its frontiers, and as far into the heart of it as a man dare go. Not the law, but the land sets the limit. Desert is the name it wears upon the maps, but the Indian's is the better word. Desert is a loose term to indicate land that supports no man; whether the land can be bitted and broken to that purpose is not proven. Void of life it never is, however dry the air and villainous the soil.

This is the nature of that country. There are hills, rounded, blunt, burned, squeezed up out of chaos, chrome and vermilion painted, aspiring to the snowline. Between the hills lie high level-looking plains full of intolerable sun glare, or narrow valleys drowned in a blue haze. The hill surface is streaked with ash drift and black, unweathered lava flows. After rains water accumulates in the hollows of small closed valleys, and, evaporating, leaves hard dry levels of pure desertness that get the local name of dry lakes. Where the mountains are steep and the rains heavy, the pool is never quite dry, but dark and bitter, rimmed about with the efflorescence of alkaline deposits. A thin crust of it lies along the marsh over the vegetating area, which has neither beauty nor freshness. In the broad wastes open to the wind the sand drifts in hummocks about the stubby shrubs, and between them the soil shows saline traces. The sculpture of the hills here is more wind than water work, though the quick storms do sometimes scar them past many a year's redeeming. In all the Western desert edges there are essays in miniature at the famed, terrible Grand Canon, to which, if you keep on long enough in this country, you will come at last.

Since this is a hill country one expects to find springs, but not to depend upon them; for when found they are often brackish and unwholesome, or maddening, slow dribbles in a thirsty soil. Here you find the hot sink of Death Valley, or high rolling districts where the air has always a tang of frost. Here are the long heavy winds and breathless calms on the tilted mesas where dust devils dance, whirling up into a wide, pale sky. Here you have no rain when all the earth cries for it, or quick downpours called cloud-bursts for violence. A land of lost rivers, with little in it to love; yet a land that once visited must be come back to inevitably. If it were not so there would be little told of it.

This is the country of three seasons. From June on to November it lies hot, still, and unbearable, sick with violent unrelieving storms; then on until April, chill, quiescent, drinking its scant rain and scanter snows; from April to the hot season again, blossoming, radiant, and seductive. These months are only approximate; later or earlier the rain-laden wind may drift up the water gate of the Colorado from the Gulf, and the land sets its seasons by the rain.

The desert floras shame us with their cheerful adaptations to the seasonal limitations. Their whole duty is to flower and fruit, and they do it hardly, or with tropical luxuriance, as the rain admits. It is recorded in the report of the Death Valley expedition that after a year of abundant rains, on the Colorado desert was found a specimen of Amaranthus ten feet high. A year later the same species in the same place matured in the drought at four inches. One hopes the land may breed like qualities in her human offspring, not tritely to "try," but to do. Seldom does the desert herb attain the full stature of the type. Extreme aridity and extreme altitude have the same dwarfing effect, so that we find in the high Sierras and in Death Valley related species in miniature that reach a comely growth in mean temperatures. Very fertile are the desert plants in expedients to prevent evaporation, turning their foliage edge-wise toward the sun, growing silky hairs, exuding viscid gum. The wind, which has a long sweep, harries and helps them. It rolls up dunes about the stocky stems, encompassing and protective, and above the dunes, which may be, as with the mesquite, three times as high as a man, the blossoming twigs flourish and bear fruit.

There are many areas in the desert where drinkable water lies within a few feet of the surface, indicated by the mesquite and the bunch grass (Sporobolus airoides). It is this nearness of unimagined help that makes the tragedy of desert deaths. It is related that the final breakdown of that hapless party that gave Death Valley its forbidding name occurred in a locality where shallow wells would have saved them. But how were they to know that? Properly equipped it is possible to go safely across that ghastly sink, yet every year it takes its toll of death, and yet men find there sun-dried mummies, of whom no trace or recollection is preserved. To underestimate one's thirst, to pass a given landmark to the right or left, to find a dry spring where one looked for running water—there is no help for any of these things.

Along springs and sunken watercourses one is surprised to find such water-loving plants as grow widely in moist ground, but the true desert breeds its own kind, each in its particular habitat. The angle of the slope, the frontage of a hill, the structure of the soil determines the plant. South-looking hills are nearly bare, and the lower tree-line higher here by a thousand feet. Canons running east and west will have one wall naked and one clothed. Around dry lakes and marshes the herbage preserves a set and orderly arrangement. Most species have well-defined areas of growth, the best index the voiceless land can give the traveler of his whereabouts.

If you have any doubt about it, know that the desert begins

with the creosote. This immortal shrub spreads down into Death Valley and up to the lower timberline, odorous and medicinal as you might guess from the name, wandlike, with shining fretted foliage. Its vivid green is grateful to the eye in a wilderness of gray and greenish white shrubs. In the spring it exudes a resinous gum which the Indians of those parts know how to use with pulverized rock for cementing arrow points to shafts. Trust Indians not to miss any virtues of the plant world!

Nothing the desert produces expresses it better than the unhappy growth of the tree yuccas. Tormented, thin forests of it stalk drearily in the high mesas, particularly in that triangular slip that fans out eastward from the meeting of the Sierras and coastwise hills where the first swings across the southern end of the San Joaquin Valley. The yucca bristles with bayonet-pointed leaves, dull green, growing shaggy with age, tipped with panicles of fetid, greenish bloom. After death, which is slow, the ghostly hollow network of its woody skeleton, with hardly power to rot, makes the moonlight fearful. Before the yucca has come to flower, while yet its bloom is a creamy cone-shaped bud of the size of a small cabbage, full of sugary sap, the Indians twist it deftly out of its fence of daggers and roast it for their own delectation.

So it is that in those parts where man inhabits one sees young plants of Yucca arborensis infrequently. Other yuccas, cacti, low herbs, a thousand sorts, one finds journeying east from the coastwise hills. There is neither poverty of soil nor species to account for the sparseness of desert growth, but simply that each plant requires more room. So much earth must be preempted to extract so much moisture. The real struggle for existence, the real brain of the plant, is underground; above there is room for a rounded perfect growth. In Death Valley, reputed the very core of desolation, are nearly two hundred identified species.

Above the lower tree-line, which is also the snowline, mapped out abruptly by the sun, one finds spreading growth of pinon, juniper, branched nearly to the ground, lilac and sage, and scattering white pines.

There is no special preponderance of self-fertilized or wind-fertilized plants, but everywhere the demand for and evidence of insect life. Now where there are seeds and insects there will be birds and small mammals and where these are, will come the slinking, sharp-toothed kind that prey on them. Go as far as you dare in the heart of a lonely land, you cannot go so far that life and death are not before you. Painted lizards slip in and out of rock crevices, and pant on the white hot sands. Birds, hummingbirds even, nest in the cactus scrub; woodpeckers befriend the demoniac yuccas; out of the stark, treeless waste rings the music of the night-singing mockingbird. If it be summer and the sun well down, there will be a burrowing owl to call. Strange, furry, tricksy things dart across the open places, or sit motionless in the conning towers of the creosote. The poet may have "named all the birds without a gun," but not the fairy-footed, ground-inhabiting, furtive, small folk of the rainless regions. They are too many and too swift; how many you would not believe without seeing the footprint tracings in the sand. They are nearly all night workers, finding the days too hot and white. In mid-desert where there are no cattle, there are no birds of carrion, but if you go far in that direction the chances are that you will find yourself shadowed by their tilted wings. Nothing so large as a man can move unspied upon in that country, and they know well how the land deals with strangers. There are hints to be had here of the way in which a land forces new habits on its dwellers. The quick increase of suns at the end of spring sometimes overtakes birds in their nesting and effects a reversal of the ordinary manner of incubation. It becomes necessary to keep eggs cool rather than warm. One hot, stifling spring in the Little Antelope I had occasion to pass and repass frequently the nest of a pair of meadowlarks, located unhappily in the shelter of a very slender weed. I never caught them sitting except near night, but at mid-day they stood, or drooped above it, half fainting with pitifully parted bills, between their treasure and the sun. Sometimes both of them together with wings spread and half lifted continued a spot of shade in a temperature that constrained me at last in a fellow feeling to spare them a bit of canvas for permanent shelter. There was a fence in that country shutting in a cattle range, and along its fifteen miles of posts one could be sure of finding a bird or two in every strip of shadow; sometimes the sparrow and the hawk, with wings trailed and beaks parted, drooping in the white truce of noon.

If one is inclined to wonder at first how so many dwellers came to be in the loneliest land that ever came out of God's hands, what they do there and why stay, one does not wonder so much after having lived there. None other than this long brown land lays such a hold on the affections. The rainbow hills, the tender bluish mists, the luminous radiance of the spring, have the lotus charm. They trick the sense of time, so that once inhabiting there you always mean to go away without quite realizing that you have not done it. Men who have lived there, miners and cattlemen, will tell you this, not so fluently, but emphatically, cursing the land and going back to it. For one thing there is the divinest, cleanest air to be breathed anywhere in God's world. Some day the world will understand that, and the little oases on the windy tops of hills will harbor for healing its ailing, house-weary broods. There is promise there of great wealth in ores and earths, which is no wealth by reason of being so far removed from water and workable conditions, but men are bewitched by it and tempted to try the impossible.

You should hear Salty Williams tell how he used to drive eighteen and twenty-mule teams from the borax marsh to Mojave, ninety miles, with the trail wagon full of water barrels. Hot days the mules would go so mad for drink that the clank of the water bucket set them into an uproar of hideous, maimed noises, and a tangle of harness chains, while Salty would sit on the high seat with the sun glare heavy in his eyes, dealing out curses of pacification in a level, uninterested voice until the clamor fell off from sheer exhaustion. There was a line of

160

shallow graves along that road; they used to count on dropping a man or two of every new gang of coolies brought out in the hot season. But when he lost his swamper, smitten without warning at the noon halt, Salty quit his job; he said it was "too durn hot." The swamper he buried by the way with stones upon him to keep the coyotes from digging him up, and seven years later I read the penciled lines on the pine head-board, still bright and unweathered.

But before that, driving up on the Mojave stage, I met Salty again crossing Indian Wells, his face from the high seat, tanned and ruddy as a harvest moon, looming through the golden dust above his eighteen mules. The land had called him.

The palpable sense of mystery in the desert air breeds fables, chiefly of lost treasure. Somewhere within its stark borders, if one believes report, is a hill strewn with nuggets; one seamed with virgin silver; an old clayey water-bed where Indians scooped up earth to make cooking pots and shaped them reeking with grains of pure gold. Old miners drifting about the desert edges, weathered into the semblance of the tawny hills, will tell you tales like these convincingly. After a little sojourn in that land you will believe them on their own account. It is a question whether it is not better to be bitten by the little horned snake of the desert that goes sidewise and strikes without coiling, than by the tradition of a lost mine.

And yet—and yet—is it not perhaps to satisfy expectation that one falls into the tragic key in writing of desertness? The more you wish of it the more you get, and in the mean time lose much of pleasantness. In that country which begins at the foot of the east slope of the Sierras and spreads out by less and less lofty hill ranges toward the Great Basin, it is possible to live with great zest, to have red blood and delicate joys, to pass and repass about one's daily performance an area that would make an Atlantic seaboard State, and that with no peril, and, according to our way of thought, no particular difficulty. At any rate, it was not people who went into the desert merely to write it up who invented the fabled Hassaympa, of whose waters, if any drink, they can no more see fact as naked fact, but all radiant with the color of romance. I, who must have drunk of it in my twice seven years' wanderings, am assured that it is worth while.

For all the toll the desert takes of a man it gives compensations, deep breaths, deep sleep, and the communion of the stars. It comes upon one with new force in the pauses of the night that the Chaldeans were a desert-bred people. It is hard to escape the sense of mastery as the stars move in the wide clear heavens to risings and settings unobscured. They look large and near and palpitant; as if they moved on some stately service not needful to declare. Wheeling to their stations in the sky, they make the poor world-fret of no account. Of no account you who lie out there watching, nor the lean coyote that stands off in the scrub from you and howls and howls.

A CHAPTER FROM
The Land of Little Rain, 1903

RURAL RIDES

By William Henry Hudson

"A-birding on a Broncho" is the title of a charming little book published some years ago, and probably better known to readers on the other side of the Atlantic than in England. I remember reading it with pleasure and pride on account of the author's name, Florence Merriam, seeing that, on my mother's side, I am partly a Merriam myself (of the branch on the other side of the Atlantic), and having been informed that all of that rare name are of one family, I took it that we were related, though perhaps very distantly. "A-birding on a Broncho" suggested an equally alliterative title for this chapter—"Birding on a Bike"; but I will leave it to others, for those who go a-birding are now very many and are hard put to find fresh titles to their books. For several reasons it will suit me better to borrow from Cobbett and name this chapter "Rural Rides."

Sore of us do not go out on bicycles to observe the ways of birds. Indeed, some of our common species have grown almost too familiar with the wheel: it has become a positive danger to them. They not infrequently mistake its rate of speed and injure themselves in attempting to fly across it. Recently I had a thrush knock himself senseless against the spokes of my forewheel, and cycling friends have told me of similar experiences they have had, in some instances the heedless birds getting killed. Chaffinches are like the children in village streets—they will not get out of your way; by and by in rural places the merciful man will have to ring his bell almost incessantly to avoid running over them. As I do not travel at a furious speed I manage to avoid most things, even the wandering loveless oil-beetle and the small rose-beetle and that slow-moving insect tortoise the tumbledung. Two or three seasons ago I was so unfortunate as to run over a large and beautifully bright grass snake near Aldermaston, once a snake sanctuary. He writhed and wriggled on the road as if I had broken his back, but on picking him up I was pleased to find that my wind-inflated rubber tyre had not, like the brazen chariot wheel, crushed his delicate vertebra; he quickly recovered, and when released glided swiftly and easily away into cover. Twice only have I deliberately tried to run down, to tread on coat-tails so to speak, of any wild creature. One was a weasel, the other a stoat, running along at a hedge-side before me. In both instances, just as the front wheel was touching the tail, the little flat-headed rascal swerved quickly aside and escaped.

Even some of the less common and less tame birds care as little for a man on a bicycle as they do for a cow. Not long ago a peewit trotted leisurely across the road not more than ten yards from my front wheel; and on the same day I came upon a green woodpecker enjoying a dust-bath in the public road. He declined to stir until I stopped to watch him, then merely flew about a dozen yards away and attached himself to the trunk of a fir tree at the roadside and waited there for me to go. Never in all my wanderings afoot had I seen a yaffingale dusting himself like a barn-door fowl!

It is not seriously contended that birds can be observed narrowly in this easy way; but even for the most conscientious field naturalist the wheel has its advantages. It carries him quickly over much barren ground and gives him a better view of the country he traverses; finally, it enables him to see more birds. He will sometimes see thousands in a day where, walking, he would hardly have seen hundreds, and there is joy in mere numbers. It was just to get this general rapid sight of the bird life of the neighbouring hilly district of Hampshire that I was at Newbury on the last day of October. The weather was bright though very cold and windy, and towards evening I was surprised to see about twenty swallows in Northbrook Street flying languidly to and fro in the shelter of the houses, often fluttering under the eaves and at intervals sitting on ledges and projections. These belated birds looked as if they wished to hibernate, or find the most cosy holes to die in, rather than to emigrate. On the following day at noon they came out again and flew up and down in the same feeble aimless manner.

Undoubtedly a few swallows of all three species, but mostly house-martins, do "lie up" in England every winter, but probably very few survive to the following spring. We should have said that it was impossible that any should survive but for one authentic instance in recent years, in which a barn-swallow lived through the winter in a semi-torpid state in an outhouse at a country vicarage. What came of the Newbury birds I do not know, as I left on the 2nd of November—tore myself away, I may say, for, besides meeting with people I didn't know who treated a stranger with sweet friendliness, it is a town which quickly wins one's affections. It is built of bricks of a good deep rich red—not the painfully bright red so much in use now—and no person has had the bad taste to spoil the harmony by introducing stone and stucco. Moreover, Newbury has, in Shaw House, an Elizabethan mansion of the rarest beauty. Let him that is weary of the ugliness and discords in our town buildings go and stand by the ancient cedar at the gate and look across the wide green lawn at this restful house, subdued by time to a tender rosy-red colour on its walls and a deep dark red on its roof, clouded with grey of lichen.

From Newbury and the green meadows of the Kennet the Hampshire hills may be seen, looking like the South Down range at its highest point viewed from the Sussex Weald. I made for Coombe Hill, the highest hill in Hampshire, and found it a considerable labour to push my machine up from the pretty tree-hidden village of East Woodhay at its foot. The top is a league-long tableland, with stretches of green elastic turf, thickets of furze and bramble, and clumps of ancient noble beeches—a beautiful lonely wilderness with rabbits and birds for only inhabitants. From the highest point where a famous gibbet stands for ever a thousand feet above the sea and where there is a dew-pond, the highest in England, which has never dried up although a large flock of sheep drink in it every summer day, one looks down into an immense hollow, a Devil's Punch Bowl very many times magnified,—and spies, far away and far below, a few lonely houses half hidden by trees at the bottom. This is the romantic village of Coombe, and hither I went and found the vicar busy in the garden of the small old picturesque parsonage. Here a very pretty little bird comedy was in progress: a pair of stock-doves which had been taken from a rabbit-hole in the hill and reared by hand had just escaped from the large cage where they had always lived, and all the family were excitedly engaged in trying to recapture them. They were delightful to see—those two pretty blue birds with red legs running busily about on the green lawn, eagerly searching for something to eat and finding nothing. They were quite tame and willing to be fed, so that anyone could approach them and put as much salt on their tails as he liked, but they refused to be touched or taken; they were too happy in their new freedom, running and flying about in that brilliant sunshine, and when I left towards the evening they were still at large.

But before quitting that small isolated village in its green basin—a human heart in a chalk hill, almost the highest in England—I wished the hours I spent in it had been days, so much was there to see and hear. There was the gibbet on the hill, for example, far up on the rim of the green basin, four hundred feet above the village; why had that memorial, that symbol of a dreadful past, been preserved for so many years and generations? and why had it been raised so high—was it because the crime of the person put to death there was of so monstrous a nature that it was determined to suspend him, if not on a gibbet fifty cubits high, at all events higher above the earth than Haman the son of Hammedatha the Agagite? The gruesome story is as follows.

Once upon a time there lived a poor widow woman in Coombe, with two sons, aged fourteen and sixteen, who worked at a farm in the village. She had a lover, a middle-aged man, living at Woodhay, a carrier who used to go on two or three days each week with his cart to deliver parcels at Coombe. But he was a married man, and as he could not marry the widow while his wife remained alive, it came into his dull Berkshire brain that the only way out of the difficulty was to murder her, and to this course the widow probably consented. Accordingly, one day, he invited or persuaded her to accompany him on his journey to the remote village, and on the way he got her out of the cart and led her into a close thicket to show her something he had discovered there. What he wished to show her (according to one version of the story) was a populous hornets' nest, and having got her there he suddenly flung her against it and made off, leaving the cloud of infuriated hornets to sting her to death. That night he slept at Coombe, or stayed till a very late hour at the widow's cottage and told her what he had done. In telling her he had spoken in his ordinary voice, but by and by it occurred to him that the two boys, who were sleeping close by in the living-room, might have been awake and listening. She assured him that they were both fast asleep, but he was not satisfied, and said that if they had heard him he would kill them both, as he had no wish to swing, and he could not trust them to hold their tongues. Thereupon they got up and examined the faces of the two boys, holding a candle over them, and saw that they were in a deep sleep, as was natural after their long day's hard work on the farm, and the murderer's fears were set at rest. Yet one of the boys, the younger, had been wide awake all the time, listening, trembling with terror, with wide eyes to the dreadful tale, and only when they first became suspicious instinct came to his aid and closed his eyes and stilled his tremors and gave him the appearance of being asleep. Early next morning, with his terror still on him, he told what he had heard to his brother, and by and by, unable to keep the dreadful secret, they related it to someone—a carter or ploughman on the farm. He in turn told the farmer, who at once gave information, and in a short time the man and woman were arrested. In due time they were tried, convicted, and sentenced to be hanged in the parish where the crime had been committed.

Everybody was delighted, and Coombe most delighted of all, for it happened that some of their wise people had been diligently examining into the matter and had made the discovery that the woman had been murdered just outside their borders in the adjoining parish of Inkpen, so that they were going to enjoy seeing the wicked punished at somebody else's expense. Inkpen was furious and swore that it would not be saddled with the cost of a great public double execution. The line dividing the two parishes had always been a doubtful one; now they were going to take the benefit of the doubt and let Coombe hang its own miscreants!

As neither side would yield, the higher authorities were compelled to settle the matter for them, and ordered the cost to be divided between the two parishes, the gibbet to be erected on the boundary line, as far as it could be ascertained. This was accordingly done, the gibbet being erected at the highest point crossed by the line, on a stretch of beautiful smooth elastic turf, among prehistoric earthworks—a spot commanding one of the finest and most extensive views in Southern England. The day appointed for the execution brought the greatest concourse of people ever witnessed at that lofty spot, at all events since prehistoric times. If some of the ancient Britons had come out of their graves to look on, seated on their earthworks, they would have probably rubbed their ghostly hands together and remarked to each other that it reminded them of old times. All classes were there, from the nobility and gentry, on horseback and in great coaches in which they carried their own provisions, to the meaner sort who had trudged from all the country round on foot, and those who had not brought their own food and beer were catered for by traders in carts. The crowd was a hilarious one, and no doubt that grand picnic on the beacon was the talk of they country for a generation or longer. The two wretches having been hanged in chains on one gibbet were left to be eaten by ravens, crows, and magpipes, and dried by sun and winds, until, after long years, the swinging, creaking skeletons with their chains on fell to pieces and were covered with the turf, but the gibbet itself was never removed.

Then a strange thing happened. The sheep on a neighbouring farm became thin and sickly and yielded little wool and died before their time. No remedies availed and the secret of their malady could not be discovered; but it went on so long that the farmer was threatened with utter ruin. Then, by chance, it was discovered that the chains in which the murderers had been hanged had been thrown by some evil-minded person into a dew-pond on the farm. This was taken to be the cause of the malady in the sheep; at all events, the chains having been taken out of the pond and buried deep in the earth, the flock recovered: it was supposed that the person who had thrown the chains in the water to poison it had done so to ruin the farmer in revenge for some injustice or grudge. But even now we are not quite done with the gibbet! Many, many years had gone by when Inkpen discovered from old documents that their little dishonest neighbour, Coombe, had taken more land than she was entitled to, that not only a part but the whole of that noble hill-top belonged to her! It was Inkpen's turn to chuckle now; but she chuckled too soon, and Coombe, running out to look, found the old rotten stump of the gibbet still in the ground. Hands off! she cried. Here stands a post, which you set up yourself, or which we put up together and agreed that this should be the boundary line for ever. Inkpen sneaked off to hide herself in her village, and Coombe, determined to keep the subject in mind, set up a brand-new stout gibbet in the place of the old rotting one. That too decayed and fell to pieces in time, and the present gibbet is therefore the third, and nobody has ever been hanged on it.

Coombe is rather proud of it, but I am not sure that Inkpen is.

That was one of three strange events in the life of the village which I heard: the other two must be passed by; they would take long to tell and require a good pen to do them justice. To me the best thing in or of the village was the vicar himself, my put-upon host, a man of so blithe a nature, so human and companionable, that when I, a perfect stranger without an introduction or any excuse for such intrusion came down like a wolf on his luncheon-table, he received me as if I had been an old friend or one of his own kindred, and freely gave up his time to me for the rest of that day. To count his years he was old: he had been vicar of Coombe for half a century, but he was a young man still and had never had a day's illness in his life—he did not know what a headache was. He smoked with me, and to prove that he was not a total abstainer he drank my health in a glass of port wine—very good wine. It was Coombe that did it—its peaceful life, isolated from a distracting world in that hollow hill, and the marvellous purity of its air. "Sitting there on my lawn," he said, "you are six hundred feet above the sea, although in a hollow four hundred feet deep." It was an ideal open-air room, round and green, with the sky for a roof. In winter it was sometimes very cold, and after a heavy fall of snow the scene was strange and impressive from the tiny village set in its stupendous dazzling white bowl. Not only on those rare arctic days, but at all times it was wonderfully quiet. The shout of a child or the peaceful crow of a cock was the loudest sound you heard. Once a gentleman from London town came down to spend a week at the parsonage. Towards evening on the very first day he grew restless and complained of the abnormal stillness. "I like a quiet place well enough," he exclaimed, "but this tingling silence I can't stand!" And stand it he wouldn't and didn't, for on the very next morning he took himself off. Many years had gone by, but the vicar could not forget the Londoner who had come down to invent a new way of describing the Coombe silence. His tingling phrase was a joy for ever.

He took me to the church—one of the tiniest churches in the country, just the right size for a church in a tiny village and assured me that he had never once locked the door in his fifty years—day and night it was open to any one to enter. It was a refuge and shelter from the storm and the Tempest, and many a poor homeless wretch had found a dry place to sleep in that church during the last half a century. This man's feeling of pity and tenderness for the very poor, even the outcast and tramp, was a passion. But how strange all this would sound in the ears of many country clergymen! How many have told me when I have gone to the parsonage to "borrow the key" that it had been found necessary to keep the church door locked, to prevent damage, thefts, etc. "Have you never had anything stolen?" I asked him. Yes, once, a great many years ago, the church plate had been taken away in the night. But it was recovered: the thief had taken it to the top of the hill and thrown it into the dewpond there, no doubt intending to take it out and dispose of it at some more convenient time. But it was found, and had ever since then been kept safe at the vicarage. Nothing of value to tempt a man to steal was kept in the church. He had never locked it, but once in his fifty years it had been locked against him by the churchwardens. This happened in the days of the Joseph Arch agitation, when the agricultural labourer's condition was being hotly discussed throughout the country. The vicar's heart was stirred, for he knew better than most how hard these conditions were at Coombe and in the surrounding parishes. He took up the subject and preached on it in his own pulpit in a way that offended the landowners and alarmed the farmers in the district. The church wardens, who were farmers, then locked him out of his church, and for two or three weeks there was no public worship in the parish of Coombe. Doubtless their action was applauded by all the substantial men in the neighbourhood; the others who lived in the cottages and were unsubstantial didn't matter. That storm blew over, but its consequences endured, one being that the inflammatory parson continued to be regarded with cold disapproval by the squires and their larger tenants. But the vicar himself was unrepentant and unashamed; on the contrary, he gloried in what he had said and done, and was proud to be able to relate that a quarter of a century later one of the two men who had taken that extreme course said to him, "We locked you out of your own church, but years have brought me to another mind about that question. I see it in a different light now and know that you were right and we were wrong."

Towards evening I said good-bye to my kind friend and entertainer and continued my rural ride. From Coombe it is five miles to Hurstbourne Tarrant, another charming "highland" village, and the road, sloping down the entire distance, struck me as one of the best to be on I had travelled in Hampshire, running along a narrow green valley, with oak and birch and bramble and thorn in their late autumn colours growing on the slopes on either hand. Probably the beauty of the scene, or the swift succession of beautiful scenes, with the low sun flaming on the "coloured shades," served to keep out of my mind something that should have been in it. At all events, it was odd that I had more than once promised myself a visit to the very village I was approaching solely because William Cobbett had described and often stayed in it, and now no thought of him and his ever-delightful Rural Rides was in my mind.

Arrived at the village I went straight to the "George and Dragon," where a friend had assured me I could always find good accommodations. But he was wrong: there was no room for me, I was told by a weird-looking, lean, white-haired old woman with whity-blue unfriendly eyes. She appeared to resent it that any one should ask for accommodation at such a time, when the "shooting gents" from town required all the rooms available. Well, I had to sleep somewhere, I told her: couldn't she direct me to a cottage where I could get a bed? No, she couldn't—it is always so; but after the third time of asking she unfroze so far as to say that perhaps they would take me in at a cottage close by. So I went, and a poor kind widow who lived there with a son consented to put me up. She made a nice fire in the sitting-room, and after warming myself before it, while watching the firelight and shadows playing on the dim walls and ceiling, it came to me that I was not in a cottage, but in a large room with an oak floor and wainscoting. "Do you call this a cottage?" I said to the woman when she came in with tea. "No, I have it as a cottage, but it is an old farm-house called the Rookery," she returned. Then, for the first time, I remembered Rural Rides. "This then is the very house where William Cobbett used to stay seventy or eighty years ago," I said. She had never heard of William Cobbett; she only knew that at that date it had been tenanted by a farmer named Blount, a Roman Catholic, who had some curious ideas about the land.

That settled it. Blount was the name of Cobbett's friend, and I had come to the very house where Cobbett was accustomed to stay. But how odd that my first thought of the man should have come to me when sitting by the fire where Cobbett himself had sat on many a cold evening! And this was November the second, the very day eighty-odd years ago when he paid his first visit to the Rookery; at all events, it is the first date he gives in Rural Rides. And he too had been delighted with the place and the beauty of the surrounding country with the trees in their late autumn colours. Writing on November 2nd, 1821, he says: "The place is commonly called Uphusband, which is, I think, as decent a corruption of names as one could wish to meet with. However, Uphusband the people will have it, and Uphusband it shall be for me." That is indeed how he names it all through his book, after explaining that "husband" is a corruption of Hurstbourne, and that there are two Hurstbournes, this being the upper one.

I congratulated myself on having been refused accommodation at the "George and Dragon," and was more than satisfied to pass an evening without a book, sitting there alone listening to an imaginary conversation between those two curious friends. "Lord Carnarvon," says Cobbett, "told a man, in

1820, that he did not like my politics. But what did he mean by my politics? I have no politics but such as he ought to like. To be sure I labour most assiduously to destroy a system of distress and misery; but is that any reason why a Lord should dislike my politics? However, dislike them or like them, to them, to those very politics, the Lords themselves must come at last."

Undoubtedly he talked like that, just as he wrote and as he spoke in public, his style, if style it can be called, being the most simple, direct, and colloquial ever written. And for this reason, when we are aweary of the style of the stylist, where the living breathing body becomes of less consequence than its beautiful clothing, it is a relief, and refreshment, to turn from the precious and delicate expression, the implicit word, sought for high and low and at last found, the balance of every sentence and perfect harmony of the whole work—to go from it to the simple vigorous unadorned talk of Rural Rides. A classic, and as incongruous among classics as a farmer in his smock-frock, leggings, and stout boots would appear in a company of fine gentlemen in fashionable dress. The powerful face is the main thing, and we think little of the frock and leggings and how the hair is parted or if parted at all. Harsh and crabbed as his nature no doubt was, and bitter and spiteful at times, his conversation must yet have seemed like a perpetual feast of honeyed sweets to his farmer friend. Doubtless there was plenty of variety in it: now he would expatiate on the beauty of the green downs over which he had just ridden, the wooded slopes in their glorious autumn colours, and the rich villages between; this would remind him of Malthus, that blasphemous monster who had dared to say that the increase in food production did not keep pace with increase of population; then a quieting down, a breathing-space, all about the turnip crop, the price of eggs at Weyhill Fair, and the delights of hare coursing, until politics would come round again and a fresh outburst from the glorious demagogue in his tantrums.

At eight o'clock Cobbett would say good night and go to bed, and early next morning write down what he had said to his friend, or some of it, and send it off to be printed in his paper. That, I take it, is how Rural Rides was written, and that is why it seems so fresh to us to this day, and that to take it up after other books is like going out from a luxurious room full of fine company into the open air to feel the wind and rain on one's face and see the green grass. But I very much regret that Cobbett tells us nothing of his farmer friend. Blount, I imagine, must have been a man of a very fine character to have won the heart and influenced such a person. Cobbett never loses an opportunity of vilifying the parsons and expressing his hatred of the Established Church; and yet, albeit a Protestant, he invariably softens down when he refers to the Roman Catholic faith and appears quite capable of seeing the good that is in it.

It was Blount, I think, who had soothed the savage breast of the man in this matter. The only thing I could hear about Blount and his "queer notions" regarding the land was his idea that the soil could be improved by taking the flints out. "The soil to look upon," Cobbett truly says, "appears to be more than half flint, but is a very good quality." Blount thought to make it better, and for many years employed all the aged poor villagers and the children in picking the flints from the ploughed land and gathering them in vast heaps. It does not appear that he made his land more productive, but his hobby was a good one for the poor of the village; the stones, too, proved useful afterwards to the road-makers, who have been using them these many years. A few heaps almost clothed over with a turf which had formed on them in the course of eighty years were still to be seen on the land when I was there.

The following day I took no ride. The weather was so beautiful it seemed better to spend the time sitting or basking in the warmth and brightness or strolling about. At all events, it was a perfect day at Hurstbourne Tarrant, though not everywhere, for on that third of November the greatest portion of Southern England was drowned in a cold dense white fog. In

London it was dark, I heard. Early in the morning I listened to a cirl-bunting singing merrily from a bush close to the George and Dragon Inn. This charming bird is quite common in the neighbourhood, although, as elsewhere in England, the natives know it not by its book name, nor by any other, and do not distinguish it from its less engaging cousin, the yellowhammer.

After breakfast I strolled about the common and in Doles Wood, on the down above the village, listening to the birds, and on my way back encountered a tramp whose singular appearance produced a deep impression on my mind. We have heard of a work by some modest pressman entitled "Monarchs I have met", and I sometimes think that one equally interesting might be written on "Tramps I have met". As I have neither time nor stomach for the task, I will make a present of the title to any one of my fellow-travellers, curious in tramps, who cares to use it. This makes two good titles I have given away in this chapter with a borrowed one.

But if it had been possible for me to write such a book, a prominent place would be given in it to the one tramp I have met who could be accurately described as gorgeous. I did not cultivate his acquaintance; chance threw us together and we separated after exchanging a few polite commonplaces, but his big flamboyant image remains vividly impressed on my mind.

At noon, in the brilliant sunshine, as I came loiteringly down the long slope from Doles Wood to the village, he overtook me. He was a huge man, over six feet high, nobly built, suggesting a Scandinavian origin, with a broad blond face, good features, and prominent blue eyes, and his hair was curly and shone like gold in the sunlight. Had he been a mere labourer in a workman's rough clay-stained clothes, one would have stood still to look at and admire him, and say perhaps what a magnificent warrior he would have looked with sword and spear and plumed helmet, mounted on a big horse! But alas! he had the stamp of the irreclaimable blackguard on his face; and that same handsome face was just then disfigured with several bruises in

176

three colours—blue, black, and red. Doubtless he had been in a drunken brawl on the previous evening and had perhaps been thrown out of some low public-house and properly punished.

In his dress he was as remarkable as in his figure. Bright blue trousers much too small for his stout legs, once the property, no doubt, of some sporting young gent of loud tastes in colours; a spotted fancy waistcoat, not long enough to meet the trousers, a dirty scarlet tie, long black frock-coat, shiny in places, and a small dirty grey cap which only covered the topmost part of his head of golden hair.

Walking by the hedge-side he picked and devoured the late blackberries, which were still abundant. It was a beautiful unkept hedge with scarlet and purple fruit among the many-coloured fading leaves and silver-grey down of old-man's-beard.

I too picked and ate a few berries and made the remark that it was late to eat such fruit in November. The Devil in these parts, I told him, flies abroad in October to spit on the bramble bushes and spoil the fruit. It was even worse further north, in Norfolk and Suffolk, where they say the Devil goes out at Michaelmas and shakes his verminous trousers over the bushes.

He didn't smile; he went on sternly eating blackberries, and then remarked in a bitter tone, "That Devil they talk about must have a busy time, to go messing about blackberry bushes in addition to all his other important work."

I was silent, and presently, after swallowing a few more berries, he resumed in the same tone: "Very fine, very beautiful all this"—waving his hand to indicate the hedge, its rich tangle of purple-red stems and coloured leaves, and scarlet fruit and silvery oldman's-beard. "An artist enjoys seeing this sort of thing, and it's nice for all those who go about just for the pleasure of seeing things. But when it comes to a man tramping twenty or thirty miles a day on an empty belly, looking for work which he can't find, he doesn't see it quite in the same way."

"True," I returned, with indifference.

But he was not to be put off by my sudden coldness, and he

177

proceeded to inform me that he had just returned from Salisbury Plain, that it had been noised abroad that ten thousand men were wanted by the War Office to work in forming new camps. On arrival he found it was not so—it was all a lie—men were not wanted—and he was now on his way to Andover, penniless and hungry and—

By the time he had got to that part of his story we were some distance apart, as I had remained standing still while he, thinking me still close behind, had gone on picking blackberries and talking. He was soon out of sight.

At noon the following day, the weather still being bright and genial, I went to Crux Easton, a hilltop village consisting of some low farm buildings, cottages, and a church not much bigger than a cottage. A great house probably once existed here, as the hill has a noble avenue of limes, which it wears like a comb or crest. On the lower slope of the hill, the old unkept hedges were richer in colour than in most places, owing to the abundance of the spindle-wood tree, laden with its loose clusters of flame-bright, purple-pink and orange berries.

Here I saw a pretty thing: a cock cirl-bunting, his yellow breast towards me, sitting quietly on a large bush of these same brilliant berries, set amidst a mass of splendidly coloured hazel leaves, mixed with bramble and tangled with ivy and silver-grey traveller's-joy. An artist's heart would have leaped with joy at the sight, but all his skill and oriental colours would have made nothing of it, for all visible nature was part of the picture, the wide wooded earth and the blue sky beyond and above the bird, and the sunshine that glorified all.

On the other side of the hedge there were groups of fine old beech trees and, strange to see, just beyond the green slope and coloured trees, was the great whiteness of the fog which had advanced thus far and now appeared motionless. I went down and walked by the side of the bank of mist, feeling its clammy coldness on one cheek while the other was fanned by the warm bright air. Seen at a distance of a couple of hundred yards, the appearance was that of a beautiful pearly-white cloud resting upon the earth. Many fogs had I seen, but never one like this, so substantial-looking, so sharply defined, standing like a vast white wall or flat-topped hill at the foot of the green sunlit slope! I had the fancy that if I had been an artist in sculpture, and rapid modeller, by using the edge of my hand as a knife I could have roughly carved out a human figure, then drawing it gently out of the mass proceeded to press and work it to a better shape, the shape, let us say, of a beautiful woman. Then, if it were done excellently, and some man-mocking deity, or power of the air, happened to be looking on, he would breathe life and intelligence into it, and send it, or her, abroad to mix with human kind and complicate their affairs. For she would seem a woman and would be like some women we have known, beautiful with blue flower-like eyes, pale gold or honey-coloured hair; very white of skin, Leightonian, almost diaphanous, so delicate as to make all other skins appear coarse and made of clay. And with her beauty and a mysterious sweetness not of the heart, since no heart there would be in that mist-cold body, she would draw all hearts, ever inspiring, but never satisfying passion, her beauty and alluring smiles being but the brightness of a cloud on which the sun is shining.

Birds, driven by the fog to that sunlit spot, were all about me in incredible numbers. Rooks and daws were congregating on the bushes, where their black figures served to intensify the red-gold tints of the foliage. At intervals the entire vast cawing multitude simultaneously rose up with a sound as of many waters, and appeared now at last about to mount up into the blue heavens, to float circling there far above the world as they are accustomed to do on warm windless days in autumn. But in a little while their brave note would change to one of trouble; the sight of that immeasurable whiteness covering so much of the earth would scare them, and led by hundreds of clamouring daws they would come down again to settle once more in black masses on the shining yellow trees.

Close by a ploughed field of about forty acres was the camping-ground of an army of peewits; they were travellers from the north perhaps, and were quietly resting, sprinkled over the whole area. More abundant were the small birds in mixed flocks or hordes—finches, buntings, and larks in thousands on thousands, with a sprinkling of pipits and pied and grey wagtails, all busily feeding on the stubble and fresh ploughed land. Thickly and evenly distributed, they appeared to the vision ranging over the brown level expanse as minute animated and variously coloured clods—black and brown and grey and yellow and olive-green.

It was a rare pleasure to be in this company, to revel in their astonishing numbers, to feast my soul on them as it were—little birds in such multitudes that ten thousand Frenchmen and Italians might have gorged to repletion on their small succulent bodies—and to reflect that they were safe from persecution so long as they remained here in England. This is something for an Englishman to be proud of.

After spending two hours at Crux Easton, with that dense immovable fog close by, I at length took the plunge to get to Highclere. What a change! I was at once where all form and colour and melody had been blotted out. My clothes were hoary with clinging mist, my fingers numb with cold, and Highclere, its scattered cottages appearing like dim smudges through the whiteness, was the dreariest village on earth. I fled on to Newbury in quest of warmth and light, and found it indoors, but the town was deep in the fog.

The next day I ventured out again to look for the sun, and found it not, but my ramble was not without its reward. In a pine wood three miles from the town I stood awhile to listen to the sound as of copious rain of the moisture dropping from the trees, when a sudden tempest of loud, sharp metallic notes—a sound dear to the ornithologist's ears—made me jump; and down into the very tree before which I was standing dropped a flock of about twenty crossbills. So excited and noisy when coming down, the instant they touched the tree they became perfectly silent and motionless. Seven of their number had settled on the outside shoots, and sat there within forty feet of me, looking like painted wooden images of small green and greenish-yellow parrots; for a space of fifteen minutes not the slightest movement did they make, and at length, before going, I waved my arms about and shouted to frighten them, and still they refused to stir.

Next morning that memorable fog lifted, to England's joy, and quitting my refuge I went out once more into the region of high sheep-walks, adorned with beechen woods and traveller's-joy in the hedges, rambling by Highclere, Burghclere, and Kingsclere. The last—Hampshire's little Cuzco—is a small and village-like old red brick town, unapproached by a railroad and unimproved, therefore still beautiful, as were all places in other, better, less civilized days. Here in the late afternoon a chilly grey haze crept over the country and set me wishing for a fireside and the sound of friendly voices, and I turned my face towards beloved Silchester. Leaving the hills behind me I got away from the haze and went my devious way by serpentine roads through a beautiful, wooded, undulating country. And I wish that for a hundred, nay, for a thousand years to come, I could on each recurring November have such an afternoon ride, with that autumnal glory in the trees. Sometimes, seeing the road before me carpeted with pure yellow, I said to myself, now I am coming to elms; but when the road shone red and russet-gold before me I knew it was overhung by beeches. But the oak is the common tree in this place, and from every high point on the road I saw far before me and on either hand the woods and copses all a tawny yellow gold—the hue of the dying oak leaf. The tall larches were lemon-yellow, and when growing among tall pines produced a singular effect. Best of all was it where beeches grew among the firs, and the low sun on my left hand shining through the wood gave the coloured translucent leaves an unimaginable splendour. This was the very effect which men, inspired by a sacred passion, had sought to reproduce in their noblest work—the Gothic cathedral and church, its dim interior lit by many-coloured stained glass. The only choristers in these natural fanes were the robins and the small lyrical wren; but on passing through the rustic village of Wolverton I stopped for a couple of minutes to listen to the lively strains of a cirl-bunting among some farm buildings.

Then on to Silchester, its furzy common and scattered village and the vast ruinous walls, overgrown with ivy, bramble, and thorn, of ancient Roman Calleva. Inside the walls, at one spot, a dozen men were still at work in the fading light; they were just finishing—shovelling earth in to obliterate all that had been opened out during the year. The old flint foundations that had been revealed; the houses with porches and corridors and courtyards and pillared hypocausts; the winter room with its wide beautiful floor—red and black and white and grey and yellow, with geometric pattern and twist and scroll and flower and leaf and quaint figures of man and beast and bird—all to be covered up with earth so that the plough may be driven over it again, and the wheat grow and ripen again as it has grown and ripened there above the dead city for so many centuries. The very earth within those walls had a reddish cast owing to the innumerable fragments of red tile and tessera mixed with it. Larks and finches were busily searching for seeds in the reddish-brown soil. They would soon be gone to their roosting-places and the tired men to their cottages, and the white owl coming from his hiding-place in the walls would have old Silchester to himself, as he has had it since the cries and moans of the conquered died into silence so long ago.

A Chapter from
Afoot in England, 1909

NATURE AND ETERNITY

By Richard Jefferies

The goldfinches sing so sweetly hidden in the topmost boughs of the apple-trees that heart of man cannot withstand them. These four walls, though never so well decorated with pictures, this flat white ceiling, feels all too small, and dull and tame. Down with books and pen, and let us away with the goldfinches, the princes of the birds. For thirty of their generations they have sung and courted and built their nests in those apple-trees, almost under the very windows—a time in their chronology equal to a thousand years. For they are so very busy, from earliest morn till night—a long summer's day is like a year. Now flirting with a gaily-decked and coy lady-love, chasing her from tree to tree; now splashing at the edge of a shallow stream till the golden feathers glisten and the red topknot shines. Then searching in and out the hedgerow for favourite seeds, and singing, singing all the while, verily a 'song without an end.' The wings never still, the bill never idle, the throat never silent, and the tiny heart within the proud breast beating so rapidly that, reckoning time by change and variety, an hour must be a day. A life all joy and freedom, without thought, and full of love. What a great god the sun must be to the finches from whose wings his beams are reflected in glittering gold! The abstract idea of a deity apart, as they feel their life-blood stirring, their eyelids opening, with the rising sun; as they fly to satisfy their hunger with those little fruits they use; as they revel in the warm sunshine, and utter soft notes of love to their beautiful mates, they cannot but feel a sense, unnamed, indefinite, of joyous gratitude towards that great orb which is very nearly akin to the sensual worship of ancient days. Darkness and cold are Typhon and Ahriman, light and warmth, Osiris and Ormuzd, indeed to them; with song they welcome the spring and celebrate the awakening of Adonis. Lovely little idolaters, my heart goes with them. Deep down in the mysteries of organic life there are causes for the marvellously extended grasp which the worship of light once held upon the world, hardly yet guessed at, and which even now play a part unsuspected in the motives of men. Even yet, despite our artificial life, despite railroads, telegraphs, printing-press, in the face of firm monotheistic convictions, once a year the old, old influence breaks forth, driving thousands and thousands from cities and houses out into field and forest, to the seashore and mountain-top, to gather fresh health and strength from the Sun, from the Air—Jove—and old Ocean. So the goldfinches rejoice in the sunshine, and who can sit within doors when they sing?

Foolish fashion has banished the orchard from the mansion— the orchard which Homer tells us kings once valued as part of their demesne—and has substituted curious evergreens to which the birds do not take readily. But this orchard is almost under the windows, and in summer the finches wake the sleeper with their song, and in autumn the eye looks down upon the yellow and rosy fruit. Up the scaling bark of the trunks the brown tree-climbers run, peering into every cranny, and few are the insects which escape those keen eyes. Sitting on a bench under a pear-tree, I saw a spider drop from a leaf fully nine feet above the ground, and disappear in the grass, leaving a slender rope of web, attached at the upper end to a leaf, and at the lower to a fallen pear. In a few minutes a small white caterpillar, barely an inch long, began to climb this rope. It grasped the thread in the mouth and drew up its body about a sixteenth of an inch at a time, then held tight with the two fore-feet, and, lifting its head, seized the rope a sixteenth higher; repeating this operation incessantly, the rest of the body swinging in the air. Never pausing, without haste and without rest, this creature patiently worked its way upwards, as a man might up a rope. Let anyone seize a beam overhead and attempt to lift the chest up to a level with it, the expenditure of strength is very great; even with long practice, to 'swarm' up a pole or rope to any distance is the hardest labour the human muscles are capable of. This despised 'creeping thing,' without the slightest apparent effort, without once pausing to take breath, reached the leaf overhead in rather under half an hour, having climbed a rope fully 108 times its own length. To equal this a man must climb 648 feet, or more than half as high again as St. Paul's. The insect on reaching the top at once commenced feeding, and easily bit through the hard pear-leaf: how delicately then it must have grasped the slender spider's web, which a touch would destroy! The thoughts which this feat call forth do not end here, for there was no necessity to go up the thread; the insect could to all appearance have travelled up the trunk of the tree with ease, and it is not to be supposed that its mouth and feet were specially adapted to climb a web, a thing which I have never seen done since, and which was to all appearance merely the result of the *accident* of the insect coming along just after the spider had left the thread. Another few minutes, and the first puff of wind would have carried the thread away—as a puff actually did soon afterwards. I claim a wonderful amount of *original* intelligence—as opposed to the ill-used term instinct—of patience and perseverance for this creature. It is so easy to imagine that because man is big, brain power cannot exist in tiny organizations; but even in man the seat of thought is so minute that it escapes discovery, and his very life may be said to lie in the point of contact of two bones of the neck. Put the mind of man within the body of the caterpillar—what more could it have done? Accustomed to bite and eat its way through hard leaves, why did not the insect snip off and destroy its rope? These are matters to think over dreamily while the finches sing overhead in the apple-tree.

They are not the only regular inhabitants, still less the only visitors. As there are wide plains even in thickly populated

England where man has built no populous city, so in bird-life there are fields and woods almost deserted by the songsters, who at the same time congregate thickly in a few favourite resorts, where experience gathered in slow time has shown them they need fear nothing from human beings. Such a place, such a city of the birds and beasts, is this old orchard. The bold and handsome bullfinch builds in the low hawthorn hedge which bounds it upon one side. In the walls of the arbour formed of thick ivy and flowering creepers, the robin and thrush hide their nests. On the topmost branches of the tall pear-trees the swallows rest and twitter. The noble blackbird, with full black eye, pecks at the decaying apples upon the sward, and takes no heed of a footstep. Sometimes the loving pair of squirrels who dwell in the fir-copse at the end of the meadow find their way down the hedges—staying at each tree as an inn by the road—into the orchard, and play their fantastic tricks upon the apple-boughs. The flycatchers perch on a branch clear from the tree, and dart at the passing flies. Merriest of all, the tomtits chatter and scold, hanging under the twigs, head downwards, and then away to their nest in the crumbling stone wall which encloses one side of the orchard. They have worked their way by a cranny deep into the thick wall. On the other side runs the king's highway, and ever and anon the teams go by, making music with their bells. One day a whole nation of martins savagely attacked this wall. Pressure of population probably had compelled them to emigrate from the sand quarry, and the chinks in the wall pleased their eyes. Five-and-thirty brown little birds went to work like miners at twelve or fourteen holes, tapping at the mortar with their bills, scratching out small fragments of stone, twittering and talking all the time, and there undoubtedly they would have founded a colony had not the jingling teams and now and then a barking dog disturbed them. Resting on the bench and leaning back against an apple-tree, it is easy to watch the eager starlings on the chimney-top, and see them tear out the straw of the thatch to form their holes. They are all orators born. They live in a democracy, and fluency of speech leads the populace. Perched on the edge of the chimney, his bronze-tinted wings flapping against his side to give greater emphasis—as a preacher moves his hands—the starling pours forth a flood of eloquence, now rising to screaming-pitch, now modulating his tones to soft persuasion, now descending to deep, low, complaining, regretful sounds—a speech without words—addressed to a dozen birds gravely listening on the ash-tree yonder. He is begging them to come with him to a meadow where food is abundant. In the ivy close under the window there, within reach of the hand, a water-wagtail built its nest. To this nest one lovely afternoon came a great bird like a hawk, to the fearful alarm and intense excitement of all the bird population. It was a cuckoo, and after three or four visits, despite a curious eye at the window, there was a strange egg in that nest. Inside that window, huddled fearfully in the darkest corner of the room, there was once a tiny heap of blue and yellow feathers. A tomtit straying through the casement had been chased by the cat till it dropped exhausted, and the cat was fortunately frightened by a footstep. The bird was all but dead—the feathers awry and ruffled, the eyelids closed, the body limp and helpless—only a faint fluttering of the tiny heart. When placed tenderly on the ledge of the casement, where the warm sunshine fell and the breeze came softly, it dropped listlessly on one side. But in a little while the life-giving rays quickened the blood, the eyelids opened, and presently it could stand perched upon the finger. Then, lest with returning consciousness fear should again arise, the clinging claws were transferred from the finger to a twig of wall-pear. A few minutes more, and with a chirp the bird was gone into the flood of sunlight. What intense joy there must have been in that little creature's heart as it drank the sweet air and felt the loving warmth of its great god Ra, the Sun!

Throwing open the little wicket-gate, by a step the greensward of the meadow is reached. Though the grass has been mown and the ground is dry, it is better to carry a thick rug, and cast it down in the shadow under the tall horse-chestnut-tree. It is only while in a dreamy, slumbrous, half-mesmerized state that nature's ancient papyrus roll can be read—only when the mind is at rest, separated from care and labour; when the body is at ease, luxuriating in warmth and delicious languor; when the soul is in accord and sympathy with the sunlight, with the leaf, with the slender blades of grass, and can feel with the tiniest insect which climbs up them as up a mighty tree. As the genius of the great musicians, without an articulated word or printed letter, can carry with it all the emotions, so now, lying prone upon the earth in the shadow, with quiescent will, listening, thoughts and feelings rise respondent to the sunbeams, to the leaf, the very blade of grass. Resting the head upon the hand, gazing down upon the ground, the strange and marvellous inner sight of the mind penetrates the solid earth, grasps in part the mystery of its vast extension upon either side, bearing its majestic mountains, its deep forests, its grand oceans, and almost feels the life which in ten thousand thousand forms revels upon its surface. Returning upon itself, the mind joys in the knowledge that it too is a part of this wonder—akin to the ten thousand thousand creatures, akin to the very earth itself. How grand and holy is this life! how sacred the temple which contains it!

Out from the hedge, not five yards distant, pours a rush of deep luscious notes, succeeded by the sweetest trills heard by man. It is the nightingale, which tradition assigns to the night only, but which in fact sings as loudly, and to my ear more joyously, in the full sunlight, especially in the morning, and always close to the nest. The sun has moved onward upon his journey, and this spot is no longer completely shaded, but the foliage of a great oak breaks the force of his rays, and the eye can even bear to gaze at his disc for a few moments. Living for this brief hour at least in unalloyed sympathy with nature, apart from all disturbing influences, the sight of that splendid disc carries the soul with it till it feels as eternal as the sun. Let the memory call up a picture of the desert sands of Egypt—upon the kings with the double crown, upon Rameses, upon Sesostris, upon Assurbanipal the burning beams of this very sun descended, filling their veins with tumultuous life, three thousand years ago. Lifted up in absorbing thought, the mind feels that these three thousand years are in truth no longer past than the last beat of the pulse. It throbbed—the throb is gone; their pulse throbbed, and it seems but a moment since, for to thought, as to the sun, there is no time. This little petty life of seventy years, with its little petty aims and hopes, its despicable fears and contemptible sorrows, is no more the life with which the mind is occupied. This golden disc has risen and set, as the graven marks of man alone record, full eight thousand years. The hieroglyphs of the rocks speak of a fiery sun shining inconceivable ages before that. Yet even this almost immortal sun had a beginning—perhaps emerging as a ball of incandescent gas from chaos: how long ago was that? And onwards, still onwards goes the disc, doubtless for ages and ages to come. It is time that our measures should be extended; these paltry divisions of hours and days and years—aye, of centuries—should be superseded by terms conveying some faint idea at least of the vastness of space. For in truth, when thinking thus, there is no *time* at all. The mind loses the sense of time and reposes in eternity. This hour, this instant is eternity; it extends backwards, it extends forwards, and we are in it. It is a grand and an ennobling feeling to know that at this moment illimitable time extends on either hand. No conception of a supernatural character formed in the brain has ever or will ever surpass the mystery of this endless existence as exemplified—as made manifest by the physical sun—a visible sign of immortality. This—this hour is part of the immortal life. Reclining upon this rug under the chestnut-tree, while the graceful shadows dance, a passing bee hums and the nightingale sings, while the oak foliage sprinkles the sunshine over us, we are really and in truth in the midst of eternity. Only by walking hand in hand with nature, only by a reverent and loving study of the mysteries for ever around us, is it possible to disabuse the mind of the narrow view, the contracted belief that time is now and eternity to-morrow. Eternity is to-day. The goldfinches and the tiny caterpillars, the brilliant sun, if looked at lovingly and thoughtfully, will lift the soul out of the smaller life of human care that is of selfish aims, bounded by seventy years, into the greater, the limitless life which has been going on over universal space from endless ages past, which is going on now, and which will for ever and for ever, in one form or another, continue to proceed.

Dreamily listening to the nightingale's song, let us look down upon the earth as the sun looks down upon it. In this meadow how many millions of blades of grass are there, each performing wonderful operations which the cleverest chemist can but poorly indicate, taking up from the earth its sap, from the air its gases, in a word living, living as much as ourselves, though in a lower form? On the oak-tree yonder, how many leaves are doing the same? Just now we felt the vastness of the earth—its extended majesty, bearing mountain, forest, and sea. Not a blade of grass but has its insect, not a leaf; the very air as it softly woos the cheek bears with it living germs, and upon all those mountains, within those forests, and in every drop of those oceans, life in some shape moves and stirs. Nay, the very solid earth itself, the very chalk and clay and stone and rock has been built up by once living organisms. But at this instant, looking down upon the earth as the sun does, how can words depict the glowing wonder, the marvellous beauty of all the plant, the insect, the animal life, which presses upon the mental eye? It is impossible. But with these that are more immediately around us—with the goldfinch, the caterpillar, the nightingale, the blades of grass, the leaves—with these we may feel, into their life we may in part enter, and find our own existence thereby enlarged. Would that it were possible for the heart and mind to enter into *all* the life that glows and teems upon the earth—to feel with it, hope with it, sorrow with it—and thereby to become a grander, nobler being. Such a being, with such a sympathy and larger existence, must hold in scorn the feeble, cowardly, selfish desire for an immortality of pleasure only, whose one great hope is to escape pain! No. Let me joy with all living creatures; let me suffer with them all—the reward of feeling a deeper, grander life would be amply sufficient.

What wonderful patience the creatures called 'lower' exhibit! Watch this small red ant travelling among the grass-blades. To it they are as high as the oak-trees to us, and they are entangled and matted together as a forest overthrown by a tornado. The insect slowly overcomes all the difficulties of its route— now climbing over the creeping roots of the buttercups, now struggling under a fallen leaf, now getting up a bennet, up and down, making one inch forward for three vertically, but never pausing, always onwards at racing speed. A shadow sweeps rapidly over the grass—it is that of a rook which has flown between us and the sun. Looking upwards into the deep azure of the sky, intently gazing into space and forgetting for a while the life around and beneath, there comes into the mind an intense desire to rise, to penetrate the height, to become part and parcel of that wondrous infinity which extends overhead as it extends along the surface. The soul full of thought grows concentrated in itself, marvels only at its own destiny, labours to behold the secret of its own existence, and, above all, utters without articulate words a prayer forced from it by the bright sun, by the blue sky, by bird and plant:—Let me have wider feelings, more extended sympathies, let me feel with all living things, rejoice and praise with them. Let me have deeper knowledge, a nearer insight, a more reverent conception. Let me see the mystery of life—the secret of the sap as it rises in the tree—the secret of the blood as it courses through the vein. Reveal the broad earth and the ends of it—make the majestic ocean open to the eye down to its inmost recesses. Expand the mind till it grasps the idea of the unseen forces which hold the globe suspended and draw the vast suns and stars through space. Let it see the life, the organisms which dwell in those great worlds, and feel with them their hopes and joys and sorrows. Ever upwards, onwards, wider, deeper, broader, till capable of all—all. Never did vivid imagination stretch out the powers of deity with such a fulness, with such intellectual grasp, vigour, omniscience as the human mind could reach to, if only its organs, its means, were equal to its thought. Give us, then, greater strength of body, greater length of days; give us more vital energy, let our limbs be mighty as those of the giants of old. Supplement such organs with nobler mechanical engines—with extended means of locomotion; add novel and more minute methods of analysis and discovery. Let us become as demi-gods. And why not? Whoso gave the gift of the mind gave also an infinite space, an infinite matter for it to work upon, an infinite time in which to work. Let no one presume to define the boundaries of that divine gift—that mind—for all the experience of eight thousand years proves beyond a question that the limits of its powers will never be reached, though the human race dwell upon the globe for eternity. Up, then, and labour: and let that labour be sound and holy. Not for immediate and petty reward, not that the appetite or the vanity may be gratified, but that the sum of human perfection may be advanced; labouring as consecrated priests, for true science is religion. All is possible. A grand future awaits the world. When man has only partially worked out his own conceptions—when only a portion of what the mind foresees and plans is realized—then already earth will be as a paradise.

Full of love and sympathy for this feeble ant climbing over grass and leaf, for yonder nightingale pouring forth its song, feeling a community with the finches, with bird, with plant, with animal, and reverently studying all these and more—how is it possible for the heart while thus wrapped up to conceive the desire of crime? For ever anxious and labouring for perfection, shall the soul, convinced of the divinity of its work, halt and turn aside to fall into imperfection? Lying thus upon the rug under the shadow of the oak and horse-chestnut-tree, full of the joy of life—full of the joy which all organisms feel in living alone—lifting the eye far, far above the sphere even of the sun, shall we ever conceive the idea of murder, of violence, of aught that degrades ourselves? It is impossible while in this frame. So thus reclining, and thus occupied, we require no judge, no prison, no law, no punishment—and, further, no army, no monarch. At this moment, did neither of these institutions exist our conduct would be the same. Our whole existence at this moment is permeated with a reverent love, an aspiration—a desire of a more perfect life; if the very name of religion was extinct, our hopes, our wish would be the same. It is but a simple transition to conclude that with more extended knowledge, with wider sympathies, with greater powers—powers more equal to the vague longings of their minds, the human race would be as we are at this moment in the shadow of the chestnut-tree. No need of priest and lawyer; no need of armies or kings. It is probable that with the progress of knowledge it will be possible to satisfy the necessary wants of existence much more easily than now, and thus to remove one great cause of discord. And all these thoughts because the passing shadow of a rook caused the eye to gaze upwards into the deep azure of the sky. There is no limit, no number to the thoughts which the study of nature may call forth, any more than there is a limit to the number of the rays of the sun.

This blade of grass grows as high as it can, the nightingale there sings as sweetly as it can, the goldfinches feed to their full desire and lay down no arbitrary rules of life; the great sun above pours out its heat and light in a flood unrestrained. What is the meaning of this hieroglyph, which is repeated in a thousand thousand other ways and shapes, which meets us at every turn? It is evident that all living creatures, from the zoophyte upwards, plant, reptile, bird, animal, and in his natural state—in his physical frame—man also, strive with all their powers to obtain as perfect an existence as possible. It is the one great law of their being, followed from birth to death. All the efforts of the plant are put forth to obtain more light, more air, more moisture—in a word, more food—upon which to grow, expand, and become more beautiful and perfect. The aim may be unconscious, but the result is evident. It is equally so with the animal; its lowest appetites subserve the one grand object of its advance. Whether it be eating, drinking, sleeping, procreating, all tends to one end, a fuller development of the individual, a higher condition of the species; still further, to the production of new races capable of additional progress. Part and parcel as we are of the great community of living beings, indissolubly connected with them from the lowest to the highest by a thousand ties, it is impossible for us to escape from the operation of this law; or if, by the exertion of the will, and the resources of the intellect, it is partially suspended, then the individual may perhaps pass away unharmed, but the race must suffer. It is, rather, the province of that inestimable gift, the mind, to aid nature, to smooth away the difficulties, to assist both the physical and mental man to increase his powers and widen his influence. Such efforts have been made from time to time, but unfortunately upon purely empirical principles, by arbitrary interference, without a long previous study of the delicate organization it was proposed to amend. If there is one thing our latter-day students have demonstrated beyond all reach of cavil, it is that both the physical and the mental man are, as it were, a mass of inherited structures—are built up of partially absorbed rudimentary organs and primitive conceptions, much as the trunks of certain trees are formed by the absorption of the leaves. He is made up of the Past. This is a happy and an inspiriting discovery, insomuch as it holds out a resplendent promise that there may yet come a man of the future made out of our present which will then be the past. It is a discovery which calls upon us for new and larger moral and physical exertion, which throws upon us wider and nobler duties, for upon us depends the future. At one blow this new light casts aside those melancholy convictions which, judging from the evil blood which seemed to stain each new generation alike, had elevated into a faith the depressing idea that man could not advance. It explains the causes of that stain, the reason of those imperfections, not necessary parts of the ideal man, but inherited from a lower order of life, and to be gradually expunged.

But this marvellous mystery of inheritance has brought with it a series of mental instincts, so to say; a whole circle of ideas of moral conceptions, in a sense belonging to the Past—ideas which were high and noble in the rudimentary being, which were beyond the capacity of the pure animal, but which are now in great part merely obstructions to advancement. Let these perish. We must seek for enlightenment and for progress, not in the dim failing traditions of a period but just removed from the time of the rudimentary or primeval man—we must no longer allow the hoary age of such traditions to blind the eye and cause the knee to bend—we must no longer stultify the mind by compelling it to receive as infallible what in the very nature of things must have been fallible to the highest degree. The very plants are wiser far. They seek the light of to-day, the heat of the sun which shines at this hour; they make no attempt to guide their life by the feeble reflection of rays which were extinguished ages ago. This slender blade of grass, beside the edge of our rug under the chestnut-tree, shoots upwards in the fresh air of to-day; its roots draw nourishment from the moisture of the dew which heaven deposited this morning. If it does make use of the past—of the soil, the earth that has accumulated in centuries—it is to advance its present growth. Root out at once and for ever these primeval, narrow, and contracted ideas; fix the mind upon the sun of the present, and prepare for the sun that must rise to-morrow. It is our duty to develop both mind and body and soul to the utmost: as it is the duty of this blade of grass and this oak-tree to grow and expand as far as their powers will admit. But the blade of grass and the oak have this great disadvantage to work against—they can only labour in the lines laid down for them, and unconsciously; while man can think, foresee, and plan. The greatest obstacle to progress is the lack now beginning to be felt all over the world, but more especially in the countries most highly civilized, of a true ideal to work up to. It is necessary that some far-seeing master-mind, some giant intellect, should arise, and sketch out in bold, unmistakable outlines the grand and noble future which the human race should labour for. There have been weak attempts—there are contemptible makeshifts now on their trial, especially in the new world—but the whole of these, without exception, are simply diluted reproductions of systems long since worn out. These can only last a little while; if anything, they are worse than the prejudices and traditions which form the body of wider-spread creeds. The world cries out for an intellect which shall draw its inspiration from the unvarying and infallible laws regulating the universe; which shall found its faith upon the teaching of grass, of leaf, of bird, of beast, of hoary rock, great ocean, star and sun; which shall afford full room for the development of muscle, sense, and above all of the wondrous brain; and which without fettering the individual shall secure the ultimate apotheosis of the race. No such system can spring at once, complete, perfect in detail, from any one mind. But assuredly when once a firm basis has been laid down, when an outline has been drawn, the converging efforts of a thousand thousand thinkers will be brought to bear upon it, and it will be elaborated into something approaching a reliable guide. The faiths of the past, of the ancient world, now extinct or feebly lingering on, were each inspired by one mind only. The faith of the future, in strong contrast, will spring from the researches of a thousand thousand thinkers, whose minds, once brought into a focus, will speedily burn up all that is useless and worn out with a fierce heat, and evoke a new and brilliant light. This converging thought is one of the greatest blessings of our day, made possible by the vastly extended means of communication, and almost seems specially destined for this very purpose. Thought increases with the ages. At this moment there are probably as many busy brains studying, reflecting, collecting scattered truths, as there were thinkers—effectual thinkers—in all the recorded eighty centuries gone by. Daily and hourly the noble army swells its numbers, and the sound of its mighty march grows louder; the inscribed roll of its victories fills the heart with exultation.

There is a slight rustle among the bushes and the fern upon the mound. It is a rabbit who has peeped forth into the sunshine. His eye opens wide with wonder at the sight of us; his nostrils work nervously as he watches us narrowly. But in a little while the silence and stillness reassure him; he nibbles in a desultory way at the stray grasses on the mound, and finally ventures out into the meadow almost within reach of the hand. It is so easy to make the acquaintance—to make friends with the children of Nature. From the tiniest insect upwards they are so ready to dwell in sympathy with us—only be tender, quiet, considerate, in a word, *gentlemanly*, towards them and they will freely wander around. And they have all such marvellous tales to tell—intricate problems to solve for us. This common wild rabbit has an ancestry of almost unsearchable antiquity. Within that little body there are organs and structures which, rightly studied, will throw a light upon the mysteries hidden in our own frames. It is a peculiarity of this search that nothing is despicable; nothing can be passed over—not so much as a fallen leaf, or a grain of sand. Literally everything bears stamped upon it characters in the hieratic, the sacred handwriting, not one word of which shall fall to the ground.

Sitting indoors, with every modern luxury around, rich carpets, artistic furniture, pictures, statuary, food and drink brought from the uttermost ends of the earth, with the telegraph, the printing-press, the railway at immediate command, it is easy to say, 'What have *I* to do with all this? I am neither an animal nor a plant, and the sun is nothing to me. This is *my* life which I have created; I am apart from the other inhabitants of the earth.' But go to the window. See—there is but a thin, transparent sheet of brittle glass between the artificial man and the air, the light, the trees, and grass. So between him and the other innumerable organisms which live and breathe there is but a thin feeble crust of prejudice and social custom. Between him and those irresistible laws which keep the sun upon its course there is absolutely no bar whatever. Without air he cannot live. Nature cannot be escaped. Then face the facts, and having done so, there will speedily arise a calm pleasure beckoning onwards.

The shadows of the oak and chestnut-tree no longer shelter our rug; the beams of the noonday sun fall vertically on us; we will leave the spot for a while. The nightingale and the goldfinches, the thrushes and blackbirds, are silent for a time in the sultry heat. But they only wait for the evening to burst forth in one exquisite chorus, praising this wondrous life and the beauties of the earth.

An Essay from
The Hills and the Vale, 1909

ONE GREEN FIELD

By Edward Thomas

Happiness is not to be pursued, though pleasure may be; but I have long thought that I should recognise happiness could I ever achieve it. It would be health, or at least unthwarted intensity of sensual and mental life, in the midst of beautiful or astonishing things which should give that life full play and banish expectation and recollection. I never achieved it, and am fated to be almost happy in many different circumstances, and on account of my forethought to be contemptuous or even disgusted at what the beneficent designs of chance have brought—refusing, for example, to abandon my nostrils frankly to the "musk and amber" of revenge; or polluting, by the notice of some trivial accident, the remembrance of past things, both bitter and sweet, in the company of an old friend. Wilfully and yet helplessly I coin mere pleasures out of happiness. And yet herein, perhaps, a just judge would declare me to be at least not more foolish than those men who are always pointing out the opportunities and just causes of happiness which others have. Also, the flaw in my happiness which wastes it to a pleasure is in the manner of my looking back at it when it is past. It is as if I had made a great joyous leap over a hedge, and then had looked back and seen that the hedge was but four feet high and not dangerous. Is it perhaps true that those are never happy who know what happiness is? The shadow of it I seem to see every day in entering a little idle field in a sternly luxuriant country.

It is but five grassy acres, and yet as the stile admitting you to it makes you pause—to taste the blackberries or to see how far the bryony has twined—you salute it in a little while as a thing of character. Many of the fields around are bounded by straight-ruled hedges, as if they had been cut up by a tyrant or a slave, with only a few of such irregularities as a stream or a pond may enforce. Not one of the five hedges of this field makes a straight line. The hedge up to your right from the stile is of a noble and fascinating unruliness. So winds a mountain stream down its ladders of crag in Cardigan; into some such form would the edge of a phalanx be worn by long swaying in the height of battle. The other hedges are equally fretted. Here, there is a deep indentation where the cattle lie and wear the blackthorn stems until they are polished for ever; and there the knitted stoles and roots of ash jut out and encroach, fierce and antique and stony, like a strange beast left there to lie in the sweet grass—like a worn effigy over a grave where knight and hound have become mingled in monstrous ambiguity. The surface of the field is of the same wildness. It does not rise and fall in a few sea-like heavings, or in many little waves, nor is it level or in one long, gradual slope, but rising sleepily from west to east it is broken by sudden hollows and mounds. In one place the furze on a mound makes a little world for two or three pairs of linnets and white-throats, and there are the largest and sweetest blackberries; there also a hundred young stems of brier spend spring and summer in perfecting the curves of their long leaps—curves that are like the gush of water over a dam, and yet crossing in multitudes without crowding, in all ways without discord, like the paths of the flight of swallows when they embroider the twilight air. In another place it is always marshy, the home of marigold and reed. One corner used to be dominated by a tall tented oak, of so majestic balance that when sawn through it stood long in the wind; there the pheasants are proud among bugle or centaury flowers. Here and there a smooth boulder protrudes, guarded by hundreds of blue scabious flowers which welcome butterflies of their own hue, and sometimes a peacock butterfly displays himself on the naked stone.

At the eastern and higher end the field becomes so narrow that it is like a lane, through which the hunt gloriously decants itself among the knolls. It is narrowed still more by a small pond, and round that a tall holly of solid shadow with glancing edges, an oak, an overhanging thicket of bramble and thorn and three old butts of ash, where the fairy gold of toadstools is scattered abundantly as if sown by one sweep of a generous hand. The pond is the home of one moorhen, which is always either swimming there or hastening to it from the field. It is but as large as a farmhouse kitchen, and yet the moorhen will not desert it, finding the eaves among the roots as pleasing as attics to a boy; content with her seeming security though the road passes just above, and rich in her share of sun and moon and stars. To see the moorhen swimming in the narrow pond on a silent and misty autumn morning is to think, now with joy, now with pain, of solitude, but always with a reverie at last that is entangled among the dim, late stars—she possessing the solitary pond, in the solitary autumn country on a planet that is but an element in the solitude of the infinite; and her liquid hoot dwells long in the brain.

It is worth while to watch the pool at dawn, because, though it might seem to be but one of the myriad waters that light candles of adoration and celebration to every dawn, it has then the air, as the mist drips and tingles at the edge, of being a grey priest who has not yet done serving other gods than the dawn, and, until it puts on its white robes and glimmers altogether, it makes with the oak tree a group of pathetic revolt against the day—the oak might be a Saturn or a Lear, the pool in its gradual surrender to the light a Druid sheltering dear and unprosperous mysteries yet a little longer from the proud sun. Then the thrush sings on the holly crest with such blitheness as cannot, nevertheless, excel the water's glory in the fully risen light.

But whatever conversion the little pond undergoes on dawn after dawn, the field as a whole retains the same antiquity, which it announces so powerfully that I knew it on first crossing the stile. Perhaps the lawless shape of the field, its unusual undulations, its unkemptness in the midst of a land all rich with crops—perhaps these things suggested antiquity; but I think not—at least they do not explain it for it was then strange, and now with all its familiarity it has rather gained than lost its power. It is the same when its outlines are concealed by mist and all I can see is the clover rough with silver dew, white mushrooms, and perhaps one red yoke of maple in the hollow air, and when the snow covers all but the myriad thistles blossoming with blue tits. Enter it in spring—the linnets sprinkle a song like audible sunlight—and yet the field is old. But November is its notable month. Its trees are all oaks and they have hardly lost a leaf; the leaves are falling continually from those smouldering sunset clouds of foliage, which, kingly rich, look as if they would never be poor. One skylark sings high over the field in the rainy sky. The blue rooks unsheathe themselves heavily from the branches and shine silverly and caw with genial voices. A pheasant explodes from a grass tussock underfoot. The air smells like the musky white wild rose; coming from the west it blows gently, laden with all the brown and golden savours of Wales and Devon and Wiltshire and Surrey which I know, and the scent lifts the upper lip so that you snuff deeply as a dog snuffs. A stoat goes with uplifted tail across the field. But the field itself—was there a great house here once and is it dead and yet vocal? Are its undulations and rude edges all that remain of an old wood? Or was there a battle here, and is the turf alive with death? Certainly there is death somewhere speaking eloquently to mortal men. It is not alive, but it laments something, and where there is sorrow there is life.

For just one day in September the goldfinches come and twitter, and are happy among the thistles, and fly away.

A CHAPTER FROM
The Heart of England, 1909

SUMMER

A DIARY

By Susan Fenimore Cooper

Friday, June 1st.—Beautiful day. Pleasant walk. The whole country is green at this moment, more so than at any other period of the year. The earth is completely decked in delicate verdure of varied shades: the fruit-trees have dropped their blossoms, and the orchards and gardens are green; the forest has just put on its fresh foliage, the meadows are yet uncolored by the flowers, and the young grain-fields look grassy still. This fresh green hue of the country is very charming, and with us it is very fugitive, soon passing away into the warmer coloring of midsummer.

The cedar-birds have been very troublesome among the fruit blossoms, and they are still haunting the gardens. As they always move in flocks, except for a very short period when busy with their young, they leave their mark on every tree they attack, whether in fruit or flower. We saw them last week scattering the petals in showers, to get at the heart of the blossom, which, of course, destroys the young fruit. They are very much their own enemies in this way, for no birds are greater fruit-eaters than themselves; they are even voracious feeders when they find a berry to their taste, actually destroying themselves, at times, by the numbers they swallow.

There are two closely-allied varieties of this bird, very similar in general appearance and character, one coming from the extreme north, while the other is found within the tropics. Both, however, meet on common ground in the temperate regions of our own country. The larger sort—the Bohemian wax-wing—is well known in Europe, though so irregular in its flights, that in former times its visits were looked upon by superstitious people as the forerunner of some public calamity. Until lately, this bird was supposed to be unknown on the Western continent; but closer observation has shown that it is found here, within our own State, where it is said to be increasing. It bears a strong general resemblance to the cedar-bird, though decidedly larger, and differently marked in some points. It is supposed to breed very far north in arctic countries. Both birds are crested, and both have a singular appendage to their wings, little red, wax-like, tips at the extremity of their secondary wing-feathers. These vary in number, and are not found on all individuals, but they are quite peculiar to themselves. The habits of the two varieties are, in many respects, similar: they are both berry-eaters, very gregarious in their habits, and particularly affectionate in their dispositions toward one another; they crowd as near together as possible, half a dozen often sitting side by side on the same branch, caressing one another, and even feeding one another out of pure friendliness. They have been called chatterers in the Old World, but in fact they are very silent birds, though fussy and active, which perhaps made people fancy they were chatty creatures also.

The Bohemian wax-wing is rather rare, even in Europe; and yet it is believed that a small flock were in our own neighborhood this spring. On two different occasions we remarked what seemed very large cedar-birds *without* the white line about the eye, and *with* a white stripe on the wings; but they were in a thicket both times, and not being at liberty to stay and watch them, it would not do to assert positively that these were the Bohemian wax-wing. Learned ornithologists, wth a bird in the hand, have sometimes made great mistakes on such matters, and, of course, unlearned people should be very modest in expressing an opinion, especially where, instead of one bird in the hand, they can only point to two in a bush. As for the cedar-birds, everybody knows them; they are common enough throughout the country, and are also abundant in Mexico. They are sold in the markets of our large towns, in the autumn and spring, for two or three cents a piece.

Saturday, 2d.—Cloudy morning, followed by a charming afternoon. Long walk. Took a by-road which led us over the hills to a wild spot, where, in a distance of two or three miles, there is only one inhabited house, and that stands on the border of a gloomy swamp, from which the wood has been cut away, while two or three deserted log-cabins along the road only make things look more desolate. We enjoyed the walk all the more, however, for its wild, rude character, so different from our everyday rambles. Passed several beautiful springs in the borders of the unfenced woods, and saw several interesting birds. A handsome Clape, or golden-winged woodpecker, a pretty wood-pewee, and a very delicate little black-poll warbler, this last rare, and entirely confined to the forest; it was hopping very leisurely among the flowery branches of a wild cherry, and we had an excellent opportunity of observing it, for on that wild spot it was not on the look-out for human enemies, and we approached, unobserved, placing ourselves behind a bush. These three birds are all peculiar to our part of the world.

The rude fences about several fields in these new lands were prettily bordered with the Canadian violet, white and lilac; the chinks and hollows of several old stumps were also well garnished with these flowers; one does not often see so many together.

Upon one of these violets we found a handsome colored spider, one of the kind that live on flowers and take their color from them; but this was unusually large. Its body was of the size of a well-grown pea, and of a bright lemon color; its legs were also yellow, and altogether it was one of the most showy colored spiders we have seen in a long time. Scarlet, or red ones still larger, are found, however, near New York. But, in their gayest aspect, these creatures are repulsive. It gives one a chilling idea of the gloomy solitude of a prison, when we remember that spiders have actually been petted by men shut out from better companionship. They are a very common insect with us, and on that account more annoying than any other that is found here. Some of them, with great black bodies, are of a formidable size. These haunt cellars, and barns, and churches, and appear occasionally in inhabited rooms. There is a black spider of this kind, with a body said to be an inch long, and legs double that length, found in the Palace of Hampton Court, in England, which, it will be remembered, belonged to Cardinal Wolsey, and these great creatures are called "Cardinals" there, being considered by some people as peculiar to that building. A huge spider, by-the-bye, with her intricate web and snares, would form no bad emblem of a courtier and diplomatist, of the stamp of Cardinal Wolsey. He certainly took "hold with his hands, in kings' palaces," and did his share of mischief there.

Few people like spiders. No doubt these insects must have their merits and their uses, since none of God's creatures are made in vain; all living things are endowed with instincts more or less admirable; but the spider's plotting, creeping ways, and a sort of wicked expression about him, lead one to dislike him as a near neighbor. In a battle between a spider and a fly, one always sides with the fly, and yet of the two, the last is certainly the most troublesome insect to man. But the fly is frank and free in all his doings; he seeks his food openly, and he pursues his pastimes openly; suspicions of others or covert designs against them are quite unknown to him, and there is something almost confiding in the way in which he sails around you, when a single stroke of your hand might destroy him. The spider, on the contrary, lives by snares and plots; he is at the same time very designing and very suspicious, both cowardly and fierce; he always moves stealthily, as though among enemies, retreating before the least appearance of danger, solitary and morose, holding no communion with his fellows. His whole appearance corresponds with this character, and it is not surprising, therefore, that while the fly is more mischievous to us than the spider, we yet look upon the first with more favor than the last; for it is a natural impulse of the human heart to prefer that which is open and confiding to that which is wily and suspicious, even in the brute creation. The cunning and designing man himself will, at times, find a feeling of respect and regard for the guileless and generous stealing over him, his heart, as it were, giving the lie to his life.

Some two or three centuries since, when people came to this continent from the Old World in search of gold, oddly enough, it was considered a good sign of success when they met with spiders! It would be difficult to say why they cherished this fancy; but according to that old worthy, Hakluyt, when Martin Frobisher and his party landed on Cumberland Island, in quest of gold, their expectations were much increased by finding there numbers of spiders, "which, as many affirm, are signes of great store of gold."

They fancied that springs also were abundant near minerals, so that we may, in this county, cherish great hopes of a mine— if we choose.

Monday, 4th.—Very warm yesterday and to-day. Thermometer 83 in the shade at noon. Walked in the evening. The corn-fields are now well garnished with scare-crows, and it is amusing to see the different devices employed for the purpose. Bits of tin hung upon upright sticks are very general; lines of white twine, crossing the field at intervals near the soil, are also much in favor, and the crows are said to be particularly shy of this sort of network; other fields are guarded by a number of little whirligig windmills. One large field that we passed evidently belonged to a man of great resources in the way of expedients; for, among a number of contrivances, no two were alike: in one spot, large as life, stood the usual man of straw, here was a tin pan on a pole, there a sheet was flapping its full breadth in the breeze, here was a straw hat on a stick, there an old flail, in one corner a broken tin *Dutch oven* glittered in the sunshine, and at right angles with it was a tambourine! It must needs be a bold crow that will venture to attack such a camp.[3] It is strange how soon these creatures find out where maize has been planted. For two or three weeks, at this season, they are very troublesome until the grain has outgrown its seed character, and taken root. They do not seem to attack other grains much;—at least, scare-crows are never seen in other fields.

The chipmucks, or ground-squirrels, are also very mischievous in the maize-fields; and the blue-jay follows the same bad example occasionally. In autumn, the king-birds, in addition to the others, attack the ripe grain also, so that the maize has many enemies.

A thunder-shower passed over the village in the afternoon, and in the course of an hour the thermometer fell 20 degrees.

Tuesday, 5th.—Charming, cloudless day; fresh air from the west rustling among the new leaves. Stroll in the woods; flowers blooming abundantly. The wood betony, with its yellow heads, makes quite a show this season; there is more of it than usual, and it is quite ornamental on that account.

The different varieties of Solomon's seal—all elegant plants—are now in bloom. The wise King of Israel must have set his stamp upon many roots in these western forests; for the flowers of the tribe are very numerous here, especially the false spikenard, the delicate two-leaved Solomon's seal, or bead-ruby, and the Clintonia, with yellow lily-like flowers and large blue berries.

The tufted convallaria bifolia, or bead-ruby, is one of our most common wood plants, very much like that of Europe, although the flowerets are larger. It is singularly slow in the

3   This field yielded ninety-three bushels of maize to the acre the following autumn.

208

progress of its fruit. The cluster of berries forms early in June, but requires all summer to ripen; at first they are green and opaque, like wax; then, in July, they become speckled with red; in August the spots spread, and the whole berry is red; and, later still, in September, it takes a beautiful ruby color, and is nearly transparent; in which condition we have seen them as late as the first of December. The false spikenard goes through much the same process, but its fruit is more frequently blasted, and the name of bead-ruby is here confined to the smaller two-leaved plant. The pretty little lily of the valley, that charming flower of the gardens, grows wild in the Southern Alleghanies, but it is not found among the plants of these northernmost ridges of the chain.

We were walking in a beautiful grove where the wood had been only partially cleared, leaving many fine trees standing, mingled with the stumps of others long since felled. The mossy roots of these mouldering old stumps are choice places for the early flowers; one often finds the remains of an old oak, or pine, or chestnut, encircled by a beautiful border of this kind, mosses and flowers blended together in a way which art can never equal. During many successive springs, we have been in the habit of watching the flowers as they unfold upon these mossy hillocks. As usual, they are now daintily sprinkled with blossoms, for the soil is rich as possible in such spots.

We amused ourselves with counting the different kinds of flowers growing on several of these little knolls. In one instance, we found fifteen different plants, besides the grasses, in a narrow circle about the swelling roots, six or eight feet in breadth; around another we counted eighteen varieties; another showed twenty-two; and a fourth had six-and-twenty kinds. The groundwork is usually made up of mosses of three or four varieties and shades, all very beautiful, and blended with these are the silvery leaves of the pearly everlastings.

Violets, blue, white, and yellow, grow there, with rosy gay-wings,[4] cool-wort, fairy-cup, or mitella, low-cornel, May-star, strawberry, dew-drop, bead-ruby, squaw-vine, partridge-plant, pipsissiwa, pyrolas, loose-strife, ground-laurel, innocence, Michaelmas-daisies of several kinds, perhaps the coptis, or gold-thread, and three or four ferns. Such are the plants often found in these wild, posy patches, about old stumps, in half-cleared woods. Of course, they are not all in flower together; but toward the prime of the spring, one may at times find nearly a dozen kinds in blossom at the same moment. These are all native plants, gathering, as if out of affection, about the roots of the fallen forest trees.

Wednesday, 6th.—Coolish this morning. Chilly people have lighted their parlor fires. Last year we had strawberries the 6th of June, but the present season is more backward. Good walking weather to-day.

It is a pleasing part of the elegance of May, in a temperate climate, that few of the coarser weeds show themselves during that month; or, rather, at that early day, they do not appear in their true character. They are, of course, very troublesome to gardeners from the first, but they do not then obtrude themselves upon general attention. The season advances with great rapidity, however, and already these rude plants are beginning to show themselves in the forms by which we know them. The burdock and nettle, and thistle, &c., &c., are growing too plentifully under fences, and in waste spots; duckweed and purslane, &c., &c., spring up in the paths and beds so freely and so boldly, that it is the chief labor of the month to wage war upon their tribe.

It is remarkable that these troublesome plants have come very generally from the Old World; they do not belong here, but following the steps of the white man, they have crossed the

---

4   Gay-wings, Poly-gala paucifolia; Cool-wort, Tiarella cordofolia; Fairy-cup, Mitella dyphylla; May-star, Trientalis Americana; Bead-ruby, Convallaria bifolia; Squaw-vine, Mitchella repens; Partridge plant, Gualtheria; Dew-drop, Dalibaraa.

ocean with him. A very large proportion of the most common weeds in our fields and gardens, and about our buildings, are strangers to the soil. It will be easy to name a number of these:—such, for instance, as the dock and the burdock, found about every barn and outbuilding; the common plaintains and mallows—regular path-weeds; the groundsel, purslane, pigweed, goose-foot, shepherd's-purse, and lamb's-quarters, so troublesome in gardens; the chickweed growing everywhere; the prinpernel, celandine, and knawel; the lady's thumb and May-weed; the common nettles and teazel; wild flax, stickseed, burweed, doorweed; all the mulleins; the most pestilent thistles, both the common sort and that which is erroneously called the Canada thistle; the sow thistles; the chess, corn-cockle, tares, bugloss, or blue-weed, and the pigeon-weed of the grain-fields; the darnel, yarrow, wild parsnip, ox-eye daisy, the wild garlick, the acrid buttercup, and the acrid St. John's wort of the meadows; the nightshades, Jerusalem artichoke, wild radish, wild mustard, or charlock, the poison hemlock, the henbane,—ay, even the very dandelion,[5] a plant which we tread under foot at every turn. Others still might be added to the list, which were entirely unknown to the red man, having been introduced by the European race, and are now choking up all our way-sides, forming the vast throng of foreign weeds. Some of these have come from a great distance, travelling round the world. The shepherd's-purse, with others, is common in China, on the most eastern coast of Asia. One kind of mallows belongs to the East Indies; another to the coast of the Mediterranean. The gimson weed, or Datura, is an Abyssinian plant, and the Nicandra came from Peru. It is supposed that the amaranths or greenweeds, so very common here, have also been introduced, though possibly only from the more southern parts of our own country.

Some few American plants have been also carried to Europe, where they have become naturalized; but the number

5   Dr. Torrey.

is very small. The evening primrose, and the silkweed, among others, have sowed themselves in some parts of the Old World, transported, no doubt, with the tobacco, and maize, and potato, which are now so widely diffused over the Eastern continent, to the very heart of Asia. But even at home, on our own soil, the amount of native weeds is small when compared with the throngs brought from the Old World. The wild cucumber, a very troublesome plant, the great white convolvolus, the dodder, the field sorrel, the pokeweed, the silkweed, with one or two plantains and thistles, of the rarer kinds, are among the most important of those whose origin is clearly settled as belonging to this continent. It is also singular that among those tribes which are of a divided nature, some being natives, others introduced, the last are generally the most numerous; for instance, the native chickweeds, and plantains, and thistles, are less common here than the European varieties.

There are other naturalized plants frequent in neglected spots, about farm-houses, and along road-sides, which have already become so common as to be weeds; the simples and medicinal herbs, used for ages by the goodwives of England and Holland, were early brought over, and have very generally become naturalized,—catnip, mint, horehound, tansy, balm, comfrey, elecampane, &c., &c.,—immediately take root, spreading far and wide wherever they are allowed to grow. It is surprising how soon they become firmly established in a new settlement; we often observe them in this new county apart from any dwelling. At times we have found them nearly a mile from either garden or house. The seeds of naturalized plants seem, in many cases, to have floated across our lake upon the water; for we have found the European mint and catnip growing with the blue gentian immediately on the banks where the woods spread around in every direction for some distance.

The word weed varies much with circumstances; at times, we even apply it to the beautiful flower or the useful herb. A plant may be a weed, because it is noxious, or fetid, or unsightly, or troublesome, but it is rare indeed that all these faults are united in one individual of the vegetable race. Often the unsightly, or fetid, or even the poisonous plant, is useful, or it may be interesting from some peculiarity; and on the other hand, many others, troublesome from their numbers, bear pleasing flowers, taken singly. Upon the whole, it is not so much a natural defect which marks the weed, as a certain impertinent, intrusive character in these plants; a want of modesty, a habit of shoving themselves forward upon ground where they are not needed, rooting themselves in soil intended for better things, for plants more useful, more fragrant, or more beautiful. Thus the corn-cockle bears a fine flower, not unlike the mullein-pink of the garden, but then it springs up among the precious wheat, taking the place of the grain, and it is a weed; the flower of the thistle is handsome in itself, but it is useless, and it pushes forward in throngs by the way-side until we are weary of seeing it, and everybody makes war upon it; the common St. John's wort, again, has a pretty yellow blossom, and it has its uses also as a simple, but it is injurious to the cattle, and yet it is so obstinately tenacious of a place among the grasses, that it is found in every meadow, and we quarrel with it as a weed.

These noxious plants have come unbidden to us, with the grains and grasses of the Old World, the evil with the good, as usual in this world of probation—the wheat and tares together. The useful plants produce a tenfold blessing upon the labor of man, but the weed is also there, ever accompanying his steps, to teach him a lesson of humility. Certain plants of this nature—the dock, thistle, nettle, &c., &c.—are known to attach themselves especially to the path of man; in widely different soils and climates, they are still found at his door. Patient care and toil can alone keep the evil within bounds, and it seems doubtful whether it lies within the reach of human means entirely to remove from the face of the earth one single plant of this peculiar nature, much less all their varieties. Has any one, even of the more noxious sorts, ever been utterly destroyed?

Agriculture, with all the pride and power of science now at her command, has apparently accomplished but little in this way. Egypt and China are said to be countries in which weeds are comparatively rare; both regions have long been in a high state of cultivation, filled to overflowing with a hungry population, which neglects scarce a rood of the soil, and yet even in those lands, even upon the banks of the Nile, where the crops succeed each other without any interval throughout the whole year, leaving no time for weeds to extend themselves; even there, these noxious plants are not unknown, and the moment the soil is abandoned, only for a season, they return with renewed vigor.

In this new country, with a fresh soil, and a thinner population, we have not only weeds innumerable, but we observe, also, that briers and brambles seem to acquire double strength in the neighborhood of man; we meet them in the primitive forest, here and there, but they line our roads and fences, and the woods are no sooner felled to make ready for cultivation, than they spring up in profusion, the first natural produce of the soil. But in this world of mercy, the just curse is ever graciously tempered with a blessing; many a grateful fruit, and some of our most delightful flowers, grow among the thorns and briers, their fragrance and excellence reminding man of the sweets as well as the toils of his task. The sweet-briar, more especially, with its simple flower and delightful fragrance, unknown in the wilderness, but moving onward by the side of the ploughman, would seem, of all others, the husbandman's blossom.

Thursday, 7th.—There was an alarm of frost last evening, and cautious people covered their tender plants, but no harm was done. It happens frequently, that late in May or early in June, we have a return of cool weather for a day or two, with an alarm about frost, at a very critical moment, when all our treasures are lying exposed; some seasons, much mischief is done to the gardens and crops, but frequently the alarm passes over and we are spared the evil. It seldom happens, even after heavy frosts at such unseasonable times, that the blight is half as severe as people at first suppose; things usually turn out much better than our fears, the plants reviving and yielding a portion of their fruits, if not a full crop. Happily, this year we have had nothing of the kind—the cool moment came earlier—before vegetation was sufficiently advanced to be injured. To-day the air is very pleasant and summer-like.

Walked on Hannah's Height; gathered azaleas in abundance; they are in their prime now, and very beautiful; we have known them, however, to blossom three weeks earlier. Our Dutch ancestors used to call these flowers *Pinxter Blumejies*, from their being usually in bloom about Whit-Sunday; under this name, they figured annually at the great holyday of the negroes, held in old colonial times at Albany and New Amsterdam. The blacks were allowed full liberty to frolic, for several days in Whitsunweek, and they used to hold a fair, building booths, which they never failed to ornament with the *Pinxter Blumejies*. The flowers are very abundant this year, and their deep rose-colored clusters seem to light up the shady woods.

We were in good luck, for we found also a little troop of moccasin plants in flower; frequently, the season has passed without our seeing one, but this afternoon we gathered no less than eighteen of the purple kind, the *Cyprepedium acaule* of botanists. The small yellow, the large yellow, and the showy ladyslipper have also been found here, but they are all becoming more rare.

Friday, 8th.—Rainy morning. It appears that yesterday we missed a fine sight: about dawn it was foggy; a large flock of wild pigeons passing over the valley, became bewildered in the mist, and actually alighted in the heart of the village, which we have never known them to do before. The trees in the churchyard, those in our own grounds, and several other gardens, were loaded with them; unfortunately, no one in the house was aware of their visit at the time. At that early hour, the whole village was quiet, and only a few persons saw them. They were not molested, and remained some little time, fluttering about the trees, or settling on them in large parties. When the fog rose, they took flight again. What a pity to have missed so unusual a sight!

Saturday, 9th.—Charming day. Pleasant row on the lake, which looks very inviting this warm weather; the views are always pleasing: hills and forest, farms and groves, encircling a beautiful sheet of water.

There is certainly no natural object, among all those which make up a landscape, winning so much upon our affection, as water. It is an essential part of prospects, widely different in character. Mountains form a more striking and imposing feature, and they give to a country a character of majesty which cannot exist without them; but not even the mountains, with all their sublime prerogative, can wholly satisfy the mind, when stripped of torrent, cascade, or lake; while, on the other hand, if there be only a quiet brook running through a meadow in some familiar spot, the eye will often turn, unconsciously, in that direction, and linger with interest upon the humble stream. Observe, also, that the waters in themselves are capable of the highest degree of beauty, without the aid of any foreign element to enhance their dignity; give them full sway, let them spread themselves into their widest expanse, let them roll into boundless seas, enfolding the earth in their embrace, with half the heavens for their canopy, and assuredly they have no need to borrow from the mountain or the forest.

Even in a limited water-view, there is a flow of life, a ceaseless variety, which becomes a perpetual source of delight; every passing hour throws over the transparent countenance of the lake, or river, some fresh tint of coloring, calls up some new play of expression beneath the changing influences of the sun, the winds, the clouds, and we are all but cheated into the belief that the waters know something of the sorrows and joys of our own hearts; we turn to them with more than admiration—with the partiality with which we turn to the face of a friend. In the morning, perhaps, we behold the waves charged with the wild power of the storm, dark and threatening, and the evening sun of the same day finds the flood lulled to rest, calmly reflecting the intelligent labors of man, and the sublime works of the Almighty, as though in conscious repose.

Our own highland lake can lay no claim to grandeur; it has no broad expanse, and the mountains about cannot boast of any great height, yet there is a harmony in the different parts of the picture which gives it much merit, and which must always excite a lively feeling of pleasure. The hills are a charming setting for the lake at their feet, neither so lofty as to belittle the sheet of water, nor so low as to be tame and commonplace; there is abundance of wood on their swelling ridges to give the charm of forest scenery, enough of tillage to add the varied interest of cultivation; the lake, with its clear, placid waters, lies gracefully beneath the mountains, flowing here into a quiet little bay, there skirting a wooded point, filling its ample basin, without encroaching on its banks by a rood of marsh or bog.

And then the village, with its buildings and gardens covering the level bank to the southward, is charmingly placed, the waters spreading before it, a ridge of hills rising on either side, this almost wholly wooded, that partly tilled, while beyond lies a background, varied by nearer and farther heights. The little town, though an important feature in the prospect, is not an obtrusive one, but quite in proportion with surrounding objects. It has a cheerful, flourishing aspect, yet rural and unambitious, not aping the bustle and ferment of cities; and certainly one may travel many a mile without finding a village more prettily set down by the water-side.

A collection of buildings always shows well rising immediately from the water; the liquid plain, in its mobile play of expression, and the massive piles of building, with the intricate medley of outline which make up the perspective of a town, when brought naturally into one view, form an admirable contrast, the mind unconsciously delighting in the opposite characters of these chief objects of the scene, each heightening, and yet relieving, the beauty of the other.

217

Monday, 11*th.*—Warm day, with soft, hazy sunshine; this sort of atmosphere is always especially fine in a hilly country, shading all the distances so beautifully, from the nearest wooded knoll, to the farthest height. Walked to the Cliffs; found the views very fine. The woods are in great beauty, the foliage very rich, without having lost, as yet, anything of its spring freshness. The hemlocks are still clearly marked with their lighter and darker greens of different years' growth. The old cones are hanging on the pines; many of these remain on the trees all summer. There were very few flowers in the wood where we walked, though I do not know why this should be so; it was composed of fine chestnut and beech, of primitive growth, mingled, as usual, with evergreens. The young seedling forest trees are now springing up everywhere, taking the place of the fading violets. On some of the little beeches and aspens, the growth of one or two seasons, we found the new leaves colored in tender pink, or a shade of red, which is remarkable in trees which do not show any traces of this coloring at other times; even in autumn their brightest tint is usually yellow.

The fire-flies are gleaming about the village gardens this evening—the first we have seen this year.

Tuesday, 12*th.*—Fine day. The roses are opening at length; they are a fortnight later than last year. This morning we were delighted to find a few May-roses in full bloom; by evening, others will have unfolded—to-morrow, many more will have opened—and in a few days, the village gardens will be thronged with thousands of these noble flowers.

How lavishly are the flowers scattered over the face of the earth! One of the most perfect and delightful works of the Creation, there is yet no other form of beauty so very common. Abounding in different climates, upon varying soils—not a few here to cheer the sad, a few there to reward the good—but countless in their throngs, infinite in their variety, the gift of measureless beneficence—wherever man may live, there grow the flowers.

Wednesday, 13*th.*—Pale, hazy sunshine. Heard of a dish of wild strawberries; we have not yet seen them ourselves.

Thursday, 14*th.*—The whip-poor-wills are now heard every evening, from some particular points on the skirts of the village. They arrive here about the first week in May, and continue their peculiar nocturnal note until toward the last of June: "most musical, most melancholy" of night-sounds known in our region. From some houses on the bank of the lake and near the river, they are heard every night; probably the sound comes over the water from the wooded hills beyond, for they are said to prefer high and dry situations. Once in a while, but not very frequently, they come into the village, and we have heard them when they must have been in our own grounds. It is only natural, perhaps, that some lingering shade of superstition should be connected with this singular bird—so often heard, so seldom seen; thousands of men and women in this part of the world have listened to the soft wailing whistle, from childhood to old age, through every summer of a long life, without having once laid their eyes on the bird. Until quite lately, almost every one believed the night-hawk and the whip-poor-will to be the same, merely because the first is often seen by daylight, while the last, which much resembles it, is wholly nocturnal, and only known to those who search for him in the shady woods by day, or meet him by moonlight at night. These birds will soon cease their serenading; after the third week in June, they are rarely heard, in which respect they resemble the nightingale, who sings only for a few weeks in May and June; early in September, they go to the southward. Forty years since, they are said to have been much more numerous here than they are to-day.

Friday, 10*th.*—Very warm; various sorts of weather in the course of the day. Cloudy morning, brilliant mid-day, and in the afternoon a sudden shower. It rained heavily, with thunder and lightning, for an hour, then cleared again, and we had a charming evening.

Saw a number of humming-birds—they are particularly

partial to the evening hours. One is sure to find them now toward sunset, fluttering about their favorite plants; often there are several together among the flowers of the same bush, betraying themselves, though unseen, by the trembling of the leaves and blossoms. They are extremely fond of the Missouri currant—of all the early flowers, it is the greatest favorite with them; they are fond of the lilacs also, but do not care much for the syringa; to the columbine they are partial, to the bee larkspur also, with the wild bergamot or Oswego tea, the speckled jewels, scarlet trumpet-flower, red clover, honeysuckle, and the lychnis tribe. There is something in the form of these tube-shape blossoms, whether small or great, which suits their long, slender bills, and possibly, for the same reason, the bees cannot find such easy access to the honey, and leave more in these than in the open flowers. To the lily the humming-bird pays only a passing compliment, and seems to prefer the great tiger-lily to the other varieties; the rose he seldom visits; he will leave these stately blossoms any day for a head of the common red clover, in which he especially delights. Often of a summer's evening have we watched the humming-birds flitting about the meadows, passing from one tuft of clover to another, then resting a moment on a tall spear of timothy grass, then off again to fresh clover, scarcely touching the other flowers, and continuing frequently in the same field until the very latest twilight.

Mr. Tupper, in his paper on "Beauty," pays a pretty compliment to the humming-bird. Personifying Beauty, he says, she

"Fluttereth into the tulip with the humming-bird."

But, although these little creatures are with us during the tulip season, it may be doubted if they feed on these gaudy blossoms. On first reading the passage, this association struck us as one with which we were not familiar; had it been the trumpet-flower, nothing would have been more natural, for these dainty birds are forever fluttering about the noble scarlet blossoms of that plant, as we all know, but the tulip did not seem quite in place in this connection. Anxious to know whether we had deceived ourselves, we have now watched the humming-birds for several seasons, and, as yet, have never seen one in a tulip, while we have often observed them pass these for other flowers. Possibly this may have been accidental, or other varieties of the humming-bird may have a different taste from our own, and one cannot positively assert that this little creature never feeds on the tulip, without more general examination. But there is something in the upright position of that flower which, added to its size, leads one to believe that it must be an inconvenient blossom for the humming-bird, who generally seems to prefer nodding or drooping flowers, if they are at all large, always feeding on the wing as he does, and never alighting, like butterflies and bees, on the petals. Altogether, we are inclined to believe that if the distinguished author of Proverbial Philosophy had been intimate with our little neighbor, he would have placed him in some other native plant, and not in the Asiatic tulip, to which he seems rather indifferent. The point is a very trifling one, no doubt, and it is extremely bold to find fault with our betters; but in the first place, we are busying ourselves wholly with trifles just now, and then the great work in question has been a source of so much pleasure and advantage to half the world, that no one heeds the misplaced tulip, unless it be some rustic bird-fancier. By supposing the flower of the *tulip-tree* to be meant, the question would be entirely settled to the satisfaction of author, reader, and humming-bird also, who is very partial to those handsome blossoms of his native woods.

It is often supposed that our little friend seeks only the most fragrant flowers; the blossoms on the Western Prairies, those of Wisconsin at least, and probably others also, are said to have but little perfume, and it is observed that the humming-bird is a stranger there, albeit those wilds are a perfect sea of flowers during the spring and summer months. But the amount of honey in a plant has nothing to do with its perfume, for we daily see the humming-birds neglecting the rose and the white lily, while many of their most favorite flowers, such as the scarlet honeysuckle, the columbine, the lychnis tribe, the trumpet flower, and speckled jewels, have no perfume at all. Other pet blossoms of theirs, however, are very fragrant, as the highly-scented Missouri currant, for instance, and the red clover, but their object seems to be quite independent of this particular quality in a plant.

The fancy these little creatures have for perching on a dead twig is very marked; you seldom see them alight elsewhere, and the fact that a leafless branch projects from a bush, seems enough to invite them to rest; it was but yesterday we saw two males sitting upon the same dead branch of a honeysuckle beneath the window. And last summer, there chanced to be a little dead twig, at the highest point of a locust-tree, in sight from the house, which was a favorite perching spot of theirs for some weeks; possibly it was the same bird, or the same pair, who frequented it, but scarcely a day passed without a tiny little creature of the tribe being frequently seen there. Perhaps there may have been a nest close at hand, but they build so cunningly, making their nests look so much like a common bunch of moss or lichen, that they are seldom discovered, although they often build about gardens, and usually at no great height; we have known a nest found in a lilac-bush, and sometimes they are even satisfied with a tall coarse weed; in the woods, they are said to prefer a white oak sapling, seldom building, however, more than ten feet from the ground.

Though so diminutive, they are bold and fearless, making very good battle when necessary, and going about generally in a very careless, confident way. They fly into houses more frequently than any other bird, sometimes attracted by plants or flowers within, often apparently by accident, or for the purpose of exploring. The country people have a saying that when a humming-bird flies in at a window he brings a love message for some one in the house; a pretty fancy, certainly, for Cupid himself could not have desired a daintier *avant courier*. Unfortunately, this trick of flying in at the windows is often a very serious and fatal one to the poor little creatures themselves, whatever felicity it may bring to the Romeo and Juliet of the neighborhood ; for they usually quiver about against the ceiling until quite stunned and exhausted, and unless they are caught and set at liberty, soon destroy themselves in this way. We have repeatedly known them found dead in rooms little used, that had been opened to air, and which they had entered unperceived.

They are not so very delicate in constitution as one might suppose. Mr. Wilson remarks that they are much more numerous in this country than the common wren is in England. It is well known that we have but one variety in this part of the continent; there is another in Florida, and there are several more on the Pacific coast, one reaching as far north as Nootka Sound. They frequently appear with us before the chimney-swallows, and I have seen one about our own flower-borders, during a mild autumn, as late as the first of December; they usually disappear, however, much earlier, remaining, perhaps, a month or six weeks later than the swallows. They winter in the tropics, and are said to make their long journeys in pairs, which looks as though they mated for life, like some other birds.

Saturday, 16th.—Warm; thermometer 79 in the shade at five o'clock. Long drive down the valley toward evening. The farms are looking very pleasantly: the young grain waving in the breeze is headed, but not yet colored; the meadows are becoming tinged with their own proper blossoms, the red sorrel flowers, golden buttercups, daisies, and clover appearing successively, until the whole field is gay. The crops generally look very well, promising a good return to the husbandman for his labor. In low grounds, about the brooks, the purple flags are now blooming in profusion, and the thorn-trees are still in flower on many banks.

There is a tradition that during the war of the Revolution the long spines of the thorn were occasionally used by the American women for pins, none of which were manufactured in the country; probably it was the cockspur variety, which bears the longest and most slender spines, and is now in flower. The peculiar condition of the colonies rendered privations of this kind a great additional evil of that memorable struggle; almost everything in the shape of the necessaries and luxuries of life came then from the Old World. Several native plants were prepared at that time to take the place of the prohibited *souchong* and *bohea*; the "New Jersey tea," for instance, a pretty shrub, and the "Labrador tea," a low evergreen with handsome white flowers. Certainly it was only fair that the women should have their share of privations in the shape of pins and tea, when Washington and his brave army were half clad, half armed, half starved, and never paid; the soldiers of that remarkable war, both officers and men, if not literally using the spines of the thorn-tree, like their wives, often went about looking something like Spenser's picture of Despair:

> "His garments naught but many ragged clouts,
> With *thorns* together pinned, and patched was."

In some farm-houses where much knitting and spinning is going on, one occasionally sees a leafless branch of a thorn-bush hanging in a corner, with a ball of yarn on each spine: quite a pretty, rustic device. We saw one the other day which we admired very much.

Monday, 18th.—Lovely day; thermometer 82 in the shade at dinner-time. The wild roses are in flower. We have them of three varieties: the early rose, with reddish branches, which seldom blooms here until the first week in June; the low rose, with a few large flowers; and the tall many-flowered swamp rose, blooming late in the summer. They are quite common about us, and although the humblest of their tribe, they have a grace all their own; there is, indeed, a peculiar modesty about the wild rose which that of the gardens does not always possess. There is one caprice of the gardening art to-day which a rustic finds it difficult to admire, and that is the tall grafted tree roses taking a form which nature assuredly never yet gave to a rose-bush. The flowers themselves may be magnificent as flowers, but one stares at them with curiosity, one does not turn to them with affection; moreover, they look as though they enjoyed being stared at, thereby losing much of their attractiveness; in short, they are not thoroughly rose-like. It is a cruel thing in a gardener to pervert, as it were, the very nature of a plant, and one could sooner forgive the clipping a yew-tree into a peacock, according to the quaint fancy of our forefathers, than this stripping the modest rose of her drapery of foliage—it reminds one of the painful difference between the gentle, healthy-hearted daughter of home, the light of the house, and the meretricious dancer, tricked out upon the stage to dazzle and bewilder, and be stared at by the mob. The rose has so long been an emblem of womanly loveliness, that we do not like to see her shorn of one feminine attribute; and modesty in every true-hearted woman is, like affection, a growth of her very nature, whose roots are fed with her life's blood. No; give back her leaves to the rose, that her flowers may open amid their native branches. This veil of verdure, among whose folds the starry blossoms bud, and bloom, and die, has been given to every plant—the lowly dew-drop, as well as the gorgeous martagon; nay, it is the inheritance of the very rudest weeds; and yet the rose, the noblest flower on earth, you would deprive of this priceless grace!

We are very fortunate in having the wild roses about our own haunts; they are not found everywhere. M. de Humboldt mentions that in his travels in South America he never saw one, even in the higher and cooler regions, where other brambles and plants of a temperate climate were common.

Tuesday, 9th.—Fine strawberries from the fields this evening for tea. Warm, bright weather; thermometer 85—lovely evening, but too warm for much exercise. Strolled in the lane, enjoying the fragrant meadows, and the waving corn-fields on the skirts of the village.

A meadow near at hand would seem to give more pleasure than a corn-field. Grain, to appear to full advantage, should be seen at a little distance, where one may note the changes in its coloring with the advancing season, where one may enjoy the play of light when the summer clouds throw their shadows there, or the breezes chase one another over the waving lawn. It is like a piece of shaded silk which the salesman throws off a little, that you may better appreciate the effect. But a meadow is a delicate embroidery in colors, which you must examine closely to understand all its merits; the nearer you are, the better. One must bend over the grass to find the blue violet in May, the red strawberry in June; one should be close at hand to mark the first appearance of the simple field-blossoms, clover, red and white, buttercup and daisy, with the later lily, and primrose, and meadow-tuft; one should be nigh to breathe the sweet and fresh perfume, which increases daily until the mowers come with their scythes.

The grasses which fill our meadows are very many of them foreign plants; among these are the vernal-grass, which gives such a delightful fragrance to the new-mown hay. The timothy is also an imported grass; so is the meadow-grass considered as the best of all for pasture; the orchard-grass much esteemed also; and the canary-grass, which yields a seed for birds. Some of the most troublesome weeds of this tribe are naturalized, as the darnel in pastures, the chess or cheat of the grain-fields; quaking-grass, quitch-grass, yard-grass, and crab-grass, also. Altogether, there are some thirty varieties of these imported grasses enumerated by botanists in this part of the country.

A number more are common to both continents, like the Vanilla-grass, often gathered for its perfume, and which in Northern Europe is called holy-grass, from its being scattered before church-doors on holydays; and the manna-grass, bearing sweet grains, which are eaten in Holland and some other countries; the dent-grasses, also, good for cattle, several of which are natives, while others have been introduced. There seem to be some twenty varieties which thus belong to both continents.

In addition to the preceding, there are upwards of a hundred more grasses belonging strictly to the soil; many of these are mere weeds, though others are very useful. Among the native plants of this kind are nimble-will, a great favorite with the Kentucky farmers, and found as far east as this State; several useful kinds of fescue-grass, and soa, one of which has something of the fragrance of the vernal-grass, and the reed canary-grass, of which the ribbon-grass of gardeners is a variety; the salt grasses of the coast, also, very important to the sea-shore farmers. Among the native plants of this tribe we have the wild oat, wild rye, wild barley, mountain rice, and wild rice, found in many of the waters of this State, both fresh and brackish.

Altogether, of some hundred and fifty grasses, about one-fifth of the number seem of foreign origin; but if we consider their importance to the farmer, and the extent of cultivated soil they now cover, we must take a different view of them; probably in this sense the native grasses scarcely rank more than as one to four in our meadows and cultivated lands.

The clovers, also, though thoroughly naturalized, are most of them imported plants: the downy "rabbit-foot," or "stone-clover," the common red variety; the "zig-zag," and the "hop clovers," are all introduced. The question regarding the white clover has not been clearly settled, but it is usually considered, I believe, as indigenous, though some botanists mark the point as doubtful. The buffalo clover found in the western part of this State, and common still farther westward, is the only undoubtedly native variety we posses.

Wednesday, 20th.— Very warm day; thermometer 93 in the shade at three o'clock. The locust flowers are perfuming the village; one perceives their fragrance within doors, throughout the house. In many parts of the country these beautiful trees have been very much injured of late years by a worm called the *borer*, which is very destructive wherever it appears. In the pleasant villages at the westward, where locusts are so much in favor for planting in the streets, they have been very much injured, and their blighted branches give quite a melancholy look to some of these towns. Fortunately for us, the trees in our neighborhood are yet unscathed; these *borers* have not, I believe, appeared anywhere in the county.[6]

Thursday, 21st.—Extremely warm; thermometer 92. Happily, there have been pleasant western breezes through these warm days. Strolled about the village in the evening; saw an old neighbor of threescore and fifteen at work in his garden, hoeing his dozen corn-hills, and weeding his cucumber vines.

One always loves a garden; labor wears its pleasantest aspect there. From the first days of spring, to latest autumn, we move about among growing plants, gay flowers, and cheerful fruits; and there is some pretty change to note by the light of every sun. Even the narrowest cottage patch looks pleasantly to those who come and go along the highway; it is well to stop now and then when walking, and look over the paling of such little gardens, and note what is going on there.

Potatoes, cabbages, and onions are grown here by every family as first requisites. Indian corn and cucumbers are also thought indispensable, for Americans of all classes eat as much maize as their Indian predecessors. And as for cucumbers, they are required at every meal of which a thorough-going Yankee partakes, either as salad in summer, or pickled in winter. We sometimes see men about the villages eating them unseasoned like apples. Peas and beans rank next in favor; some of each are generally found in the smallest gardens. Beets, turnips, and carrots are not so very common; they are not thought absolutely necessary; one sees gardens without them. Radishes do not thrive well in this soil, but the light green leaves of the lettuce are seen everywhere. There is usually a pumpkin-vine running about the corn-hills, its large yellow flowers and golden fruit

---

6   These borers are the young of different beetles, some of which
     live several years in the wood before their transformation.

showing, as a matter of course, below the glossy leaves of the maize; a part of the fruit is made into pies, the rest goes to the cow or pig. Sometimes you find squashes, also, in these small gardens, with a few tomatoes, perhaps; but these last are difficult to raise here, on account of the occasional frosts of May.

Flowers are seldom forgotten in the cottage garden; the widest walk is lined with them, and there are others beneath the low windows of the house. You have rose-bushes, sun-flowers, and holly-hocks, as a matter of course; generally a cluster of pinks, bachelor's buttons, also, and a sweet pea, which is a great favorite; plenty of marigolds, a few poppies, large purple china asters, and a tuft of the lilac phlox. Such are the blossoms to be seen before most doors; and each is pretty in its own time and place; one has a long-standing regard for them all, including the homely sun-flower, which we should be sorry to miss from its old haunts. Then the scarlet flowering bean, so intimately connected with childish recollections of the hero Jack and his wonderful adventure, may still be seen flourishing in the cottage garden, and it would seem to have fallen from a pod of the identical plant celebrated in nursery rhyme, for it has a great inclination for climbing, which is generally encouraged by training it over a window. We do not hear, however, of any in these parts reaching the roof in a single night's growth. You must go to the new lands on the prairies for such marvels now-a-days. They tell a wonderful story of a cucumber-vine somewhere beyond the great lakes, in the last "new settlement," probably; the seed having been sowed one evening in a good bit of soil, the farmer, going to his work next morning, found it not only out of the ground, but grown so much that he was curious to measure it; "he followed it to the end of his garden, over a fence, along an Indian trail, through an oak opening, and then seeing it stretch some distance beyond, he went back for his horse, but while he was saddling old Bald the vine had so much the advantage of him that it reached the next clearing before he did; there he left it to go back to dinner; and how much farther it ran that day

Ebenezer could not tell for certain."

We have no such wonders hereabouts; and even the ambitious bean seldom reaches higher than a low roof; nor is its growth always sufficiently luxuriant to shade the window, for it often shares that task with a morning-glory. The plan of these leafy blinds is a pretty one, but they are too often trained in stiff and straight lines; a poetical idea, *tirée à quatre épingles*. Frequently we see a cottage with a door in the centre, and one window on each side, and vines trained over the sashes in this way, which gives it an odd look, like a house in green spectacles, as it were. When hop-vines are used for screening the windows, which is often the case, the plant is not so easily restrained; and throwing out its luxuriant branches right and left, takes care of itself.

Currants are almost the only fruit seen in the smaller gardens of our neighborhood; even gooseberries are not so general; both raspberries and strawberries grow wild here in such profusion that few persons cultivate them. Currants, by-the-by, both black and red, are also native plants; the black currant is by no means rare in this State, and very much resembles the varieties cultivated in gardens; the wild red currant is chiefly confined to the northern parts of the country, and it is precisely like that which we cultivate. Both purple and green gooseberries are also found wild in our woods.

It is often a matter of surprise and regret that fruit should not be more cultivated among us in gardens of all sizes; but the indifferent common cherry is almost the only fruit-tree found here in cottage gardens. Even the farmers neglect cherries, and plums, and pears, surprisingly. Peaches and grapes seldom ripen here in the open air; they might probably be cultivated as wall fruit, but it is so easy now to procure them by railroad from other counties, that few persons care to try experiments of this kind. Peaches, and melons, and plums, brought from a distance, are carried about the village for sale, throughout the season, as a matter of course.

There is, unhappily, a very serious objection to cultivating fruit in our village gardens; fruit-stealing is a very common crime in this part of the world; and the standard of principle on such subjects is as low as it well can be in our rural communities. Property of this kind is almost without protection among us; there are laws on the subject, but these are never enforced, and of course people are not willing to throw away money, and time, and thought, to raise fruit for those who might easily raise it for themselves, if they would take the pains to do so. There can be no doubt that this state of things is a serious obstacle to the cultivation of choice fruit in our villages; horticulture would be in a much higher condition here if it were not for this evil. But the impunity with which boys, and men, too, are allowed to commit thefts of this kind, is really a painful picture, for it must inevitably lead to increase a spirit of dishonesty throughout the community.

It is the same case with flowers. Many people seem to consider them as public property, though cultivated at private expense. It was but the other day that we saw a little girl, one of the village Sunday-scholars, moreover, put her hand within the railing of a garden and break off several very fine plants, whose growth the owner had been watching with care and interest for many weeks, and which had just opened to reward his pains. Another instance of the same kind, but still more flagrant in degree, was observed a short time since: the offender was a full-grown man, dressed in fine broadcloth to boot, and evidently a stranger; he passed before a pretty yard, gay with flowers, and unchecked by a single scruple of good manners, or good morals, proceeded to make up a handsome bouquet, without so much as saying by your leave to the owner; having selected the flowers most to his fancy, he arranged them tastefully, and then walked off with a free and jaunty air, and an expression of satisfaction and self-complacency truly ridiculous under the circumstances. He had made up his nosegay with so much pains, eyed it so tenderly as he carried it before him, and moved along with such a very mincing and dainty manner, that he was probably on the way to present himself and his trophy to his sweetheart; and we can only hope that he met with just such a reception as was deserved by a man who had been committing petty larceny. As if to make the chapter complete, the very same afternoon, the village being full of strangers, we saw several young girls, elegantly flounced, put their hands through the railing of another garden, facing the street, and help themselves in the same easy manner to their neighbor's prettiest flowers: what would they have thought if some one had stepped up with a pair of scissors and cut half a yard from the ribbon on their hats, merely because it was pretty, and one had a fancy for it? Neither the little girl, nor the strangers in broadcloth and flowers, seem to have learned at common school, or at Sunday school, or at home, that respect for the pleasures of others is simple good manners, regard for the rights of others, common honesty.

No one who had a flower border of his own would be likely to offend in this way; he would not do so unwittingly, at least; and if guilty of such an act, it would be premeditated pilfering. When people take pains to cultivate fruits and flowers themselves, they have some idea of their value, which can only be justly measured by the owner's regard for them. And then, moreover, gardening is a civilizing and improving occupation in itself; its influences are all beneficial; it usually makes people more industrious, and more amiable. Persuade a careless, indolent man to take an interest in his garden, and his reformation has begun. Let an idle woman honestly watch over her own flower-beds, and she will naturally become more active. There is always work to be done in a garden, some little job to be added to yesterday's task, without which it is incomplete; books may be closed with a mark where one left off, needlework may be thrown aside and resumed again; a sketch may be left half finished, a piece of music half practiced; even attention to household matters may relax in some measure for a while; but regularity and method are constantly required, are absolutely indispensable, to the well-being of a garden. The occupation itself is so engaging, that one commences readily, and the interest increases so naturally, that no great share of perseverance is needed to continue the employment, and thus labor becomes a pleasure, and the dangerous habit of idleness is checked. Of all faults of character, there is not one, perhaps, depending so entirely upon habit as indolence; and nowhere can one learn a lesson of order and diligence more prettily and more pleasantly than from a flower-garden.

But another common instance of the good effect of gardening may be mentioned:—it naturally inclines one to be open-handed. The bountiful returns which are bestowed, year after year, upon our feeble labors, shame us into liberality. Among all the misers who have lived on earth, probably few have been gardeners. Some cross-grained churl may set out, perhaps, with a determination to be niggardly with the fruits and flowers of his portion; but gradually his feelings soften, his views change, and before he has housed the fruits of many summers, he sees that these good things are but the free gifts of Providence to himself, and he learns at last that it is a pleasure, as well as a duty, to give. This head of cabbage shall be sent to a poor neighbor; that basket of refreshing fruit is reserved for the sick; he has pretty nosegays for his female friends; he has apples or peaches for little people; nay, perhaps in the course of years, he at length achieves the highest act of generosity—he bestows on some friendly rival a portion of his rarest seed, a shoot from his most precious root! Such deeds are done by gardeners.

Horticulture is not carried on upon a great scale anywhere in this county. We regret that this should be so. A large garden, where taste and knowledge have full scope, is indeed a noble work, full of instruction and delight. The rare trees and plants brought with toil, and cost, and patience, from distant regions; the rich variety of fruits and vegetables; the charming array of flowers, are among the most precious and the most graceful trophies of commerce, and industry, and adventure. Such gardens, whether public or private, are always desirable in a neighborhood. They are among the best gifts of wealth, and scatter abroad too many benefits to deserve the doubtful name of a luxury. If we have none near enough to bring good to our own rural village, it is at least pleasant to remember that other communities are more fortunate than ourselves. When one cannot enjoy some particular good thing one's self, a very little charity, and a very little philosophy, lead one to be glad, at least, that others may profit by it.

A very striking proof of the civilizing effect of large gardens may be seen any day in the great towns on the Continent of Europe, whether in France, Italy, Germany, &c., &c. In those old countries, where grounds of this kind have been more or less open to the public for generations, the privilege is never abused by any disgraceful act. The flowers, the trees, the statuary, remain uninjured year after year; it never seems to occur to the most reckless and abandoned to injure them. The general population of those towns is, in many respects, inferior to our own; but in this particular point their tone of civilization rises far above the level of this country.

Friday, 22*d*.—Still very warm; thermometer 90 in the shade. Although the heat has been greater and more prolonged than usual in this part of the country, still there is a sort of corrective in our highland air which is a great relief; the same degree of the thermometer produces much more suffering in the lower counties, particularly in the towns. Extreme lassitude from the heat is seldom felt here; and our nights are almost always comparatively cool, which is a very great advantage.

Saturday, 23*d*.—Bright, warm day; thermometer 89. Fine air from the west.

Pleasant walk in the evening. Met a party of children coming from the woods with wild flowers. In May or June, one often meets little people bringing home flowers or berries from the hills; and if you stop to chat with them, they generally offer you a share of their nosegay or their partridge-berries; they are as fond of these last as the birds, and they eat the young aromatic leaves also. Their first trip to the woods, after the snow has gone, is generally in quest of these berries; a week or two later, they go upon the hills for our earliest flowers—ground-laurel and squirrel-cups; a little later, they gather violets, and then again, the azalea, or "wild honeysuckle," as they call it, to which they are very partial.

But, though pleased with the flowers, the little creatures seldom know their names. This seems a pity; but we have often asked them what they called this or that blossom in their hands, and they seldom could give an answer, unless it happened to be a rose, perhaps, or a violet, or something of that sort, familiar to every one. But their elders are generally quite as ignorant as themselves in this way; frequently, when we first made acquaintance with the flowers of the neighborhood, we asked grown persons—learned, perhaps, in many matters—the common names of plants they must have seen all their lives, and we found they were no wiser than the children or ourselves. It is really surprising how little the country people know on such subjects. Farmers and their wives, who have lived a long life in the fields, can tell you nothing on these matters. The men are even at fault among the trees on their own farms, if these are at all out of the common way; and as for the smaller native plants, they know less about them than Buck or Brindle, their own oxen. Like the children, they sometimes pick a pretty flower to bring home, but they have no name for it. The women have some little acquaintance with herbs and simples, but even in such cases they frequently make strange mistakes; they also are attracted by the wild flowers; they gather them, perhaps, but they cannot name them. And yet, this is a day when flower borders are seen before every door, and every young girl can chatter largely about "bouquets," and the "Language of Flowers" to boot.

It is true, the common names of our wild flowers are, at best, in a very unsatisfactory state. Some are miscalled after European plants of very different characters. Very many have one name here, another a few miles off, and others again have actually, as yet, no English names whatever. They are all found in botanical works under long, clumsy, Latin appellations, very little fitted for every-day uses, just like the plants of our gardens, half of which are only known by long-winded Latin polysyllables, which timid people are afraid to pronounce. But, annoying as this is in the garden, it is still worse in the fields. What has a dead language to do on every-day occasions with the living blossoms of the hour? Why should a strange tongue sputter its uncouth, compound syllables upon the simple weeds by the way-side? If these hard words were confined to science and big books, one would not quarrel with the roughest and most pompous of them all; but this is so far from being the case, that the evil is spreading over all the woods and meadows, until it actually perverts our common speech, and libels the helpless blossoms, turning them into so many "precieuses ridicules." Happy is it for the rose that she was named long ago; if she had chanced to live until our day, by some prairie stream, or on some remote ocean island, she would most assuredly have been called Tom, Dick, or Harry, in Greek or Latin.

Before people were overflowing with science—at a time when there was some simplicity left in the world, the flowers received much better treatment in this way. Pretty, natural names were given them in olden times, as though they had been called over by some rural party—cherry-cheeked maidens, and merry-hearted lads—gone a-Maying, of a pleasant spring morning. Many of those old names were thoroughly homely and rustic, such as the ox-eye, crow-foot, cowslip, butter-cup, pudding-grass, which grew in every meadow; then there was the hare-bell, which loved to hang its light blue bells about the haunts of the timid hare; the larkspur; the bindweed, winding about shrubs and bushes; the honeysuckle, which every child has stolen many a time from the bees; spicy gilliflowers, a corruption of July-flowers, from the month in which they blossomed; daffadowndillies, a puzzle for etymologists; pennyroyal; holly-hock, or holy-oak, as it was sometimes written; paigle, another name for cowslips; primrose, from the early season when the flower blooms; carnation, or "coronation," from the custom of wearing them in wreaths. These last were also called *sops-in-wine*, from their being thrown into wine to improve its flavor, a custom which seems to have prevailed formerly in England; the old Greeks had a practice of the same kind, for l'Abbé Bartholemi tells us that they threw roses and violets into their wine-casks, for the purpose of flavoring their wines. May not this ancient custom prove the origin of the common French phrase—*le bouquet du vin?*

There were other names, again, given to the plants in those good old times, showing a touch of quaint humor—like Bouncing-Bet, Ragged-Robin, bachelor's-button, snap-dragon, foxglove, monks-hood. Others bore names which showed there had been lovers in the fields—like Sweet-Cicely, Sweet-William, heart's-ease, pansies, truelove. Even mere personal names, such as are so often given to-day, were far better managed then—as for instance, Herb-Robert, Good King-Henry, Marietts, Bartram, Angelica. Others, again, were imaginative or fanciful—as morning-glory, night-shade, flag, loose-strife, wake-robin, simpler's-joy, thrift, speedwell, traveller's-joy, snow-drop, winter's pale foundling, wayfaring-tree, eye-bright, shepherd's-purse, pink meaning *eye*, in Dutch, like the French *œillet*; marigold, lady's-smock—from the white leaves of these flowers blooming in the grass, like bleaching linen; the wall-flower, which loved the shade of knightly banners and pennons, and still clings faithfully to falling ruins; king's-spears, flower-gentle, goldilocks, yellow-golds, the flower de luce, flower of light, which great painters have placed in the hands of saintly personages in many a noble work of art; the sweet-daisy or day's-eye, the "eye of day," as Chaucer has called it.

After such names as these, ought we not to be thoroughly ashamed of appellations like Batschia, Schoberia, Buchnera, Goodyera, Brugmannsia, Heuchera, Scheuzeria, Schizanthus, and as many more to match as you please? Names remarkably well adapted to crocodiles, and rattlesnakes, and scorpions, but little suited, one would think, to the flowers gentle of the field.

There is a modest little blossom known to all the world as having been highly honored in different countries. *La Marguerite* was probably first named in the *chansons* of some lover troubadour, some noble brother-in-arms, perhaps, of him who sang Blanche of Castille so sweetly:

> "Las! si j'avais pouvoir d'oublier
> Sa beauté, son bien-dire
> Et son tres-doux regarder,
> Finirait mon martyre!"

We may well believe it to have been some such knightly poet who first felt the charm of that simple flower, and blending its name and image with that of his lady-love, sang: *"Si douce est la Marguerite!"* So long as knights wore arms, and couched lances in behalf of ladies fair, so long was la Marguerite a favored flower of chivalry, honored by all *preux chevaliers*; knight and squire bore its fame over the sea to merry England, over Alps and Pyrenees also; in Spain it is still *la Margarita*; in Italy, *la Margherettina*. The Italians, by-the-by, have also a pretty rustic name of their own for it, *la pratellina*, the little fielding. And now, when the old towers of feudal castles are falling to the ground, when even the monumental statues of knight and dame are crumbling into dust where they lie in the churches, now at this very day, you may still find the name of *la Marguerite* upon the lips of the peasant girls of France; you may see them measuring the love of their swains by the petals of these flowers, pulling them, one after another, and repeating, as each falls, *un peu, beaucoup, passionément,* pas du tout; *the last leaflet deciding the* all-important question by the word that accompanies it; alas! that it must sometimes prove *pas du tout!* Oddly enough, in Germany, the land of sentiment and *Vergiessmeinnicht*, this flower of love and chivalry has been degraded into——shall we say it,—*Gänseblume,*—Goose-blossom! Such, at least, is one of its names; we hasten, however, to call it, with others, *Masliebe,* or love-measure: probably from the same fancy of pulling the petals to try lovers' hearts by. In England, the Saxon *daisy* has always been a great favorite with rural poets and country-folk, independently of its knightly honors, as *la Marguerite.* Chaucer, as we all know, delighted in it; he rose before the sun, he went a-field, he threw himself on the ground to watch the daisy—

> "To seen this flour so yong, so fresh of hew,
> till it unclosed was
> Upon the smal, soft, swete gras."

Now can one believe that if the daisy, or the *Marguerite,* had been called *Caractacussia,* or *Chlodovigia,* it would have been sung by knightly troubadours and minstrels, in every corner of feudal Europe? Can you fancy this flower, "so yong, so fresh of hew," to have delighted Chaucer, under the title of *Sirhumphreydavya,* or *Sirwilliamherschellia,* or *Doctorjohnsonia?* Can you imagine the gentle Emilie, in the garden gathering flowers—

> "To make a sotel garland for her hed,
> While as an angel, hevonlich, she song:—"

Can you imagine this gentle creature, or any other, of whom it might be said,

> "Her cheare was simple as bird in bower,
> As white as lilly, or rose in rise:"

Can you picture to yourself such maidens, weaving in their golden tresses, *Symphoricarpus vulgaris, Tricochloa, Tradescantia, Calopogon?* &c., &c. Or conceive for a moment some Perdita of the present day, singing in her sweetest tones:

"Here's flowers for you—
Pyxidanthera, Rudbeekia, Sclerolepis,
Escholtzia, that goes to bed with the sun," &e., &c.

Fancy her calling for fragrant blossoms to bestow on her young maiden friends: "Spargonophorus, Rhododendron, Sabbatia, Schizea, Schollera, Schistidium, Waldsteinia, and the tall Vernonia, Noveborences," &c., &c. Do you suppose that if she had gone on in that style, Florizel would have whispered: "When you speak sweet, I'd have you do it ever?" No, indeed! he would have stopped his ears, and turned to Mopsa and Dorcas. Fancy poor Ophelia prattling to Laertes about the wreath she had woven; instead of her "rosemary," and "pansies," and "herb-o'grace," hear her discourse about "Plantanthera Blepharoglottis, or Psycodes, Ageratum, Syntheris, Houghtoniana, Banksia, and Jeffersonia," &c., &c. Could her brother in that case have possibly called her "O, rose of May, dear maid, kind sister, sweet Ophelia?" No, indeed! And we may rest assured, that if the daisy, the *douce Marguerite*, had borne any one of these names, Chaucer would have snapped his fingers at it. We may feel confident that Shakspeare would then have showed it no mercy; all his fairies would have hooted at it; he would have tossed it to Sycorax and Caliban; he would not have let either Perdita or Ophelia touch it, nor Miranda, with her *très doux regarder*, look at it once.

Neither daisy, nor cowslip, nor snow-drop is found among the fields of the New World, but blossoms just as sweet and pretty are not wanting here, and it is really a crying shame to misname them. Unhappily, a large number of our plants are new discoveries—new, at least, when compared with Chaucer's daisy, Spenser's coronation flower, or Shakspeare's "pansies and herb-o'grace"—and having been first gathered since the days of Linnaeus, as specimens, their names tell far more of the musty hortus siccus, than of the gay and fragrant May-pole. But if we wish those who come after us to take a natural, unaffected pleasure in flowers, we should have names for the blossoms that mothers and nurses can teach children before they are "in Botany;" if we wish that American poets should sing our native flowers as sweetly and as simply as the daisy, and violets, and celandine have been sung from the time of Chaucer or Herrick, to that of Burns and Wordsworth, we must look to it that they have natural, pleasing names.

Monday, 25th.—Pleasant day; much cooler; thermometer 75. Yesterday, Sunday, we had a shower, which has very much refreshed the air for us here. No thunder or lightning, however, in spite of the previous heat. Long walk this afternoon. Passing through a wheat-field, heard a full chorus of crickets and other insects; they have begun their summer song in earnest. Goldfinches were flying about in little flocks; they are very social creatures, always pleased to be together.

Tuesday, 26th.—Fine day; soft breeze from the north, the wind much warmer than usual from that quarter. Thermometer 78. Walked in the woods. The dogmackie is in flower, and being so common, its white blossoms look very cheerfully in the woods. These flowering shrubs, which live and bloom in shady groves, are scarcely ever touched by the sunbeams; but they are none the less beautiful for the subdued light which plays about them. The dogmackie, like others of the same family, is also called arrow-wood; probably their branches and stems have been employed, at some period or other in the history of arms, for making arrows. We have never heard whether the Indians used the wood in this way.

It was a pretty sight, coming home, to see the women and children scattered about the meadows, gathering wild strawberries. This delightful fruit is very abundant here, growing everywhere, in the woods, along the road-sides, and in every meadow. Happily for us, the wild strawberries rather increase than diminish in cultivated lands; they are even more common among the foreign grasses of the meadows than within the woods. The two varieties marked by our botanists are both

241

found about our lake.

This wild harvest of fruit, a blessing to all, is an especial advantage to the poor; from the first strawberries in June, there is a constant succession until the middle of September. In a week or two we shall have raspberries: both the red and the black varieties are very abundant, and remarkably good. Then come the blackberries—plenty here as in the neighborhood of Falstaff; the running kind, or vine-blackberry, bearing the finest fruit of all its tribe, and growing abundantly on Long Island and in Westchester, is not, however, found in our hills. Whortleberries abound in our woods, and on every waste hillside. Wild gooseberries are common, and last summer we met a man with a pail of them, which he was carrying to the village for sale. Wild plums are also common, and frequently brought to market. The large purple flower of the rose-raspberry yields a fruit of a beautiful color and pleasant, acid taste, but it is seldom eaten in quantities. Wild grape-vines are very common, and formerly the fruit used to be gathered for sale, but of late years we have not seen any. All these lesser kinds of wild fruits, strawberries, raspberries, blackberries, and whortleberries, are gathered, to a very great extent, for sale; women, children, and occasionally men also, find it a profitable employment to bring them to market; an industrious woman has made in this way, during the fruit season, thirty dollars, without neglecting her family, and we have known an old man who made forty dollars in one summer; children also, if well disposed, can easily support themselves by the same means. Strawberries sell in the village at a shilling a quart; blackberries for three or four cents; raspberries, and whortleberries also, from three to five cents a quart.

Wednesday, 27th.—Charming day; thermometer 80. Toward sunset strolled in the lane.

The fields which border this quiet bit of road are among the oldest in our neighborhood, belonging to one of the first farms cleared near the village; they are in fine order, and to look at them, one might readily believe these lands had been under cultivation for ages. But such is already very much the character of the whole valley; a stranger moving along the highway looks in vain for any striking signs of a new country; as he passes from farm to farm in unbroken succession, the aspect of the whole region is smiling and fruitful. Probably there is no part of the earth, within the limits of a temperate climate, which has taken the aspect of an old country so soon as our native land; very much is due, in this respect, to the advanced state of civilization in the present age, much to the active, intelligent character of the people, and something, also, to the natural features of the country itself. There are no barren tracts in our midst, no deserts which defy cultivation; even our mountains are easily tilled— arable, many of them, to their very summits—while the most sterile among them are more or less clothed with vegetation in their natural state. Altogether, circumstances have been very much in our favor.

While observing, this afternoon, the smooth fields about us, it was easy, within the few miles of country in sight at the moment, to pick out parcels of land in widely different conditions, and we amused ourselves by following upon the hill-sides the steps of the husbandman, from the first rude clearing, through every successive stage of tillage, all within range of the eye at the same instant. Yonder, for instance, appeared an opening in the forest, marking a new clearing still in the rudest state, black with charred stumps and rubbish; it was only last winter that the timber was felled on that spot, and the soil was first opened to the sunshine, after having been shaded by the old woods for more ages than one can tell. Here, again, on a nearer ridge, lay a spot not only cleared, but fenced, preparatory to being tilled; the decayed trunks and scattered rubbish having been collected in heaps and burnt. Probably that spot will soon be ploughed, but it frequently happens that land is cleared of the wood, and then left in a rude state, as wild pasture-ground; an indifferent sort of husbandry this, in which neither the soil nor the wood receives any attention; but there is more land about us in this condition than one would suppose. The broad hill-side, facing the lane in which we were walking, though cleared perhaps thirty years since, has continued untilled to the present hour. In another direction, again, lies a field of new land, ploughed and seeded for the first time within the last few weeks; the young maize plants, just shooting out their glossy leaves, are the first crop ever raised there, and when harvested, the grain will prove the first fruits the earth has ever yielded to man from that soil, after lying fallow for thousands of seasons. Many other fields in sight have just gone through the usual rotation of crops, showing what the soil can do in various ways; while the farm before us has been under cultivation from the earliest history of the village, yielding every season, for the last half century, its share of grass and grain. To one familiar with the country, there is a certain pleasure in thus beholding the agricultural history of the neighborhood unfolding before one, following upon the farms in sight these progressive steps in cultivation.

The pine stumps are probably the only mark of a new country which would be observed by a stranger. With us, they take the place of rocks, which are not common; they keep possession of the ground a long while—some of those about us are known to have stood more than sixty years, or from the first settlement of the country, and how much longer they will last, time alone can tell. In the first years of cultivation, they are a very great blemish, but after a while, when most of them have been burnt or uprooted, a gray stump here and there, among the grass of a smooth field, does not look so very much amiss, reminding one, as it does, of the brief history of the country. Possibly there may be something of partiality in this opinion, just as some lovers have been found to admire a freckled face, because the rosy cheek of their sweetheart was mottled with brown freckles; people generally may not take the same view of the matter, they may think that even the single stump had better be uprooted. Several ingenious machines have been invented for getting rid of these enemies, and they have already done good service in the county. Some of them work by levers, others by wheels; they usually require three or four men and a yoke of oxen, or a horse, to work them, and it is really surprising what large stumps are drawn out of the earth by these contrivances, the strongest roots cracking and snapping like threads. Some digging about the stump is often necessary as a preliminary step, to enable the chain to be fastened securely, and occasionally the axe is used to relieve the machine; still, they work so expeditiously, that contracts are taken to clear lands in this way, at the rate of twenty or thirty cents a stump, when, according to the old method, working by hand, it would cost, perhaps, two or three dollars to uproot a large one thoroughly. In the course of a day, these machines will tear up from twenty to fifty stumps, according to their size. Those of the pine, hemlock, and chestnut are the most difficult to manage, and these last longer than those of other trees. When uprooted, the stumps are drawn together in heaps and burnt, or frequently they are turned to account as fences, being placed on end, side by side, their roots interlocking, and a more wild and formidable barrier about a quiet field cannot well be imagined. These rude fences are quite common in our neighborhood, and being peculiar, one rather likes them; it is said that they last much longer than other wooden fences, remaining in good condition for sixty years.

But although the stumps remaining here and there may appear to a stranger the only sign of a new country to be found here, yet closer observation will show others of the same character. Those wild pastures upon hill-sides, where the soil has never been ploughed, look very differently from other fallows. Here you observe a little hillock rounding over a decayed stump, there a petty hollow where some large tree has been uprooted by the storm; fern and brake also are seen in patches, instead of the thistle and the mullein. Such open hill-sides, even when rich and grassy, and entirely free from wood or bushes, bear a kind of heaving, billowy character, which, in certain lights, becomes very distinct; these ridges are formed by the roots of old trees, and remain long after the wood has entirely decayed. Even on level ground there is always an elevation about the root of an old tree and upon a hill-side, these petty knolls show more clearly as they are thrown into relief by the light; they become much bolder, also, from the washing of the soil, which accumulates above, and is carried away from the lower side of the trunk, leaving, often, a portion of the root bare in that direction. Of course, the older a wood and the larger its trees, the more clearly will this billowy character be marked. The tracks of the cattle also make the formation more ridge-like, uniting one little knoll with another, for when feeding, they generally follow one another, their heads often turned in one direction, and upon a hill-side they naturally take a horizontal course, as the most convenient. Altogether, the billowy face of these rude hill-sides is quite striking and peculiar, when seen in a favorable light.

But there are softer touches also, telling the same story of recent cultivation. It frequently happens, that walking about our farms, among rich fields, smooth and well worked, one comes to a low bank, or some little nook, a strip of land never yet cultivated, though surrounded on all sides by ripening crops of eastern grains and grasses. One always knows such places by the pretty native plants growing there. It was but the other day we paused to observe a spot of this kind in a fine meadow, near the village, neat and smooth, as though worked from the days of Adam. A path made by the workmen and cattle crosses the field, and one treads at every step upon plantain, that regular path-weed of the Old World; following this track, we come to a little runnel, which is dry and grassy now, though doubtless at one time the bed of a considerable spring; the banks are several feet high, and it is filled with native plants; on one side stands a thorn-tree, whose morning shadow falls upon grasses and clovers brought from beyond the seas, while in the afternoon, it lies on gyromias and moose-flowers, sarsaparillas and cahoshes, which bloomed here for ages, when the eye of the red man alone beheld them. Even within the limits of the village spots may still be found on the bank of the river, which are yet unbroken by the plough, where the trailing arbutus, and squirrel-cups, and May-wings tell us so every spring; in older regions, these children of the forest would long since have vanished from all the meadows and villages, for the plough would have passed a thousand times over every rood of such ground.

The forest flowers, the gray stumps in our fields, and the heaving surface of our wild hill-sides, are not, however, the only way-marks to tell the brief course of cultivation about us. These speak of the fallen forest; but here, as elsewhere, the waters have also left their impression on the face of the earth, and in these new lands the marks of their passage is seen more clearly than in older countries. They are still, in many places, sharp and distinct, as though fresh from the workman's hand. Our valleys are filled with these traces of water-work; the most careless observer must often be struck with their peculiar features, and it appears remarkable that here, at an elevation so much above the great western lakes, upon this dividing ridge, at the very fountain head of a stream, running several hundred miles to the sea, these lines are as frequent and as boldly marked as though they lay in a low country subject to floods. Large mounds rise like islands from the fields, their banks still sharply cut; in other spots a depressed meadow is found below the level of the surrounding country, looking like a drained lake, enclosed within banks as plainly marked as the works of a fortification; a shrunken brook, perhaps, running to-day where a river flowed at some period of past time. Quite near the village, from the lane where we were walking this evening, one may observe a very bold formation of this kind; the bank of the river is high and abrupt at this spot, and it is scooped out into two adjoining basins, not unlike the amphitheatres of ancient times. The central horn, as it were, which divides the two semicircles, stretches out quite a distance into a long, sharp point, very abrupt on both sides. The farther basin is the most regular, and it is also marked by successive ledges like the tiers of seats in those ancient theatres. This spot has long been cleared of wood, and used as a wild pasture; but the soil has never yet been broken by the plough, and we have often paused here to note the singular formation, and the surprising sharpness of the lines. Quite recently they have begun to dig here for sand; and if they continue the work, the character of the place must necessarily be changed. But now, as we note the bold outline of the basin, and watch the lines worked by the waters ages and ages since, still as distinct as though made last year, we see with our own eyes fresh proofs that we are in a new country, that the meadows about us, cleared by our fathers, are the first that have lain on the lap of the old earth, at this point, since yonder bank was shaped by the floods.

Thursday, 28*th.*—Thunder shower about sunrise; it continued raining until the afternoon. The shower was much needed, and every one is rejoicing over the plentiful supply.

Walked in the afternoon, though the sky was still cloudy and threatening. Obliged to follow the highway, for the woods are damp and dripping, and the grass matted after the heavy rain. But our walk proved very pleasant. It is not always those who climb in search of a commanding position, nor those who diverge from the beaten track at the beck of truant fancy, who meet with the most enjoyment. The views beneath a sober sky were still beautiful. The village lay reflected in the clear, gray waters, as though it had nothing else to do this idle afternoon but to smile upon its own image in the lake; while the valley beyond, the upland farms of Highborough, opposite, and the wooded hills above us, were all rich in the luxuriant greens and showery freshness of June. Many crows were stirring; some passing over us with their heavy flight, while others were perched on the blasted hemlocks just within the verge of the wood. They are very partial to this eastern hill; it is a favorite haunt of theirs at all seasons. Many of the lesser birds were also flitting about, very busy, and very musical after the rainy morning; they make great havoc among the worms and insects at such times, and one fancies that they sing more sweetly of a still evening, after a showery day, than at other moments. Some of the goldfinches, wrens, song-sparrows, and blue-birds, seemed to surpass themselves as they sat perched on the rails of the fences, or upon the weeds by the road-side.

There was scarcely a breath of air stirring. The woods lay in calm repose after the grateful shower, and large rain-drops were gathered in clusters on the plants. The leaves of various kinds receive the water very differently: some are completely bathed, showing a smooth surface of varnished green from stem to point—like the lilac of the garden, for instance;—on others, like the syringa, the fluid lies in flattened transparent drops, taking an emerald color from the leaf on which they rest; while the rose and the honeysuckle wear those spherical diamond-like drops, sung by poets, and sipped by fairies. The clover also, rose among the grasses, wears her crystals as prettily as the queen of the garden. Of course, it is the different texture of the leaves which produces this very pleasing effect.

Friday, 29th.—Very pleasant. Sunshine, with a warm mist on the hills; most beautiful effects of light and shade playing about the valley.

The sweet-briar is now in full blossom. It is one of the pleasantest shrubs in the whole wide world. With us it is not so very common as in most of the older counties, growing chiefly at intervals along the road-side, and in fields which border the highways. One never sees it in the woods, with the wild roses, and other brambles. The question as to its origin is considered as settled, I believe, by botanists, and, although thoroughly naturalized in most parts of the country, we cannot claim it as a native.

That old worthy, Captain Gosnold, the first Englishman who set foot in New England, landed on Cape Cod, as far back as 1602; he then proceeded to Buzzard Bay, and took up his quarters, for a time, in the largest of the Elizabeth Islands, where the first building, raised by English hands in that part of the continent, was put together. The object of his voyage was to procure a cargo of the sassafras root, which, at that time, was in high repute for medicinal purposes, and a valuable article of commerce. In relating his voyage, besides the sassafras which he found there in abundance, he mentions other plants which he had observed: the thorn, honeysuckle, wild pea, strawberries, raspberries, and grape-vines, all undoubtedly natives; but he also names the eglantine, or sweet-briar, and the tansy, both of which are generally looked upon as naturalized on this continent. Perhaps the worthy captain had his head so full of sassafras, as to care little for the rest of the vegetation, and he may have mistaken the wild rose for the eglantine, and some other plant for tansy. His wild pea was probably one of our common vetches.

Some of the most beautiful sweet-briars in the world are found growing wild along the road-sides about Fishkill, on the Hudson. They are partial to the neighborhood of the cedars which are common there, and clinging to those trees, they climb over them, untrained, to the height of twenty feet or more. When in flower the effect is very beautiful, their star-like blossoms resting on the foliage of the cedars, which is usually so dark and grave.

Saturday, 30th.—Charming weather. First dish of green peas from the garden to-day.

Came home from our walk with the village cows, this evening. Some fifteen or twenty of them were straggling along the road, going home of their own accord to be milked. Many of these good creatures have no regular pasture the summer through, but are left to forage for themselves along the road-sides, and in the unfenced woods. They go out in the morning, without any one to look after them, and soon find the best feeding ground, generally following this particular road, which has a long reach of open woods on either side. We seldom meet them in any number on the other roads. They like to pasture in the forest, where they doubtless injure the young trees, being especially fond of the tender maple shoots. Sometimes we see them feeding on the grass by the way-side, as soon as they have crossed the village bridge; other days they all walk off in a body, for a mile or more, before they begin to graze. Toward evening, they turn their heads homeward, without being sent for, occasionally walking at a steady pace without stopping; at other times, loitering and nibbling by the way. Among those we followed, this evening, were several old acquaintances, and probably they all belonged to different houses; only two of them had bells. As they came into the village, they all walked off to their owners' doors, some turning in one direction, some in another.

Of course, those cows that feed in fenced pastures are sent for, and it is only those who forage for themselves who come and go alone, in this way.

Monday, July 2d.—Clear, and cooler. New potatoes to-day. Pleasant drive, in the afternoon, on the lake shore. The mid-summer flowers are beginning to open. Yellow evening primrose, purple rose-raspberry; the showy willow-herb, with its pyramid of lilac flowers; the red and the yellow lilies. We observed, also, a handsome strawberry blite, with its singular fruit-like crimson heads; this flower is not uncommon in new lands, in the western part of the State, and is probably a native, though precisely similar to that of Europe. The track over which we passed this afternoon, and where we found the blite, has been recently opened through the forest.

Observed many birds. The goldfinches were in little flocks as usual, and purple-finches flew across our road more than once; quarrelsome king-birds were sitting on the shrubs and plants along the bank, watching the wild bees, perhaps; for they are said to devour these as greedily as those of the hive. Some of them were skimming over the lake in pursuit of other game, being very partial also to the tribe of water insects. Saw another bird not often met with, a red-start; unlike the European red-start, which often builds about houses, the American bird of the same tribe is very shy, and only seen in the forest. The one we observed this evening was flitting about in a young grove upon the borders of a brook; his red and black plumage, and flirting tail, showing here and there among the foliage.

Tuesday, 3d.— . . . We had, for several weeks, been planning a visit to Farmer B—'s; our good friend, his step-mother, having given us a very warm invitation to spend the day with her. Accordingly, we set off in the morning, after breakfast, and drove to the little village of B— Green, where we arrived about noon. Here the coachman stopped to water his horses, and make some inquiries about the road.

"Do you know where B—'s folks live?" he asked of a man in the yard.

"Yes, sir; B—'s folks live three miles from here."

"Which road must I take?"

"Straight ahead. Turn to the left when you come to the brick school-house; then take the right when you get to the gunsmith's shop, and any of the neighbors about will tell you which is B—'s house."

The directions proved correct. We soon reached the school-house; then came to the gunsmith's shop, and a few more turnings brought us in sight of the low, gray farm-house, the object of our morning's drive. Here a very cordial and simple greeting awaited us, and we passed the day most agreeably.

* * * * *

How pleasantly things look about a farm-house! There is always much that is interesting and respectable connected with every better labor, every useful or harmless occupation of man. We esteem some trades for their usefulness, we admire others for their ingenuity, but it seems natural to like a farm or a garden beyond most workshops. It needs not to be a great agricultural establishment with scientific sheds and show dairies—for knowledge and experience are necessary to appreciate the merits of such a place;—a simple body, who goes to enjoy and not to criticise, will find enough to please him about any common

252

farm, provided the goodman be sober and industrious, the housewife be neat and thrifty.

From the window of the room in which we were sitting, we looked over the whole of Mr. B—'s farm; the wheat-field, corn-field, orchard, potato-patch, and buckwheat-field. The farmer himself, with his wagon and horses, a boy and a man, were busy in a hay-field, just below the house; several cows were feeding in the meadow, and about fifty sheep were nibbling on the hillside. A piece of woodland was pointed out on the height above, which supplied the house with fuel. We saw no evergreens there; the trees were chiefly maple, birch, oak, and chestnut; with us, about the lake, every wood contains hemlock and pine.

Finding we were interested in rural matters, our good friend offered to show us whatever we wished to see, answering all our many questions with the sweet, old smile peculiar to herself. She took us to the little garden; it contained potatoes, cabbages, onions, cucumbers, and beans; a row of currant-bushes was the only fruit; a patch of catnep, and another of mint, grcAv in one corner. Our farmers, as a general rule, are proverbially indifferent about their gardens. There was no fruit on the place besides the apple-trees of the orchard; one is surprised that cherries, and pears, and plums, all suited to our hilly climate in this county, should not receive more attention; they yield a desirable return for the cost and labor required to plant and look after them.

Passing the barn, we looked in there also; a load of sweet hay had just been thrown into the loft, and another was coming up the road at the moment. Mr. B— worked his farm with a pair of horses only, keeping no oxen. Half a dozen hens and some geese were the only poultry in the yard; the eggs and feathers were carried, in the fall, to the store at B— Green, or sometimes as far as our own village.

They kept four cows; formerly they had had a much larger dairy; but our hostess had counted her threescore and ten, and being the only woman in the house, the dairy-work of four cows, she said, was as much as she could well attend to. One would think so; for she also did all the cooking, baking, washing, ironing, and cleaning for the family, consisting of three persons; besides a share of the sewing, knitting, and spinning. We went into her little buttery; here the bright tin pans were standing full of rich milk; everything was thoroughly scoured, beautifully fresh, and neat. A stone jar of fine yellow butter, whose flavor we knew of old, stood on one side, and several cheeses were in press. The wood-work was all painted red.

While our kind hostess, on hospitable thought intent, was preparing something nice for tea, we were invited to look about the little sitting-room, and see "farm ways" in that shape. It was both parlor and guest-chamber at the same time. In one corner stood a maple bedstead, with a large, plump feather bed on it, and two tiny pillows in well-bleached cases at the head. The walls of the room were whitewashed, the wood-work was unpainted, but so thoroughly scoured, that it had acquired a sort of polish and oak color. Before the windows hung colored paper blinds. Between the windows was a table, and over it hung a small looking-glass, and a green and yellow drawing in water-colors, the gift of a friend. On one side stood a cherry bureau; upon this lay the Holy Bible, and that its sacred pages had been well studied, our friend's daily life could testify. Near the Bible lay a volume of religious character from the Methodist press, and the Life of General Marion. The mantel-piece was ornamented with peacocks' feathers, and brass candlesticks, bright as gold; in the fireplace were fresh sprigs of asparagus. An open cupboard stood on one side, containing the cups and saucers, in neat array, a pretty salt-cellar, with several pieces of cracked and broken crockery, of a superior quality, preserved for ornament more than use.

Such was the "square room," as it was called. It opened into the kitchen, and as our dear hostess was coming and going, dividing her time between her biscuits and her guests, very impartially, at last we asked permission to follow her, and sit by her while she was at work, admiring the kitchen quite as much as we did the rest of her neat dwelling. The largest room in the house, and the one most used, it was just as neat as every other corner under the roof. The chimney was very large, according to the approved old custom, and it was garnished all about with flat-irons, brooms, brushes, holders, and cooking utensils, each in its proper place. In winter, they used a stove for cooking, and in the very coldest weather, they kept two fires burning, one in the chimney, another in the stove. The walls were whitewashed. There was a great deal of wood-work about the room— wainscoting, dressers, and even the ceiling being of wood— and all was painted dark red. The ceiling of a farm-kitchen, especially if it be unplastered, as this was, is often a pretty rustic sight, a sort of store-place, all kinds of things hanging there on hooks or nails driven into the beams; bundles of dried herbs, strings of red peppers and of dried apples hanging in festoons, tools of various kinds, bags of different sorts and sizes, golden ears of seed-corn ripening, vials of physic and nostrums for man and beast, bits of cord and twine, skeins of yarn and brown thread just spun, and lastly, a file of newspapers. The low red ceiling of Farmer B—'s kitchen was not quite so well garnished in July as we have seen it at other times, still, it was by no means bare, the festoons of apples, red peppers, and Indian corn being the only objects wanting. By the window hung an ink bottle and a well-fingered almanac, witty and wise, as usual. A year or two since, an edition of the almanac was printed without the usual prognostics regarding the winds and sunshine, but it proved a complete failure; an almanac that told nothing about next year's weather nobody cared to buy, and it was found expedient to restore these important predictions concerning the future snow, hail, and sunshine of the county. Public opinion demanded it.

A great spinning-wheel, with a basket of carded wool, stood in a corner, where it had been set aside when we arrived. There was a good deal of spinning done in the family; all the yarn for stockings, for flannels, for the cloth worn by the men, for the colored woolen dresses of the women, and all the thread for their coarse toweling, &c., &c., was spun in the house by our hostess, or her grand-daughter, or some neighbor hired for the purpose. Formerly, there had been six step-daughters in the family, and then, not only all the spinning, but the weaving and dying also, were done at home. They must have been notable women, those six step-daughters; we heard some great accounts of day's spinning and weaving done by them. The presses and cupboards of the house were still full to overflowing with blankets, white and colored flannels, colored twilled coverlets for bedding, besides sheets, table-cloths, and patched bed-quilts, all their own work. In fact, almost all the clothing of the family, for both men and women, and everything in the shape of bedding and toweling used by the household, was home-made. Very few dry-goods were purchased by them; hats and shoes, some light materials for caps and collars, a little ribbon, and a printed calico now and then, seemed to be all they bought. Nor was this considered at all remarkable; such is the common way of living in many farmers' families. It has been calculated that a young woman who knows how to spin and weave can dress herself with ease and comfort, as regards everything necessary, for twelve dollars a year, including the cost of the raw materials; the actual allowance for clothing made by the authorities of this county, to farmers' daughters, while the property remained undivided, has been fifteen dollars, and the estimate is said to have included everything necessary for comfort, both winter and summer clothing. The wives and daughters of our farmers are very often notable, frugal women—perhaps one may say that they are usually so until they go from home. With the young girls about our villages, the case is very different; these are often wildly extravagant in their dress, and just as restless in following the fashions as the richest fine lady in the land. They often spend all they earn in finery.

Very pretty woolen shawls were shown us, made by our friend's step-daughters, after Scotch patterns; several families of

Scotch emigrants had settled in the neighborhood some thirty years since, and had furnished their friends with the patterns of different plaids; whether these were Highland or Lowland, we could not say. Some of their twilled flannels were also remarkably good in quality and color, but these are apt to shrink in washing. They are quite skilful dyers in scarlet, orange, green, blue, and lilac. With the maple leaves, they dye a very neat gray for stockings, but most of their coloring materials were purchased in the villages, dye-stuffs being an important part of the stock in trade of all our country druggists. Most of the spinning and weaving was in cotton or wool; the clothing and bedding was wholly of cotton or woolen materials. A certain amount of tow was used for toweling, bagging, smock frocks and pantaloons, for summer working clothes for the men. From time to time, a little flax was raised, especially to make linen, chiefly for a few finer towels and tablecloths, the luxuries of the household.

Those who live in our large towns, where they buy even their bread and butter, their milk and radishes, have no idea of the large amount of domestic goods, in wool and cotton, made by the women of the rural population of the interior, even in these days of huge factories. Without touching upon the subject of political economy, although its moral aspect must ever be a highly important one, it is certainly pleasant to see the women busy in this way, beneath the family roof, and one is much disposed to believe that the home system is healthier and safer for the individual, in every way. Home, we may rest assured, will always be, as a rule, the best place for a woman; her labors, pleasures, and interests, should all centre there, whatever be her sphere of life.

The food of the family, as well as their clothing, was almost wholly the produce of their own farm; they dealt but little with either grocer or butcher. In the spring, a calf was killed; in the fall, a sheep and a couple of hogs; once in a while, at other seasons, they got a piece of fresh meat from some neighbor who had killed a beef or a mutton. They rarely eat their poultry—

the hens were kept chiefly for eggs, and their geese for feathers. The common piece of meat, day after day, was corned pork from their pork-barrel; they usually kept, also, some corned beef in brine, either from their own herd, or a piece procured by some bargain with a neighbor. The bread was made from their own wheat, and so were the hoe-cakes and griddle-cakes from the Indian meal and buckwheat of their growth. Butter and cheese from their dairy were on table at every meal, three times a day. Pies were eaten very frequently, either of apples, pumpkins, dried fruits, or coarse minced-meat; occasionally they had pie without any meat for their dinner; puddings were rare; Yankee farmers generally eating much more pastry than pudding. Mush and milk was a common dish. They ate but few eggs, reserving them for sale. Their vegetables were almost wholly potatoes, cabbage, and onions, with fresh corn and beans, when in season, and baked beans with pork in winter. Pickles were put on table at every meal. Their sugar and molasses was made from the maple, only keeping a little white sugar for company or sickness. They drank cider from their own orchard. The chief luxuries of the household were tea and coffee, both procured from the "stores," although it may be doubted if the tea ever saw China; if like much of that drunk about the country, it was probably of farm growth also.

While we were talking over these matters, and others of a more personal nature, with our gentle old hostess, several visitors arrived;—probably, on this occasion, they came less to see the mistress of the house than her carriage-load of strange company. Be that as it may, we had the pleasure of making several new acquaintances, and of admiring some very handsome strings of gold beads about their necks; a piece of finery we had not seen in a long while. Another fashion was less pleasing. We observed that a number of the women in that neighborhood had their hair cropped short like men, a custom which seems all but unnatural. Despite her seventy years and the rheumatism, our hostess had her dark hair smoothly combed and neatly rolled up under a nice muslin cap, made after the Methodist pattern. She was not one to do anything unwomanly, though all B— Green set the fashion.

A grand-daughter of our hostess, on a visit at the farm, had been in the meadow picking strawberries, and now returned with a fine bowl full, the ripest and largest in the field. The table was set; a homespun table-cloth, white as snow, laid upon it, and every vacant spot being covered by something nice, at four o'clock we sat down to tea. Why is it that cream, milk, and butter always taste better under the roof of a farm-house than elsewhere? They seem to lose something of their peculiar sweetness and richness after passing the bounds of the farm, especially if they have been rattled over the pavement of a large town to market. Country-made bread, too, is peculiar; not so light, perhaps, nor so white as that of the baker's, but much sweeter, and more nourishing. Our farmers' wives often use a little potato or Indian meal with their wheat, which gives the bread additional sweetness and *body*, as the *gourmets* call it, in speaking of their wines. With such strawberries and cream, such bread and butter, we could not do justice to half the good things on table. The cup-cake and ginger-bread, the biscuits and cheese, the various kinds of sweetmeats and stewed apples, the broiled ham and pickles, the apple-pie and mince-pie, were thrown away upon us. Our hostess put the nicest bits on a whole row of little plates and saucers before each guest, and after a long drive, one can make a very substantial meal; still, we could not eat up all the good things, and our friend was scarcely satisfied with the result, although we flattered ourselves we had been doing wonders. But such strawberries and cream, such bread and butter, ought to be enough to satisfy any reasonable tea-drinker.

As we had a drive of several miles before us, we were obliged to say good-bye early in the afternoon, taking leave of our venerable friend with those feelings of unfeigned regard and respect which the good and upright alone excite.

After such a pleasant day, we had a charming drive home, including even the long and slow ascent of Briar Hill. The birds, perched on the rails and bushes, sung us cheerfully on our way. As we stopped at the tavern, at the little hamlet of Old Oaks, to water the horses, we found a long row of empty wagons and buggies, drawn up before the house, betokening a rustic merry-making in honor of the eve of the "Fourth." A fiddle was heard from an upper room, and we had scarcely stopped before a couple of youths, in holyday attire, stepped to the carriage, offering to help us alight, "presuming the ladies had come to the dance." Being informed of their mistake, they were very civil, apologized, and expressed their regrets. "They had hoped the ladies were coming to the ball." We thanked them, but were on our way to —. They bowed and withdrew, apparently rather disappointed at the loss of a whole carriage full of merry-makers, whom they had come out to receive with so much alacrity. Dancing was going on vigorously within; the dry, ear-piercing scrape of a miserable violin was heard playing Zip Coon, accompanied by a shrill boyish voice, half screaming, half singing out his orders: "Gents, forward!"—"Ladies, same!"— "Alla-maine left!"—"Sachay all!"—"Swing to your partners!" —"Fling your ladies opposyte!"—"Prummena-a-de awl!" The directions were obeyed with great energy and alacrity; for the scraping on the floor equalled the scraping on the violin, and the house fairly shook with the general movement.

Half an hour more, over a familiar road, brought us to the village, which we entered just as the sun set.

Wednesday, 4th.—Warm and pleasant. The sun, as usual on this day, ushered in by great firing of cannon, and ringing of bells, and hoisting of flags. Many people in the village from the country, all in holyday trim. Public holydays, once in a while, are very pleasant; it does one good to see everybody looking their cleanest and gayest. It is really a cheerful spectacle to watch the family parties in wagon-loads coming into the village at such times; old and young, fathers, mothers, sons, daughters, and babies. Certainly we Americans are very partial to gatherings of all sorts; such an occasion is never thrown away upon our good folk.

There was the usual procession at noon: a prayer, reading the Declaration of Independence, a speech, and dinner. The children of the Sunday-school had also a little entertainment of their own. Frequently there is a large pick-nick party on the lake, with dancing, in honor of the day, but this year there was nothing of the kind. In the afternoon matters seemed to drag a little; we met some of the country people walking about the village, looking in rather a doubtful state of enjoyment; they reminded us of the inquiry of a pretty little French child at a party of pleasure, where things were not going off very briskly; fixing her large blue eyes earnestly on an elder sister's face, she asked anxiously, "*Eugénie, dis moi donc est ce que je m'amuse?*" About dusk, however, we were enlivened by the ascent of a paper balloon, and fire-works, rockets, serpents, fire-balls, and though not very remarkable, everybody went to see them.

Thursday, 5th.—Fine day. The locust-trees are in great beauty. Their foliage never attains its full size until the flowers have fallen; it then has an aftergrowth, the leaves become larger and richer, taking their own peculiar bluish-green. The lower branches of a group of young locusts before the door are now sweeping the grass very beautifully. These trees have never been trimmed; is not the common practice of trimming our locusts a mistake, unless one wishes for a tall tree at some particular point? Few of our trees throw out their branches so near the ground as to sweep the turf in this way, and wherever the habit is natural, the effect is very pleasing. With the locusts, it is their large pinnated leaves which cause the branches to droop in this way, or perhaps the ripening pods add their weight also, for it is only about midsummer, or just at this season, that they bend so low as to touch the grass; the same branches which are now hanging over the turf, in winter rise two or three feet above it.

The three-thorned acacia, or honey locust, as it is sometimes called, if left to its natural growth, will also follow the same fashion, its lower branches drooping gracefully, until their long leaves sweep the grass. There is a young untrimmed tree of this kind in the village, a perfect picture in its way, so prettily branched, with its foliage sweeping the ground. As a general thing, are not all our trees too much trimmed in this country?

Friday, 6th.—Warm, half-cloudy day; light, fitful airs, which set the leaves dancing here and there without swaying the branches. Of a still, summer's day, when the foliage generally is quiet, the eye is at times attracted by a solitary leaf, or a small twig dancing merrily, as though bitten by a tarantula, to say nothing of aspen leaves, which are never at rest. The leaves of the maples, on their long stalks, are much given to this trick; so are the white birches, and the scarlet oaks, and so is the fern also. This fluttering is no doubt caused by some light puff of air setting the leaf in motion, and then dying away without any regular current to follow its course; the capricious movement continues until the force of the impulse is exhausted, and the giddy leaf has tired itself out. At times the effect is quite singular, a single leaf or two in rapid movement, all else still and calm; and one might fancy Puck, or some other mischievous elf, sitting astride the stem, shaking his sides with laughter at the expense of the bewildered spectator.

Saturday, 7th.—Clear, warm weather. Thermometer 78 in the shade.

The rose-bushes about the village gardens are suffering from the same blight which attacked them last year; it has not, however, done so much mischief this season, nor have its ravages been so general. Those bushes which stand alone, surrounded by grass, escaped in many cases; those in our neighborhood have been attacked, and the richer the earth, the more they seem to have suffered.

Monday, 9th.—Brilliant, warm weather. Thermometer 80 in the shade.

Walked in the woods; went in search of the large two-leaved

orchis, a particular plant, which we have watched for several years, as it is something of a rarity, having been seen only in two places in the neighborhood. We found the large, shining leaves lying flat on the ground, in the well-known spot, but some one had been there before us and broken off the flower-stalk. The leaves of this orchis are among the largest and roundest in our woods.

The handsome, large purple-fringed orchis is also found here, but we have not seen it this summer. The country people call it soldier's plume; it is one of our most showy flowers.

Tuesday, 10th.—Warm, cloudless weather. Thermometer 84 in the shade. Pleasant row on the lake toward sunset.

The water is beautifully clear; as we rowed along we could see what was going on far below the surface. The fish kept out of view; we only observed a few small perch. The soil of the lake, if one may use the phrase, varies much in character; along the eastern shore one looks down upon a pavement of rounded gray stones, with here and there the wreck of a dead tree, lying beneath the waves it once shaded; coasting the western bank, one finds reaches of clean sand, with a few shells of fresh water muscles scattered about, and colorless leaves of last year's growth, oak and chestnut, lying near them still undecayed. Then, again, in other places, the bottom is muddy, and thickly covered with a growth of aquatic plants of various kinds. There must be a good number of these plants in our lake, judging from those we have already gathered or seen. They vary much in their construction; all springing as they do from the same watery nursery, one might expect them to be much like each other, and to differ decidedly from those of the fields; but such is not the case. Some are thick and rough, like the reeds, the water-lilies, and the pickerel-weed; but others are as fine and delicate in their foliage as those that grow in the air. Many of those which raise their flowers above the water bear handsome blossoms, like the lilies, the purple pickerel-weed, and the brilliant water-marigold, or Beck's-bidens, which is found in Canaderaga Lake, about twelve miles from us; others are dull and unsightly, and some of these form an ugly patch in shallow spots, near our wharf, for a few weeks in August.

But this fringe of reeds and plants is only seen here and there in shallow spots; a few strokes of the oar will carry a boat at once into water much too deep to be fathomed by the eye. The depth of the lake is usually given at a hundred and fifty feet. It has no tributaries beyond a few nameless brooks, and is chiefly fed by springs in its own bosom. Of course, where such is the case, the amount of water varies but little; it has never overflowed its banks, and when the water is called low, a stranger would hardly perceive the fact.

This afternoon we rowed across Black-bird Bay, and followed the shady western bank some distance. Landed and gathered wild flowers, meadow-sweet, white silk-weed, clematis, and Alleghany vine, *adlumia*. This is the season for the climbing plants to flower; they are usually later than their neighbors. The Alleghany vine, with its pale pink clusters and very delicate foliage, is very common in some places, and so is the common clematis.

Observed, also, several vines of the glycine, *Apios tuberosa*, though its handsome purple flowers have not yet appeared. This plant has been recently carried to Europe by a French gentleman, sent out to this country by his government for scientific purposes. He supposes that it may be introduced as a common article of food, to take, in some measure, the place of the potato. The root has a pleasant taste, and is said to be much eaten by some tribes of Indians. A kind of one-seeded pea, growing in the western part of the county, *Psoralea*, was also carried to France, with the view of turning it to account in the same way. This last is not found in our neighborhood; but the glycine, or ground-nut, is not uncommon in our thickets. Whether the plan of making these a part of the common food of France will succeed or not, time alone can decide. It usually takes more than one generation to make a change in national diet. Potatoes were several centuries coming into favor on the Continent of Europe; and during the last scarcity in Great Britain, the Scotch and English did not take very kindly to the Indian corn, although it is certainly one of the sweetest grains in the world. After a change of this kind has once been made, however, and people have become accustomed to the novelty, whatever it may be, there is generally a sort of reaction in its favor, until presently no one can do without it. This has been strikingly the case with potatoes, in the way of food, and with tea and coffee in the way of drinks.

Wednesday, 11*th.*—Very warm. Thermometer 89 in the coolest position. Bright sunshine, with much air. Long drive in the evening. The chestnuts are in flower, and look beautifully. They are one of our richest trees when in blossom, and being common about the lake, are very ornamental to the country, at this season; they look as though they wore a double crown of sunshine about their flowery heads. The sumachs are also in bloom, their regular yellowish spikes showing from every thicket.

The hay-makers were busy on many farms after sunset this evening. There are fewer mowers in the hay-fields with us than in the Old World. Four men will often clear a field where, perhaps, a dozen men and women would be employed in France or England. This evening we passed a man with a horse-rake gathering his hay together by himself. As we went down the valley, he had just begun his task; when we returned, an hour and a half later, with the aid of this contrivance, he had nearly done his job.

One day, as we were driving along the bank of the lake, a year or two since, we saw, for the first time in this country, several young women at work in a hay-field; they looked quite picturesque with their colored sun-bonnets, and probably they did not find the work very hard, for they seemed to take it as a frolic.

We also chanced, on one occasion, to see a woman

ploughing in this county, the only instance of the kind we have ever observed in our part of the world. Very possibly she may have been a foreigner, accustomed to hard work in the fields, in her own country. In Germany, we remember to have once seen *a woman* and *a cow* harnessed together, dragging the plough, while a man, probably the husband, was driving both. I have forgotten whether he had a whip or not. This is the only instance in which we ever saw a woman in harness, though in travelling over Europe, one often sees the poor creatures toiling so hard, and looking so wretched, that one's heart aches for them. We American women certainly owe a debt of gratitude to our countrymen for their kindness and consideration for us generally. Gallantry may not always take a graceful form in this part of the world, and mere flattery may be worth as little here as elsewhere, but there is a glow of generous feeling toward woman in the hearts of most American men, which is highly honorable to them as a nation and as individuals. In no country is the protection given to woman's helplessness more full and free—in no country is the assistance she receives from the stronger arm so general—and nowhere does her weakness meet with more forbearance and consideration. Under such circumstances, it must be woman's own fault if she be not thoroughly respected also. The position accorded to her is favorable; it remains for her to fill it in a manner worthy her own sex, gratefully, kindly, and simply; with truth and modesty of heart and life; with unwavering fidelity of feeling and principle; with patience, cheerfulness, and sweetness of temper—no unfit return to those who smooth the daily path for her.

Thursday, 12th.—Very warm and brilliant weather. Thermometer 90 in the shade. Drive in the evening over the Highborough Hills; the roads very dusty; fortunately, we left the cloud "in our wake," as the sailors say. The young fruits are getting their ruddy color in the orchards and gardens, and the grain is taking its golden tinge. The fields are looking very rich and full of promise.

266

Friday, 13th.—Very warm. Thermometer 92 in the shade, with much air from the south-west. Though very warm, and the power of the sun great, yet the weather has not been close. We have had fine airs constantly; often quite a breeze. It is, indeed, singular that so much air should collect no clouds.

Drive down the valley in the evening. The new-shorn meadows look beautifully, bordered as they are in many places by the later elder-bushes, now loaded with white flowers. The earlier kind, which blooms in May, more common in the woods, is already ripening its red berries.

About eight o'clock there was a singular appearance in the heavens: a dark bow, very clearly marked, spanned the valley from east to west, commencing at the point where the sun had just set, the sky, at the same time, being apparently cloudless. At one moment two other fainter bows were seen; the principal arch was visible, perhaps, half an hour, fading slowly away with the twilight. Neither of our party remembered to have seen anything like it. In superstitious times it would doubtless have been connected with some public calamity.

Saturday, 14th.—A light shower this morning. Just enough to lay the dust and refresh the air, which now blows cool and moist from the northward. Shaded, vapory sky; most grateful relief after the hot sun and dry air of the last ten days. No thunder or lightning.

Monday, 16th.—Rather cooler; thermometer 79. Fine day. Walked in the woods.

Found many of the Philadelphia, or orange lilies, scattered about singly, as usual. They like to grow in woods and groves, and are often found among the fern. The Canadian, or yellow lily, is also in flower, growing in lower and more open grounds; a bit of meadow-land, on the border of one of our brooks, is now brilliantly colored with these handsome flowers. The very showy Martagon, or Turk's-cap lily, also belongs to our neighborhood. Last summer a noble plant—a pyramid of twenty red blossoms on one stalk—was found growing in a marshy spot on the hill, at the Cliffs.

Brought home a beautiful bunch of these orange lilies, with the leaves of the sweet-fern, and the white flowers of the fragrant early wintergreen.

Tuesday, 17th.—Rambled about Mill Island and the woods beyond. The red wooden grist-mill, standing here, is the oldest and most important of the neighborhood. In dry seasons, when water fails in the lesser streams, grain has been brought here from farms twenty miles distant. This present summer, however, the water has been so low, that the wheels have stopped. The low saw-mill, on the farther bank, is one of half a dozen within a few miles. It does a deal of work. Some of the logs float down the lake and river; others are drawn here on the snow in winter; but the basin above the dam is generally well filled with them. As the stream runs a mere rivulet now, many of the logs are lodged on the mud, and the mill is idle. We rarely see the river so low.

We are told that for some years after the village was commenced, Mill Island was a favorite resort of the Indians, who, at that time, came frequently in parties to the new settlement, remaining here for months together. The island was then covered with wood, and they seem to have chosen it for their camp, in preference to other situations. Possibly it may have been a place of resort to their fishing and hunting parties when the country was a wilderness. Now they come very seldom, and singly, or in families, craving permission to build a shanty of boughs or boards, in order to ply their trade of basket-makers. They no longer encamp on the island itself, for the oak by the bridge is almost the only tree standing on it, and they still love the woods; but three out of the four families who have been here during the last ten years, have chosen the neighboring groves for their halting-place.

There are already many parts of this country where an Indian is never seen. There are thousands and hundreds of thousands of the white population who have never laid eyes upon a red man. But this ground lies within the former bounds of the Six Nations, and a remnant of the great tribes of the Iroquois still linger about their old haunts, and occasionally cross our path. The first group that we chance to see strike us strangely, appearing as they do in the midst of a civilized community with the characteristics of their wild race still clinging to them; and when it is remembered that the land over which they now wander as strangers, in the midst of an alien race, was so lately their own—the heritage of their fathers—it is impossible to behold them without a feeling of peculiar interest.

Standing at the window, one summer's afternoon, our attention was suddenly fixed by three singular figures approaching the house. More than one member of our household had never yet seen an Indian, and unaware that any were in the neighborhood, a second glance was necessary to convince us that these visitors must belong to the red race, whom we had long been so anxious to see. They came slowly toward the door, walking singly and silently, wrapped in blankets, bareheaded and barefooted. Without knocking or speaking, they entered the house with a noiseless step, and stood silently near the open door. We gave them a friendly greeting, and they proved to be women of the Oneida tribe, belonging to a family who had encamped in the woods the day before, with the purpose of selling their baskets in the village. Meek in countenance, with delicate forms and low voices, they had far more of the peculiarities of the red race about them than one would look for in a tribe long accustomed to intercourse with the whites, and a portion of whom have become more than half civilized. Only one of the three could speak English, and she seemed to do so with effort and reluctance. They were dressed in gowns of blue calico, rudely cut, coarsely stitched together, and so short as to show their broadcloth leggings worked with beads. Their heads were entirely bare, their straight, black hair hanging loose about their shoulders, and, although it was midsummer at the time, they were closely wrapped in coarse white blankets. We asked their names. "Wallee"—"Awa"—"Cootlee"—was the answer.

Of what tribe? "Oneida," was the reply, in a voice low and melancholy as the note of the whip-poor-will, giving the soft Italian sound to the vowels, and four syllables to the word. They were delicately made, of the usual height of American women, and their features were good, without being pretty. About their necks, arms, and ankles, they wore strings of cheap ornaments, pewter medals, and coarse glass beads, with the addition of a few scraps of tin, the refuse of some tin-shop passed on their way. One, the grandmother, was a Christian; the other two were Pagans. There was something startling and very painful in hearing these poor creatures within our own community, and under our own roof, declaring themselves heathens! They paid very little attention to the objects about them, until the youngest of the three observed a small Chinese basket on a table near her. She rose silently, took the basket in her hand, examined it carefully, made a single exclamation of pleasure, and then exchanged a few words with her companions in their own wild but musical tongue. They all seemed struck with this specimen of Chinese ingenuity. They asked, as usual, for bread and cold meat, and a supply was cheerfully given them, with the addition of some cake, about which they appeared to care very little. In the mean time a messenger had been sent to one of the shops of the village, where toys and knicknacks for children were sold, and he returned with a handful of copper rings and brooches, pewter medals, and bits of bright ribbons, which were presented to our guests; the simple creatures looking much gratified, as well as surprised, although their thanks were brief, and they still kept up the true Indian etiquette of mastering all emotion. They were, indeed, very silent, and unwilling to talk, so that it was not easy to gather much information from them; but their whole appearance was so much more Indian than we had been prepared for, while their manners were so gentle and womanly, so free from anything coarse or rude in the midst of their untutored ignorance, that we were much pleased with the visit. Later in the day we went to their camp, as they always call their halting-place; here we found several children and two men of the family. These last were evidently full-blooded Indians, with every mark of their race stamped upon them; but, alas! not a trace of the "brave" about either. Both had that heavy, sensual, spiritless expression, the stamp of vice, so painful to behold on the human countenance. They had thrown off the blanket, and were equipped in ragged coats, pantaloons, and beavers, from the cast-off clothing of their white neighbors, with the striking addition, however, of bits of tin to match those of the squaws. Some of these scraps were fastened round their hats, others were secured on their breasts and in the button-holes, where the great men of the Old World wear diamond stars and badges of honor. They were cutting bows and arrows for the boys of the village, of ash-wood, and neither of them spoke to us; they either did not, or would not understand our companion, when addressed in English. The women and children were sitting on the ground, busy with their baskets, which they make very neatly, although their patterns are all simple. They generally dye the strips of ash with colors purchased in the villages from the druggists, using only now and then, for the same purpose, the juices of leaves and berries, when these are in season, and easily procured.

Since the visit of the Oneida squaws, several other parties have been in the village. The very next season a family of three generations made their appearance at the door, claiming an hereditary acquaintance with the master of the house. They were much less wild than our first visitors, having discarded the blanket entirely, and speaking English very well. The leader and patriarch of the party bore a Dutch name, given him, probably, by some of his friends on the Mohawk Flats; and he was, moreover, entitled to write Reverend before it, being a Methodist minister—the Rev. Mr. Kunkerpott. He was notwithstanding a full-blooded Indian, with the regular copper-colored complexion, and high cheek-bones; the outline of his face was decidedly Roman, and his long, gray hair had a wave which is rare among his people; his mouth, where the savage expression is usually most strongly marked, was small, with a kindly expression about it. Altogether he was a strange mixture of the Methodist preacher and the Indian patriarch. His son was much more savage than himself in appearance—a silent, cold-looking man; and the grandson, a boy of ten or twelve, was one of the most uncouth, impish-looking creatures we ever beheld. He wore a long-tailed coat twice too large for him, with boots of the same size, and he seemed particularly proud of these last, looking at them from time to time with great satisfaction, as he went tottering along. The child's face was very wild, and he was bareheaded, with an unusual quantity of long, black hair streaming about his head and shoulders. While the grandfather was conversing about old times, the boy diverted himself by twirling round on one leg, a feat which would have seemed almost impossible, booted as he was, but which he nevertheless accomplished with remarkable dexterity, spinning round and round, his arms extended, his large black eyes staring stupidly before him, his mouth open, and his long hair flying in every direction, as wild a looking creature as one could wish to see. We expected every moment that he would fall breathless and exhausted, like a dancing dervish, supposing that the child had been taught this accomplishment as a means of pleasing his civilized friends; but no, he was only amusing himself, and kept his footing to the last.

Some farther acquaintance with the Indians, who still occupy lands reserved for them by the government in the western part of the State, has only confirmed the impressions produced by these first interviews. Civilization, in its earliest approaches, seems to produce a different effect upon the men and the women, the former losing, and the latter gaining by it. The men, when no longer warriors and hunters, lose their native character; the fire of their savage energy is extinguished, and the dull and blackened embers alone remain. Unaccustomed by habit, prejudice, hereditary instinct, to labor, they cannot work, and very generally sink into worthless, drinking idlers.

Many of them are seen in this condition in the neighborhood of their own lands. The women, on the contrary, have always been accustomed to toil while the warriors were idle, and it is much more easy for them to turn from field labors to household tasks, than for the men to exchange the excitement of war and hunting for quiet, regular, agricultural or mechanic pursuits. In the savage state, the women appear very inferior to the men, but in a half-civilized condition, they have much the advantage over the stronger sex. They are rarely beautiful, but often very pleasing; their gentle expression, meek and subdued manner, low, musical voices, and mild, dark eyes, excite an interest in their favor, while one turns with pain and disgust from the brutal, stupid, drunken countenances too often seen among the men. Many a young girl might be found to-day among the half-civilized tribes, whose manner and appearance would accord with one's idea of the gentle Pocahontas; but it is rare, indeed, that a man is seen among them who would make a Powhattan, a Philip, or an Uncas. And yet, unfavorable as their appearance is, there are few even of the most degraded who, when aroused, will not use the poetical, figurative speech, and the dignified, impressive gesture of their race. The contrast between the degraded aspect they bear every day, and these sudden instinctive flashes, is very striking. Instances are not wanting, however, in which men, of purely Indian blood, have conquered the many obstacles in their path, and now command the sympathy and respect of their white brethren by the energy and perseverance they have shown in mastering a new position among civilized men.

The dress of the women is also more pleasing than that of the men, preserving as they do something of a characteristic costume. They are generally wrapped in blankets, and bareheaded, or those of the richer families wear a round beaver, which makes them look a little like the brown peasant girls of Tuscany; they seem to be the only females in the country who do not make a profound study of the monthly fashion-plates. The men are almost always dressed in shabby clothes, cut upon white patterns. The women either dislike to speak English, or they are unable to do so, for they are very laconic indeed in conversation; many of them, although understanding what is said, will only answer you by smiles and signs; but as they do not aim as much as the men at keeping up the cold dignity of their race, this mute language is often kindly and pleasing. Many of those who carry about their simple wares for sale in the neighborhood of their own villages would be remarked for their amiable expression, gentle manner, and low, musical voices. They still carry their children tied up in a blanket at their backs, supporting them by a band passing round the forehead, which brings the weight chiefly upon the head.

It is easy to wish these poor people well; but surely something more may justly be required of us—of those who have taken their country and their place on the earth. The time seems at last to have come when their own eyes are opening to the real good of civilization, the advantages of knowledge, the blessings of Christianity. Let us acknowledge the strong claim they have upon us, not in word only, but in deed also. The native intellect of the red men who peopled this part of America surpassed that of many other races laboring under the curses of savage life; they have shown bravery, fortitude, religious feeling, eloquence, imagination, quickness of intellect, with much dignity of manner; and if we are true to our duty, now at the moment when they are making of their own accord a movement in the path of improvement, perhaps the day may not be distant when men of Indian blood may be numbered among the wise and the good, laboring in behalf of our common country.

It is painful, indeed, to remember how little has yet been done for the Indian during the three centuries since he and the white man first met on the Atlantic coast. But such is only the common course of things; a savage race is almost invariably corrupted rather than improved by its earliest contact with a civilized people; they suffer from the vices of civilization before they learn justly to comprehend its merits. It is with nations as with individuals—amelioration is a slow process, corruption a rapid one.

Wednesday, 18th.—Warm, brilliant weather. Thermometer 89, with much dry air. Walked in the woods.

That ghost-like plant, the Indian-pipe, is in flower, and quite common here—sometimes growing singly, more frequently several together. The whole plant, about a span high, is entirely colorless, looking very much as if it were cut out of Derbyshire spar; the leaves are replaced by white scales, but the flower is large and perfect, and from the root upward, it is wholly of untarnished white. One meets with it from June until late in September; at first, the flower is nodding, when it really looks something like the cup of a pipe; gradually, however, it erects itself as the seed ripens, and turns black when it decays. I have seen a whole cluster of them bordered with black—in half-mourning, as it were—though of a healthy white within this line. It was probably some blight which had affected them in this way.

The pretty little dew-drop, *Dalibarda repens* of botanists, is also in blossom—a delicate, modest little flower, opening singly among dark green leaves, which look much like those of the let; it is one of our most common wood-plants; the leaves frequently remain green through the winter. The name of dew-drop has probably been given to this flower from its blooming about the time when the summer dews are the heaviest.

The one-sided wintergreen is also in blossom, with its little greenish-white flowers all turned in the same direction; it is one of the commonest plants we tread under foot in the forest. This is a wintergreen region, all the varieties being found, I believe, in this county. Both the glossy pipsissima and the pretty spotted wintergreen, with its variegated leaves, are common here; so is the fragrant shin-leaf; and the one-flowered pyrola, rare in most parts of the country, is also found in our woods.

Observed the yellow diervilla or bush-honeysuckle still in flower. The hemlocks still show the light green of their young shoots, which grow dark very slowly.

Thursday, 19th.—Warm, clear day; thermometer 88.

It happens that the few humble antiquities of our neighborhood are all found lying together near the outlet of the lake; they consist of a noted rock, the ruins of a bridge, and the remains of a military work.

The rock lies in the lake, a stone's throw from the shore; it is a smooth, rounded fragment, about four feet high; the waters sometimes, in very warm seasons, leave it nearly dry, but they have never, I believe, overflowed it. There is nothing remarkable in the rock itself, though it is perhaps the largest of the few that show themselves above the surface of our lake; but this stone is said to have been a noted rallying-point with the Indians, who were in the habit of appointing meetings between different parties at this spot. From the Mohawk country, from the southern hunting-grounds on the banks of the Susquehannah, and from the Oneida region, they came through the wilderness to this common rendezvous at the gray rock, near the outlet of the lake. Such is the tradition; probably it is founded in truth, for it has prevailed here since the settlement of the country, and it is of a nature not likely to have been thought of by a white man, who, if given to inventing anything of the kind, would have attempted something more ambitious. Its very simplicity gives it weight, and it is quite consistent with the habits of the Indians, and their nice observation; for the rock, though unimportant, is yet the largest in sight, and its position near the outlet would make it a very natural waymark to them. Such as it is, this, moreover, is the only tradition, in a positive form, connected with the Indians preserved among us; with this single exception, the red man has left no mark here, on hill or dale, lake or stream.

From tradition we step to something more positive; from the dark ages we come to the dawn of history. On the bank of the river are found the ruins of a bridge, the first made at this point by the white man. Among the mountain streams of the Old World are many high, narrow, arches of stone, built more than a thousand years since, still standing to-day in different stages of picturesque decay. Our ruins are more rude than those. In the summer of 1786, a couple of emigrants, father and son, arrived on the eastern bank of the river, intending to cross it; there was no village here then—a single log-cabin and a deserted blockhouse stood on the spot, however, and they hoped to find at least the shelter of walls and a roof. But there was no bridge over the river, nor boat to ferry them across: some persons, under such circumstances, would have forded the stream; others might have swam across; our emigrants took a shorter course—they made a bridge. Each carried his axe, as usual, and choosing one of the tall pines standing on the bank, one of the old race which then filled the whole valley, they soon felled the tree, giving it such an inclination as threw it across the channel, and their bridge was built—they crossed on the trunk. The stump of that tree is still standing on the bank among the few ruins we have to boast of; it is fast mouldering away, but it has outlasted the lives of both the men who felled the tree—the younger of the two, the son, having died in advanced old age, a year or two since.

The military work alluded to was on a greater scale, and connected with an expedition of some importance. In 1779, when General Sullivan was ordered against the Indians in the western part of the State, to punish them for the massacres of Wyoming and Cherry Valley, a detachment of his forces, under General Clinton, was sent through this valley. Ascending the Mohawk, to what was sometimes called the "portage" over the hills to this lake, they cut a road through the forest, and transporting their boats to our waters, launched them at the head of the lake, and rowed down to the site of the present village. Here they lay encamped some little time, finding the river too much encumbered with flood-wood to allow their boats to pass. To remove this difficulty, General Clinton ordered a dam to be built at the outlet, thus raising the lake so much, that when the work was suddenly opened, the waters rushed through with such power, that they swept the channel clear; by this means, the troops were enabled to pass in their boats from these very sources of the stream to the rendezvous at Tioga Point, a distance of more than two hundred miles, by the course of this winding river. This is the only incident which has connected our secluded lake with historical events, and it is believed that upon no other occasion have troops, on a warlike errand, passed through the valley. Probably in no other instance have so large a number of boats ever floated on our quiet lake, and we can scarcely suppose that a fleet of this warlike character will ever again, to the end of time, be collected here. Some few traces of this military dam may still be seen, though every year they are becoming more indistinct.

Friday, 20th.—Warm; thermometer 85, with high wind from the southward. Light sprinkling showers through the day, barely enough to lay the dust. No thunder or lightning.

The fire-flies flitting about this evening in the rain; they do not mind a showery evening much; we have often seen them of a rainy night, carrying their little lanterns about with much unconcern; it is only a hard and driving shower which sends them home. These little creatures seem to have favorite grounds; there is a pretty valley in the county, about twenty miles from us, where they are very numerous; one sees them dancing over those meadows in larger parties than about our own.

Saturday, 21st.—Fine weather; heat not so great; thermometer 77.

Our little fruit-venders are beginning to bring whortleberries to market; they are very plenty on our hills, being common in the woods, and abundant in half-cleared lands. This little shrub, including all its numerous varieties, spreads over a broad extent of country, growing alike within the forest, in waste lands, upon hills and in swamps; it is well known that on this Western Continent it fills the place held in Europe by the heath. Though much less showy than the golden broom or the purple heather, the European plants of waste grounds, the whortleberry has the higher merit of producing an edible fruit, which we still find very pleasant, though now supplied with so many luxuries of the kind by horticulture. To the poor Indians the whortleberries must have been very precious, yielding fruit for their benefit during three months of the year, more or less.

The northern lights are brilliant this evening; for some months they have been less frequent than usual. We have them, at intervals, during all seasons.

Monday, 23d.—Just at the point where the village street becomes a road and turns to climb the hill-side, there stands a group of pines, a remnant of the old forest. There are many trees like these among the woods; far and near such maybe seen rising from the hills, now tossing their arms in the stormy winds, now drawn in still and dark relief against the glowing evening sky. Their gaunt, upright forms standing about the hill-tops, and the ragged gray stumps of those which have fallen, dotting the smooth fields, make up the sterner touches in a scene whose general aspect is smiling. But although these old trees are common upon the wooded heights, yet the group on the skirts of the village stands alone among the fields of the valley; their nearer brethren have all been swept away, and these are left in isolated company, differing in character from all about them, a monument of the past.

It is upon a narrow belt of land, a highway and a corn-field on one side, a brook and an orchard on the other, that these trees are rooted; a strip of woodland connected with the forest on the hills above, and suddenly cut off where it approaches the first buildings of the village. There they stand, silent spectators of the wonderful changes that have come over the valley. Hundreds of winters have passed since the cones which contained the seed of that grove fell from the parent tree; centuries have elapsed since their heads emerged from the topmost wave of the sea of verdure to meet the sunshine, and yet it is but yesterday that their shadows first fell, in full length, upon the sod at their feet.

Sixty years since, those trees belonged to a wilderness; the bear, the wolf, and the panther brushed their trunks, the ungainly moose and the agile deer browsed at their feet; the

279

savage hunter crept stealthily about their roots, and painted braves passed noiselessly on the war-path beneath their shade. How many successive generations of the red man have trod the soil they overshadowed, and then sat down in their narrow graves—how many herds of wild creatures have chased each other through that wood, and left their bones to bleach among the fern and moss, there is no human voice can tell. We only know that the summer winds, when they filled the canvas of Columbus and Cabot, three hundred years ago, came sweeping over these forest pines, murmuring then as we hear them murmur to-day.

There is no record to teach us even the name of the first white man who saw this sequestered valley, with its limpid lake; it was probably some bold hunter from the Mohawk, chasing the deer, or in quest of the beaver. But while towns were rising on the St. Lawrence and upon the sea-board, this inland region lay still unexplored; long after trading-houses had been opened, and fields had been tilled, and battles had been fought to the north, south, east, ay, and even at many points westward, those pines stood in the heart of a silent wilderness. This little lake lay embedded in a forest until after the great struggle of the Revolution was over. A few months after the war was brought to an honorable close, Washington made a journey of observation among the inland waters of this part of the country; writing to a friend in France, he names this little lake, the source of a river, which, four degrees farther south, flows into the Chesapeake in near neighborhood with his own Potomac. As he passed along through a half-wild region, where the few marks of civilization then existing bore the blight of war, he conceived the outline of many of those improvements which have since been carried out by others, and have yielded so rich a revenue of prosperity. It is a pleasing reflection to those who live here, that while many important places in the country were never honored by his presence, Washington has trod the soil about our lake. But even at that late day, when the great and good man came, the mountains were still clothed in wood to the water's edge, and mingled with giant oaks and ashes, those tall pines waved above the valley.

At length, nearly three long centuries after the Genoese had crossed the ocean, the white man came to plant a home on this spot, and it was then the great change began; the axe and the saw, the forge and the wheel, were busy from dawn to dusk, cows and swine fed in thickets whence the wild beasts had fled, while the ox and the horse drew away in chains the fallen trunks of the forest. The tenants of the wilderness shrunk deeper within its bounds with every changing moon; the wild creatures fled away within the receding shades of the forest, and the red man followed on their track; his day of power was gone, his hour of pitiless revenge had passed, and the last echoes of the war-whoop were dying away forever among these hills, when the pale-faces laid their hearth-stones by the lake shore. The red man, who for thousands of years had been lord of the land, no longer treads the soil; he exists here only in uncertain memories, and in forgotten graves.

Such has been the change of the last half century. Those who from childhood have known the cheerful dwellings of the village, the broad and fertile farms, the well-beaten roads, such as they are to-day, can hardly credit that this has all been done so recently by a band of men, some of whom, white-headed and leaning on their staves, are still among us. Yet such is the simple truth. This village lies just on the borders of the tract of country which was opened and peopled immediately after the Revolution; it was among the earliest of those little colonies from the sea-board which struck into the wilderness at that favorable moment, and whose rapid growth and progress in civilization have become a by-word. Other places, indeed, have far surpassed this quiet borough; Rochester, Buffalo, and others of a later date, have become great cities, while this remains a rural village; still, whenever we pause to recall what has been done in this secluded valley during the lifetime of one generation, we must needs be struck with new astonishment. And throughout every act of the work, those old pines were there. Unchanged themselves, they stand surrounded by objects over all of which a great change has passed. The open valley, the half-shorn hills, the paths, the flocks, the buildings, the woods in their second growth, even the waters in the different images they reflect on their bosom, the very race of men who come and go, all are different from what they were; and those calm old trees seem to heave the sigh of companionless age, as their coned heads rock slowly in the winds.

The aspect of the wood tells its own history, so widely does it differ in character from the younger groves waving in gay luxuriance over the valley. In the midst of smooth fields it speaks so clearly of the wilderness, that it is not the young orchard of yesterday's planting, but the aged native pines which seem the strangers on the ground. The pine of forest growth never fails to have a very marked character of its own; the gray shaft rises clear and unbroken by bend or bough, to more than half its great elevation, thence short horizontal limbs in successive fan-like growth surround the trunk to its summit, which is often crowned with a low crest of upright branches. The shaft is very fine from its great height and the noble simplicity of its lines; in coloring, it is a pure clear gray, having the lightest and the smoothest bark of all its tribe, and only occasionally mottled with patches of lichens. The white pine of this climate gathers but few mosses, unless in very moist situations; the very oldest trees are often quite free from them. Indeed, this is a tree seldom seen with the symptoms of a half-dead and decaying condition about it, like so many others; the gray line of a naked branch may be observed here and there, perhaps, a sign of age, but it generally preserves to the very last an appearance of vigor, as though keeping death at bay until struck to the heart, or laid low from the roots. It is true, this appearance may often prove deceptive; still, it is a peculiarity of our pine, that it preserves its verdure until the very last, unlike many other trees which are seen in the forest, half green, half gray, and lifeless.

The pine of the lawns or open groves and the pine of the forest differ very strikingly in outline; the usual pyramidal or conical form of the evergreen is very faintly traced on the short, irregular limbs of the forest tree; but what is lost in luxuriance and elegance is more than replaced by a peculiar character of wild dignity, as it raises its stern head high above the lesser wood, far overtopping the proudest rank of oaks. And yet, in their rudest shapes, they are never harsh; as we approach them, we shall always find something of the calm of age and the sweetness of nature to soften their aspect; there is a grace in the slow waving of their limbs in the higher air, which never fails; there is a mysterious melody in their breezy murmurs; there is an emerald light in their beautiful verdure, which lies in unfading wreaths, fresh and clear, about the heads of those old trees. The effect of light and shade on the foliage of those older forest pines is indeed much finer than what we see among their younger neighbors; the tufted branches, in their horizontal growth, are beautifully touched with circlets of a clear light, which is broken up and lost amid the confused medley of branches in trees of more upright growth. The long brown cones are chiefly pendulous, in clusters, from the upper branches; some seasons they are so numerous on the younger trees as to give their heads a decided brown coloring.

The grove upon the skirts of the village numbers, perhaps, some forty trees, varying in their girth from five or six to twelve feet; and in height, from a hundred and twenty to a hundred and sixty feet. Owing to their unscreened position and their height, these trees may be clearly distinguished for miles, whether from the lake, the hills, or the roads about the country—a land-mark overtopping the humble church-spires, and every object raised by man within the bounds of the valley. Their rude simplicity of outline, the erect, unbending trunks, their stern, changeless character, and their scanty drapery of foliage, unconsciously lead one to fancy them an image of some band of savage chiefs, emerging in a long, dark line from the glen in their rear, and gazing in wonder upon their former hunting-grounds in its altered aspect.

The preservation of those old pines must depend entirely upon the will of their owner; they are private property; we have no right to ask that they may be spared, but it is impossible to behold their hoary trunks and crested heads without feeling a hope that they may long continue unscathed, to look down upon the village which has sprung up at their feet. They are certainly one of the most striking objects in the county, and we owe a debt of gratitude to the hand which has so long preserved them, one of the honors of our neighborhood. It needs but a few short minutes to bring one of these trees to the ground; the rudest boor passing along the highway may easily do the deed; but how many years must pass ere its equal stand on the same spot! Let us pause to count the days, the months, the years; let us number the generations that must come and go, the centuries that must roll onward, ere the seed sown from this year's cones shall produce a wood like that before us. The stout arm so ready to raise the axe to-day, must grow weak with age, it must drop into the grave; its bone and sinew must crumble into dust long before another tree, tall and great as those, shall have grown from the cone in our hand. Nay, more, all the united strength of sinew, added to all the powers of mind, and all the force of will, of millions of men, can do no more toward the work than the poor ability of a single arm; these are of the deeds which time alone can perform. But allowing even that hundreds of years hence other trees were at length to succeed these with the same dignity of height and age, no other younger wood can ever claim the same connection as this, with a state of things now passed away forever; they cannot have that wild, stern character of the aged forest pines. This little town itself must fall to decay and ruin; its streets must become choked with bushes and brambles; the farms of the valley must be anew buried within the shades of a wilderness; the wild deer and the wolf, and the bear, must

284

return from beyond the great lakes; the bones of the savage men buried under our feet must arise and move again in the chase, ere trees like those, with the spirit of the forest in every line, can stand on the same ground in wild dignity of form like those old pines now looking down upon our homes.

Tuesday, 24*th*.—Thermometer 84 in the shade at three o'clock. Still, clear, and dry; the farmers very anxious for rain.

Pleasant row in the afternoon; went down the river. One cannot go far, as the mill-dam blocks the way, but it is a pretty little bit of stream for an evening row. So near its source, the river is quite narrow, only sixty or eighty feet in breadth. The water is generally very clear, and of greenish gray; after the spring thaws it sometimes has a bluish tint, and late in autumn, after heavy rains, it takes a more decided shade of dark green. It is rarely turbid, and never positively muddy. It has no great depth, except in spots; there are some deep places, however, well known to the boys of the village for feats of diving performed there, certain lads priding themselves upon walking across the bed of the river through these deep spots, while others still more daring are said to have actually played a game of "lap-stone," sitting in what they call the "Deep Hole." In general, the bottom is stony or muddy, but there are reaches of sand also. The growth of aquatic plants is thick in many places, and near the bridge there is a fine patch of water-grasses, which have a beautiful effect seen from above, their long tufts floating gracefully in the slow current of the stream, like the locks of a troop of Mermaids. One of these plants, by-the-by, bears the name of the "Canadian Water-Nymph;" but it is one of the homeliest of its tribe; there are others much more graceful to which the name would be better adapted. It will be remembered that in the northern part of the State there is quite a large stream called Grass River, from the great quantity of these grassy plants growing in its waters.

The older trees on the bank have long since been cut away; but many young elms, maples, ashes, amelanchiers, &c., stand with their roots washed by the water, while grape-vines and

Virginia creepers are climbing over them. Wild cherries and plums also line the course of our little river. Sallows and alders form close thickets lower than the forest trees. All our native willows on this continent are small; the largest is the black willow, with a dark bark, about five-and-twenty feet high. It grows some miles farther down the stream. Our alders also are mere bushes, while the European alder is a full-sized tree, tall as their elms or beeches.

Wednesday, 25th.—Warm and clear. Thermometer 83, with fine air.

Long drive. The roads very dusty, but the wind was in our favor, and it is such a busy time with the farmers, that there was little movement on the highway. In the course of a drive of several hours, we only saw three or four wagons.

The farms look very rich with the ripening grains, but rain is much wanted. The Indian corn, and hops, and potatoes, have had more sun than they need. The grass also is much drier than usual in this part of the country; but the trees are in great beauty, luxuriantly green, showing as yet no evil effects from this dry season. The maize is thought to have suffered most; the farmers say the ears are not filling as they ought to do; but the plants themselves look well, and the yellow flowers of the pumpkin-vines lying on the ground help, as usual, to make the corn-fields among the handsomest on the farms.

Vines like the pumpkin, and melon, and cucumber, bearing heavy fruits, show little inclination for climbing; it is well they do not attempt to raise themselves from the earth, since, if they did so, they could not support their own fruit. The fact that they do not seek to climb is a pleasing instance of that beautiful fitness and unity of character so striking in the vegetable world generally; the position in which they are content to lie is the one best calculated to mature their large, heavy gourds; the reflected heat of the earth aiding the sun in the task, while the moisture from the ground does not injure the thick rind, as would be the case with fruits of a more delicate covering.

Thursday, 26th.—Lowering, cloudy morning, with strong breeze from the south-east; one of those skies which promise rain every ten minutes. Dark vapors cover the heavens, and sweep over the hill-tops, but the clouds open, gleams of sunshine come and go, and no rain falls. Long drive in the morning. The mowers are still at work here and there, for there is much hay cut in our neighborhood. The wheat harvest has also commenced, and the crop is pronounced a very good one.

There are certain fancies connected with the wheat-fields prevailing among our farmers, which they are very loth to give up. There is the old notion, for instance, that a single barberry-bush will blight acres of wheat, when growing near the grain, an opinion which is now, I believe, quite abandoned by persons of the best judgment. And yet you see frequent allusions to it, and occasionally some one brings up an instance which he sagely considers as unanswerable proof that the poor barberry is guilty of this crime. In this county we have no barberries; they are a naturalized shrub in America; at least, the variety now so common in many parts of the country came originally from the other hemisphere, and they have not yet reached us. There is another kind, a native, abundant in Virginia; whether this is also accused of blighting the wheat, I do not know.

The deceitful chess, or cheat, is another object of especial aversion to the farmers, and very justly. It is not only a troublesome weed among a valuable crop, but, looking so much like the grain, its deceptive appearance is an especial aggravation. Many of our country folk, moreover, maintain that this plant is nothing but a sort of wicked, degenerate wheat; they hold that a change comes over the grain by which it loses all its virtue, and takes another form, becoming, in short, the worthless chess; this opinion some of them maintain stoutly against all opponents, at the point of scythe and pitchfork. And yet this odd notion is wholly opposed to all the positive laws, the noble order of nature; they might as well expect their raspberry bushes to turn capriciously into blackberries, their potatoes into beets, their lettuce into radishes.

Most of the weeds which infest our wheat-fields come from the Old World. This deceitful chess, the corn-cockle, the Canada thistle, tares, the voracious red-root, the blue-weed, or bugloss, with others of the same kind. There is, however, one brilliant but noxious plant found among the corn-fields of Europe which is not seen in our own, and that is the gaudy red poppy. Our farmers are no doubt very well pleased to dispense with it; they are quite satisfied with the weeds already naturalized. But so common is the poppy in the Old World that it is found everywhere in the corn-fields, along the luxuriant shores of the Mediterranean, upon the open, chequered plains of France and Germany, and among the hedged fields of England. The first wild poppies ever seen by the writer were gathered by a party of American children about the ruins of Netley Abbey, near Southampton, in England.

So common is this brilliant weed among the European grain-fields, that there is a little insect, an ingenious, industrious little creature, who invariably employs it in building her cell. This wild bee, called the upholsterer bee, from its habits, leads a solitary life, but she takes a vast deal of pains in behalf of her young. About the time when the wild poppy begins to blossom, this little insect flies into a corn-field, looks out for a dry spot of ground, usually near some pathway; here she bores a hole about three inches in depth, the lower portion being wider than the mouth; and quite a toil it must be to so small a creature to make the excavation; it is very much as if a man were to clear out the cellars for a large house with his hands only. But this is only the beginning of her task: when the cell is completed, she then flies away to the nearest poppy, which, as she very well knows, cannot be very far off in a corn-field; she cuts out a bit of the scarlet flower, carries it to the nest, and spreads it on the floor like a carpet; again she returns to the blossom and brings home another piece, which she lays over the first; when the floor is covered with several layers of this soft scarlet carpeting, she proceeds to line the sides throughout in the same way, until the whole is well surrounded with these handsome hangings. This brilliant cradle she makes for one little bee, laying only a single egg amid the flower-leaves. Honey and bee-bread are then collected and piled up to the height of an inch; and when this store is completed, the scarlet curtains are drawn close over the whole, and the cell is closed, the careful mother replacing the earth as neatly as possible, so that after she has finally smoothed the spot over, it is difficult to discover a cell you may have seen open the day before.

This constant association with the wheat, which even the insects have learned by instinct, has not remained unheeded by man. Owing to this connection with the precious grain, the poppy of the Old World received, ages ago, all the honors of a classical flower, and became blended with the fables of ancient mythology; not only was it given to the impersonation of Sleep, as one of his emblems, from the well-known narcotic influences of the plant, but it was also considered as sacred to one of the most ancient and most important deities of the system; the very oldest statues of Ceres represent her with poppies in her garlands, blended with ears of wheat, either carried in her hand, or worn on her head. The ancient poets mingled the ears of wheat and the poppy in their verses:

> "The meanest cottager
> *His poppy grows among the corn,*"

says Cowley, in his translation of Virgil; and in our own day Mr. Hood, in his pleasing picture of Ruth, introduces both plants, when describing her beautiful color:

> "And on her cheek an autumn flush
> *Like poppies grown with corn.*"

In short, so well established is this association of the poppy and wheat, by the long course of observation from time immemorial to the present season, that the very *modistes* of Paris, when they wish to trim a straw bonnet with field plants, are careful to mingle the poppy with heads of wheat in their artificial flowers. Fickle Fashion herself is content to leave these plants, year after year, entwined together in her wreaths.

But in spite of this general prevalence of the poppy throughout the grain-fields of the Old World, and its acknowledged claim to a place beside the wheat, it is quite unknown here as a weed. With us this ancient association is broken up. Never having seen it ourselves, we have frequently asked farmers from different parts of the country if they had ever found it among their wheat, and thus far the answer has always been the same; they had never seen the flower out of gardens. Among our cottage gardens it is very common. It is, however, naturalized about Westchester, in Pennsylvania, and may possibly be found in some other isolated spots; but in all this range of wheat-growing country, among the great grain-fields of the Genesee, of Ohio, of Michigan, it is said to be entirely unknown as a field plant.

It must be the comparative severity of the winters which has broken up this very ancient connection in our part of the world; and yet they have at times very severe seasons in France and Germany, without destroying the field poppies.

Friday, 21th.—Cooler; a refreshing shower last evening; no thunder or lightning.

The butterflies are very numerous now; tortoise-shell, black, and yellow, with here and there a blue; large parties of the little white kind, and the tiny tortoise-shell, also, are fluttering about the weeds. The yellow butterflies with pink markings are the most common sort we have here; they are regular roadsters, constantly seen on the highway. Last summer about this time, while driving between Penn-Yan and Seneca Lake, we found these little creatures more numerous than we had ever yet seen them; there had been a heavy rain the day before, and there were many half-dried, muddy pools along the road, which seemed to attract these butterflies more than the flowers in the meadows; they are always found hovering over such spots in summer; but on that occasion we saw so many that we attempted to count them, and in half a mile we passed seventy, so that in the course of a drive of a couple of hours we probably saw more than a thousand of these pretty creatures strung along the highway in little flocks.

There is a singular insect of this tribe, a kind of moth, seen about the flower-beds in the summer months. They are so much like humming-birds in their movements, that many of the country people consider them as a sort of cousin-german of our common rubythroat. We have been repeatedly asked if we had seen these "small humming-birds." Their size, the bird-like form of their body and tail, the rapid, quivering motion of their wings, their habit of feeding on the wing instead of alighting on the flowers, are indeed strangely like the humming-bird. Nevertheless, these are true moths, and there are, I believe, several species of them flitting about our meadows and gardens. The common green potato, or tobacco-worm, is said to become a moth of this kind; and the whole tribe of hawk-moths are now sometimes called humming-bird moths, from these same insects. They are not peculiar to this country, but are well known also in Europe, though not very common there. Altogether, they are singular little creatures; their tongues, with which they extract the honey from the flowers, just as the humming-bird does, are in some cases remarkably long, even longer than their bodies. One of the tribe is said to have a tongue six inches in length, and it coils it up like a watch-spring when not using it.

Saturday, 28th.—Passed the afternoon in the woods.

What a noble gift to man are the forests! What a debt of gratitude and admiration we owe for their utility and their beauty!

How pleasantly the shadows of the wood fall upon our heads, when we turn from the glitter and turmoil of the world of man! The winds of heaven seem to linger amid these balmy branches, and the sunshine falls like a blessing upon the green leaves; the wild breath of the forest, fragrant with bark and berry, fans the brow with grateful freshness; and the beautiful wood-light, neither garish nor gloomy, full of calm and peaceful influences, sheds repose over the spirit. The view is limited, and the objects about us are uniform in character; yet within the bosom of the woods the mind readily lays aside its daily littleness, and opens to higher thoughts, in silent consciousness that it stands alone with the works of God. The humble moss beneath our feet, the sweet flowers, the varied shrubs, the great trees, and the sky gleaming above in sacred blue, are each the handiwork of God. They were all called into being by the will of the Creator, as we now behold them, full of wisdom and goodness. Every object here has a deeper merit than our wonder can fathom; each has a beauty beyond our full perception; the dullest insect crawling about these roots lives by the power of the Almighty; and the discolored shreds of last year's leaves wither away upon the lowly herbs in a blessing of fertility. But it is the great trees, stretching their arms above us in a thousand forms of grace and strength, it is more especially the trees which fill the mind with wonder and praise.

Of the infinite variety of fruits which spring from the bosom of the earth, the trees of the wood are the greatest in dignity. Of all the works of the creation which know the changes of life and death, the trees of the forest have the longest existence. Of all the objects which crown the gray earth, the woods preserve unchanged, throughout the greatest reach of time, their native character: the works of man are ever varying their aspect; his towns and his fields alike reflect the unstable opinions, the fickle wills and fancies of each passing generation; but the forests on his borders remain to-day the same they were ages of years since. Old as the everlasting hills, during thousands of seasons they have put forth, and laid down their verdure in calm obedience to the decree which first bade them cover the ruins of the Deluge.

But, although the forests are great and old, yet the ancient trees within their bounds must each bend individually beneath the doom of every earthly existence; they have their allotted period when the mosses of Time gather upon their branches; when, touched by decay, they break and crumble to dust. Like man, they are decked in living beauty; like man, they fall a prey to death; and while we admire their duration, so far beyond our own brief years, we also acknowledge that especial interest which can only belong to the graces of life and to the desolation of death. We raise our eyes and we see collected in one company vigorous trunks, the oak, the ash, the pine, firm in the strength of maturity; by their side stand a young group, elm, and birch, and maple, their supple branches playing in the breezes, gay and fresh as youth itself; and yonder, rising in unheeded gloom, we behold a skeleton trunk, an old spruce, every branch broken, every leaf fallen,—dull, still, sad, like the finger of Death.

It is the peculiar nature of the forest, that life and death may ever be found within its bounds, in immediate presence of each other; both with ceaseless, noiseless, advances, aiming at the mastery; and if the influences of the first be the most general, those of the last are the most striking. Spring, with all her wealth of life and joy, finds within the forest many a tree unconscious of her approach; a thousand young plants springing up about the fallen trunk, the shaggy roots, seek to soften the gloomy wreck with a semblance of the verdure it bore of old; but ere they have thrown their fresh and graceful wreaths over the mouldering wood, half their own tribe wither and die with the year. We owe to this perpetual presence of death an impression calm, solemn, almost religious in character, a chastening influence, beyond what we find in the open fields. But this subdued spirit is far from gloomy or oppressive, since it never fails to be relieved by the cheerful animation of living beauty. Sweet flowers grow beside the fallen trees, among the shattered branches, the season through; and the freedom of the woods, the unchecked growth, the careless position of every tree, are favorable to a thousand wild beauties, and fantastic forms, opening to the mind a play of fancy which is in itself cheering and enlivening, like the bright sunbeams which chequer with golden light the shadowy groves. That character of rich variety also, stamped on all the works of the creation, is developed in the forest in clear and noble forms; we are told that in the field we shall not find two blades of grass exactly alike, that in the garden we shall not gather two flowers precisely similar, but in those cases the lines are minute, and we do not seize the truth at once; in the woods, however, the same fact stands recorded in bolder lines; we cannot fail to mark this great variety of detail among the trees; we see it in their trunks, their branches, their foliage; in the rude knots, the gnarled roots; in the mosses and lichens which feed upon their bark; in their forms, their coloring, their shadows. And within all this luxuriance of varied beauty, there dwells a sweet quiet, a noble harmony, a calm repose, which we seek in vain elsewhere, in so full a measure.

These hills, and the valleys at their feet, lay for untold centuries one vast forest; unnumbered seasons, ages of unrecorded time passed away while they made part of the boundless wilderness of woods. The trees waved over the valleys, they rose upon the swelling knolls, they filled the hollows, they crowded the narrow glens, they shaded the brooks and springs, they washed their roots in the lakes and rivers, they stood upon the islands, they swept over the broad hills, they crowned the heads of all the mountains. The whole land lay slumbering in the twilight of the forest. Wild dreams made up its half-conscious existence. The hungry cry of the beast of prey, or the fierce deed of savage man, whoop and dance, triumph and torture, broke in fitful bursts upon the deep silence, and then died away, leaving the breath of life to rise and fall with the passing winds.

Every rocky cliff on the hill-side, every marshy spot on the lowlands, was veiled in living, rustling folds of green. Here a dark wave of pine, hemlock, and balsam ran through a ravine, on yonder knoll shone the rich glossy verdure of oak, and maple, and chestnut; upon the breast of the mountain stood the birch, the elm, and the aspen, in light and airy tufts. Leaves of every tint of green played in the summer sunshine, leaves fluttered in the moonlight, and the showers of heaven fell everywhere upon the green leaves of the unbroken forest.

Sixty years have worked a wonderful change; the forest has fallen upon the lowlands, and there is not a valley about us which has not been opened. Another half century may find the country bleak and bare; but as yet the woods have not all been felled, and within the circle which bounds our view, there is no mountain which has been wholly shorn, none presents a bald front to the sky; upon the lake shore, there are several hills still wrapped in wood from the summit to the base. He who takes pleasure in the forest, by picking his way, and following a winding course, may yet travel many a long mile over a shady path, such as the red man loved.

The forest lands of America preserve to the present hour something that is characteristic of their wild condition, undisturbed for ages. They abound in ruins of their own. Old trees, dead and dying, are left standing for years, until at length they are shivered and broken by the winds, or they crumble slowly away to a shapeless stump. There was no forester at hand to cut them down when the first signs of decay appeared; they had no uses then, now they have no value. Broken limbs and dead bodies of great trees lie scattered through the forests; there are spots where the winds seem to have battled with the woods—at every step one treads on fallen trunks, stretched in giant length upon the earth, this still clad in its armor of bark, that bare and mouldering, stained by green mildew, one a crumbling mass of fragments, while others, again, lie shrouded in beautiful mosses, long green hillocks marking the grave of trees slowly turning to dust. Young trees are frequently found growing upon these forest ruins; if a giant pine or oak has been levelled by some storm, the mass of matted roots and earth will stand upright for years in the same position into which it was raised by the falling trunk, and occasionally a good-sized hemlock, or pine, or beech, is seen growing from the summit of the mass, which in itself is perhaps ten or twelve feet high. We have found a stout tree, of perhaps twenty years' growth, which has sprung from a chance seed, sown by the winds on the prostrate trunk of a fallen pine or chestnut, growing until its roots have stretched down the side of the mouldering log, and reached the earth on both sides, thus holding the crumbling skeleton firmly in its young embrace. The decay of these dead trees is strangely slow; prostrate pines have been known to last fifty years, undecayed, still preserving their sap; and upright gray shafts often remain standing for years, until one comes to know them as familiarly as the living trees. Instances are on record where they have thus remained erect in death for a space of forty years.[7] Amid this wild confusion, we note here and there some mark left by civilized man; the track of wheels, a rude road sprinkled over by withered leaves, or the mark of the axe, sharp and clean, upon a stump close at hand, reminding us how freely and how richly the forest contributes to the wants of our race.

Perhaps two-fifths of the woods in our neighborhood are evergreens, chiefly pine and hemlock; the proportion varies, however, in different spots; occasionally you see a whole mountain-side dark with hemlock and pine, while other hills, again, are almost entirely covered with deciduous trees; more frequently, they are pleasingly mingled in the same wood. Both hemlock and pine grow in all positions, upon the hills, in the valleys, in dry soils, and upon the banks of the streams. The balsam is less common, generally found in marshy spots, in company with its kinsman, of the tamarach, which in summer, at least, has all the appearance of an evergreen. The balsam is a beautiful tree; though not aspiring to the dignity of the pine

---

7   The trees destroyed on the Mississippi by the earthquake of 1811 are standing to-day, when nearly forty years have elapsed (Dec. 1849). And many similar instances might, no doubt, be found, if people had watched these dead inhabitants of our forests.

and hemlock, it shoots up in the most perfect and gradual spire-like form, to a height of thirty or forty feet, remarkable for its elegance; the foliage is very rich in color and quantity. It seems to delight in throwing its image into the pools and tarns about our hills, often standing on their banks, tinging the waters with its own dark green. There is no cedar very near us; the white cedar, or cypress, is found about eight or nine miles to the northward, and still farther in that direction it is very abundant, but along the course of the river, southward from the lake, to a distance of more than a hundred miles, we do not remember to have seen it. We have also but one pine, though that one is the chief of its family; the noble white pine, the pride of the Alleghanies; neither the yellow, the pitch, nor the red pine is known here, so far as one can discover. The arbor vitæ is also unknown. It has been thought by some of our neighbors that the evergreens diminish in numbers as the old woods are cut away, the deciduous trees gaining upon them; but looking about at the young thrifty groves of pine seen in every direction, there does not seem much reason to fear that they will disappear. They shoot up even in the cleared fields, here and there, and we have observed in several instances, that in spots where old pine woods had been cut down, close thickets of young trees of the same kind have succeeded them.

The oak of several varieties, white, black, the scarlet, and the red; the beech, the chestnut; black and white ashes; the lime or bass-wood; the white and the slippery elms; the common aspen, the large-leaved aspen; the downy-leaved poplar, and the balm of Gilead poplar; the white, the yellow, and the black birches, are all very common. The sumach and the alder abound everywhere. But the glossy leaves of the maple are more numerous than any others, if we include the whole family, and with the exception of the western or ash-leaved maple, they all grow here, from the fine sugar maple to the dwarf mountain maple: including them all, then, perhaps they number two for one of any other deciduous tree found here. They sow themselves very freely; in the spring one finds the little seedling maples coming up everywhere. With the exception of the chestnut, the nut trees are not so very common; yet the hickory is not rare, and both the black walnut and the butternut are met with. The sycamore, very abundant to the north of us, on the Mohawk, is rare here; it is found on the banks of a little stream two or three miles to the southward, and that is the only spot in the neighborhood where it has been observed. The pepperidge or sour-gum is found here and there only. The tulip-tree, abundant in most parts of the country, has not been seen within fifteen miles of our lake. The sweet-gum, or liquid-amber, is unknown here. The sassafras, also, is a stranger with us. That beautiful shrub, the laurel, so very common on the Hudson, is missed here; it grows in the county, however, but more than twenty miles to the southward of our village. The handsome flowering dog-wood, so ornamental to the forests in other parts of the State, is also wanting in this neighborhood.

The finest trees about the banks of our lake are remarkable rather for their height than their girth. Belonging to the old forest race, they have been closely pressed on all sides by their fellows, and the trunks rise in a branchless shaft to a commanding height; their foliage crowns the summit in full masses, and if never devoid of the native graces of each species, still it has not all the beauty developed by the free growth of the open fields. The older ashes, elms, and oaks are striking trees, much more stern and simple than their brethren of the lawns and meadows, all bearing the peculiar character of forest growth. The younger tribe of the woods, from the same cause which gives a stern simplicity to their elders, become, on the other hand, even more light and airy than their fellows in the open ground; shaded by the patriarchs of the forest, they shoot up toward the light in slender gracile stems, throwing out their branches in light and airy spray. So slight and supple are the stems of this younger race, that trees of thirty and forty, ay, even fifty feet in height, often bend low beneath the weight of the winter's snow upon their naked branches; some of them never regain their upright position, others gradually resume it as their trunks gain strength. Upon a wild wood-road near the lake shore there is a natural green archway, formed in this manner by two tall young trees accidentally bending toward each other from opposite sides of the road, until their branches meet over the track; the effect is very pretty, one of those caprices of the forest world, which in older times might have passed for the work of some elfin woodman.

It is to be feared that few among the younger generation now springing up will ever attain to the dignity of the old forest trees. Very large portions of these woods are already of a second growth, and trees of the greatest size are becoming every year more rare. It quite often happens that you come upon old stumps of much larger dimensions than any living trees about them; some of these are four, and a few five feet or more in diameter. Occasionally, we still find a pine erect of this size; one was felled the other day, which measured five feet in diameter. There is an elm about a mile from the village seventeen feet in girth, and not long since we heard of a bass-wood or linden twenty-eight feet in circumference. But among the trees now standing, even those which are sixty or eighty feet in height, many are not more than four, or five, or six feet in girth. The pines, especially, reach a surprising elevation for their bulk.

As regards the ages of the larger trees, one frequently finds stumps about two hundred years old; those of three hundred are not rare, and occasionally we have seen one which we believed to claim upward of four hundred rings. But as a rule, the largest trees are singled out very early in the history of a settlement, and many of these older stumps of the largest size have now become so worn and ragged, that it is seldom one can count the circles accurately. They are often much injured by fire immediately after the tree has been felled, and in many other instances decay has been at work at the heart, and one cannot, perhaps, count more than half the rings; measuring will help, in such cases, to give some idea; by taking fifty rings of the sound part, and allowing the same distance of the decayed portion for another fifty. But this is by no means a sure way, since the rings vary very much in the same tree, some being so broad that they must have sensibly increased the circumference of the trunk in one year, to the extent, perhaps, of an inch, while in other parts of the same shaft you will find a dozen circles crowded into that space. In short, it is seldom one has the satisfaction of meeting with a stump in which one may count every ring with perfect accuracy. It is said that some of the pines on the Pacific coast, those of Oregon and California, have numbered nine hundred rings; these were the noble Lambert pines of that region. Probably very few of our own white pines can show more than half that number of circles.

It is often said, as an excuse for leaving none standing, that these old trees of forest growth will not live after their companions have been felled; they miss the protection which one gives to another, and, exposed to the winds, soon fall to the ground. As a general rule, this may be true; but if one is inclined to believe that if the experiment of leaving a few were more frequently tried, it would often prove successful. There is an elm of great size now standing entirely alone in a pretty field of the valley, its girth, its age, and whole appearance declaring it a chieftain of the ancient race—the "Sagamore elm," as it is called—and in spite of complete exposure to the winds from all quarters of the heavens, it maintains its place firmly. The trunk measures seventeen feet in circumference, and it is thought to be a hundred feet in height; but this is only from the eye, never having been accurately ascertained. The shaft rises perhaps fifty feet without a branch, before it divides, according to the usual growth of old forest trees. Unfortunately, gray branches are beginning to show among its summer foliage, and it is to be feared that it will not outlast many winters more; but if it die to-morrow, we shall have owed a debt of many thanks to the owner of the field for having left the tree standing so long.

In these times, the hewers of wood are an unsparing race.

The first colonists looked upon a tree as an enemy, and to judge from appearances, one would think that something of the same spirit prevails among their descendants at the present hour. It is not surprising, perhaps, that a man whose chief object in life is to make money, should turn his timber into bank-notes with all possible speed; but it is remarkable that any one at all aware of the value of wood, should act so wastefully as most men do in this part of the world. Mature trees, young saplings, and last year's seedlings, are all destroyed at one blow by the axe or by fire; the spot where they have stood is left, perhaps, for a lifetime without any attempt at cultivation, or any endeavor to foster new wood. One would think that by this time, when the forest has fallen in all the valleys—when the hills are becoming more bare every day—when timber and fuel are rising in prices, and new uses are found for even indifferent woods— some forethought and care in this respect would be natural in people laying claim to common sense. The rapid consumption of the large pine timber among us should be enough to teach a lesson of prudence and economy on this subject. It has been calculated that 60,000 acres of pine woods are cut every year in our own State alone; and at this rate, it is said that in twenty years, or about 1870, these trees will have disappeared from our part of the country![8] But unaccountable as it may appear, few American farmers are aware of the full value and importance of wood. They seem to forget the relative value of the forests. It has been reported in the State of New York, that the produce of tilled lands carried to tide-water by the Erie Canal, in one year, amounted to $8,170,000 dollars worth of property; that of animals, or farm-stock, for the same year, is given at $3,230,000; that of the forests, lumber, staves, &c., &c., at $4,770,000.[9] Thus the forest yielded more than the stock, and more than half as

8   Dr. Torrey's State Botany.

9   See State Reports for 1835.

much as the farm lands; and when the comparative expense of the two is considered, their value will be brought still nearer together. Peltries were not included in this account. Our people seldom remember that the forests, while they provide food and shelter for the wildest savage tribes, make up a large amount of the wealth of the most civilized nations. The first rude devices of the barbarian are shaped in wood, and the cedar of Lebanon ranks with the gold of Ophir within the walls of palaces. How much do not we ourselves owe to the forests as regards our daily wants! Our fields are divided by wooden fences; wooden bridges cross our rivers; our village streets and highways are being paved with wood; the engines that carry us on our way by land and by water are fed with wood; the rural dwellings without and within, their walls, their floors, stairways, and roofs are almost wholly of wood; and in this neighborhood the fires that burn on our household hearths are entirely the gift of the living forest.

But independently of their market price in dollars and cents, the trees have other values: they are connected in many ways with the civilization of a country; they have their importance in an intellectual and in a moral sense. After the first rude stage of progress is past in a new country—when shelter and food have been provided—people begin to collect the conveniences and pleasures of a permanent home about their dwellings, and then the farmer generally sets out a few trees before his door. This is very desirable, but it is only the first step in the track; something more is needed; the preservation of fine trees, already standing, marks a farther progress, and this point we have not yet reached. It frequently happens that the same man who yesterday planted some half dozen branchless saplings before his door, will to-day cut down a noble elm, or oak, only a few rods from his house, an object which was in itself a hundred-fold more beautiful than any other in his possession. In very truth, a fine tree near a house is a much greater embellishment than the thickest coat of paint that could be put on its walls, or a whole row of wooden columns to adorn its front; nay, a large shady tree in a door-yard is much more desirable than the most expensive mahogany and velvet sofa in the parlor. Unhappily, our people generally do not yet see things in this light. But time is a very essential element, absolutely indispensable, indeed, in true civilization; and in the course of years we shall, it is to be hoped, learn farther lessons of this kind. Closer observation will reveal to us the beauty and excellence of simplicity, a quality as yet too little valued or understood in this country. And when we have made this farther progress, then we shall take better care of our trees. We shall not be satisfied with setting out a dozen naked saplings before our door, because our neighbor on the left did so last year, nor cut down a whole wood, within a stone's throw of our dwelling, to pay for a Brussels carpet from the same piece as our neighbor's on the right; no, we shall not care a stiver for mere show and parade, in any shape whatever, but we shall look to the general proprieties and fitness of things, whether our neighbors to the right or the left do so or not.

How easy it would be to improve most of the farms in the country by a little attention to the woods and trees, improving their appearance, and adding to their market value at the same time! Thinning woods and not blasting them; clearing only such ground as is marked for immediate tillage; preserving the wood on the hill-tops and rough side-hills; encouraging a coppice on this or that knoll; permitting bushes and young trees to grow at will along the brooks and water-courses; sowing, if need be, a grove on the bank of the pool, such as are found on many of our farms; sparing an elm or two about the spring, with a willow also to overhang the well; planting one or two chestnuts, or oaks, or beeches, near the gates or bars; leaving a few others scattered about every field to shade the cattle in summer, as is frequently done, and setting out others in groups, or singly, to shade the house—how little would be the labor or expense required to accomplish all this, and how desirable would be the result! Assuredly, the pleasing character thus given to a farm and a neighborhood is far from being beneath the consideration of a sensible man.

But there is also another view of the subject. A careless indifference to any good gift of our gracious Maker, shows a want of thankfulness, as any abuse or waste, betrays a reckless spirit of evil. It is, indeed, strange that one claiming to be a rational creature should not be thoroughly ashamed of the spirit of destructiveness, since the principle itself is clearly an evil one. Let us remember that it is the Supreme Being who is the Creator, and in how many ways do we see his gracious providence, his Almighty economy, deigning to work progressive renovation in the humblest objects when their old forms have become exhausted by Time! There is also something in the care of trees which rises above the common labors of husbandry, and speaks of a generous mind. We expect to wear the fleece from our flocks, to drink the milk of our herds, to feed upon the fruits of our fields; but in planting a young wood, in preserving a fine grove, a noble tree, we look beyond ourselves to the band of household friends, to our neighbors—ay, to the passing wayfarer and stranger who will share with us the pleasure they give, and it becomes a grateful reflection that long after we are gone, those trees will continue a good to our fellow-creatures for more years, perhaps, than we can tell.

Quite recently, two instances of an opposite character connected with this subject have accidentally fallen under our notice. At a particular point in the wilds of Oregon, near the bank of the Columbia River, there stood a single tree, of great size, one of the majestic pines of that region, and long known as a landmark to the hunters and emigrants passing over those solitary wastes. One of the expeditions sent out to explore that country by the government, arriving near the point, were on the watch for that pine to guide their course; they looked for it some time, but in vain; at length, reaching the spot where they supposed it ought to have stood—a way-mark in the wilderness—they found the tree lying on the earth. It had been felled, and left there to rot, by some man claiming, no doubt, to be a civilized being. The man who could do such an act would have been worthy to make one of the horde of Attila, barbarians who delighted to level to the ground every object over which their own horses could not leap.

Opposed to this is an instance less striking, but more pleasing, and happily much nearer to our own neighborhood. Upon the banks of the Susquehannah, not far from the little village of Bainbridge, the traveller, as he follows the road, observes a very fine tree before him, and as he approaches he will find it to be a luxuriant elm, standing actually in the midst of the highway; its branches completely cover the broad track, sweeping over the fences on either side. The tree stands in the very position where a thorough-going utilitarian would doubtless quarrel with it, for the road is turned a little out of its true course to sweep round the trunk; but in the opinion of most people, it is not only a very beautiful object in itself, but highly creditable to the neighborhood; for, not only has it been left standing in its singular position, but as far as we could see, there was not a single mark of abuse upon its trunk or branches.

Monday, 30th.—Very warm. Thermometer 80 in the house; 89 in the shade without.

Walking in the lane toward evening, saw a couple of meadowlarks in great agitation; perhaps some disaster had befallen their young; it seems rather late for them to have little ones, but they raise two broods in the summer. They were flying from one bush to another, and back again over the same ground, crying as they went quite piteously. These birds build on the ground; their nest is made of different grassy plants, quite cleverly contrived, and almost always placed in a meadow. They are decidedly larger and handsomer than the European sky-lark, but their simple note is not at all remarkable; the female sings a little as she rises and falls, like the wife of the red-wing black-bird. Their flight is very different from that of their European kinsman, being heavy and laborious; they like, however, to perch on the very highest branches of trees, which is singular in birds living so much on the ground, and moving apparently with some effort. Climate seems to affect them but little, for they reach from the tropics to 53' north latitude, and they are resident birds in the lower counties of our own State, though never remaining, I believe, among these hills.

It is to be regretted that neither of the two great singing-birds of the Old World is found in America; that both the sky-lark and the nightingale should be strangers on this side the Atlantic. In some respects the nightingale differs from the common notions regarding it in this country. We have read so much of "plaintive Philomel," that most of us fancy a solitary bird, in the deep recesses of the grove, chanting by moonlight an air "most musical, most melancholy." But this is far from being always the case; the birds sing by daylight at least as often as they do at night, and of a pleasant morning or evening, one may hear a whole choir of them singing cheerfully together. It is said that they never move about in flocks; this may be so, but they certainly live in close neighborhood—a number in the same wood. In the months of May and June, at early dawn, just about the time when the market people and chimney-sweeps are moving about the streets of Paris, the nightingales are heard singing gayly enough, a dozen at a time, perhaps, in the very heart of that great city. They live in the *maronniers*, and lindens, and elms, among the noble gardens of the town, whether public or private, and seem to mind the neighborhood of man as little as the greenlets which flit about the plane-trees of Philadelphia. It is true, that at the same season, you may, if you choose, take a moonlight walk in the country,

> "And the mute silence hist along,
> Lest Philomel will deign a song
> In her sweetest, saddest plight."

And probably this solitary song, owing partly to the moonlight, and partly to the stillness of night, will produce a much deeper effect than the choir you heard in the morning, or at sunset.

It is said that an attempt was made, some years since, to introduce the nightingale into this country, a gentleman in Virginia having imported a number and given them their liberty in the woods. But they seem to have all died; the change of climate and food was probably too great. They are delicate birds; they are said to be very rare in the northern counties of England, and to avoid also the western parts of the island. Still, the nightingale is a bird of passage, and now that the sea-voyage is so much shorter, possibly, if the experiment were repeated, it might succeed. Birds are great travellers, and they have undoubtedly spread themselves over the world as we now find them. Within our own short history, we know of well-accredited instances of changes in their course. In this very State we now have the singular Cliff-swallow, which a few years since was entirely unknown, and the first seen here were a solitary pair. The Catbirds also are said to have been unknown on the Genesee until several years after the country had been opened. Blue-birds and robins are far more numerous than they used to be, while on the other hand several birds are known to have deserted our neighborhood for regions more to their taste, such as the quail, the kill-deers, the crested woodpeckers, &c., &c.

The sky-lark is more hardy than the nightingale, and possibly might bear our climate better, though not a migratory bird. Of the two, we should perhaps prefer the lark. In the first place, he sings more or less the whole year round, and never deserts his native fields, while the nightingale is only in voice for a few weeks in May and June. And then the habits of the lark are peculiar to himself. There is no act of the eagle so noble in character as the uprising of the lark to greet the sun; it is the very sublime of action. We know nothing within the whole range of nature more eloquent. If we may believe Lafontaine, this bird likes to build his lowly nest in a grain-field—

"Les alouettes font leur nid
Dans les blès, quand ils sont en herbe."

The lark of the fable sings wittily, rather than lyrically; but all that the *bonhomme* does with the creatures which people his world of fancy, is so exquisite in its way, that we are entirely satisfied with his bird in the homely, motherly character. It is her husband who is the poet; it is he who sings those noble sunrise odes; she herself is the clever, notable—*mère de famille*—who knows the world, though Lafontaine did not. When the farmer talks of collecting first his neighbors, and then his relations, to cut the grain, she gives herself no concern whatever—why should she? But when the good-man comes with his son, and they decide to begin the work themselves, the point is settled, the lark family must take flight—

"C'est à ce coup, qu'il faut décamper, mes enfants,
Et les petits en même temps
Voletants, se culebutants
Délogèrent tous, sans trompette."

In this part of the world, Lafontaine would have been compelled to choose some other more humble bird, to teach us so cleverly the useful lesson of self-dependence; but if he had chanced to make acquaintance with the meadow-lark, the grass-bird, the bobolink, or even the modest little song-sparrow, he would have taught either of them, in a trice, to sing with more than all "l'esprit des Mortemars."

There is in this country a lark common to both continents—the horned-lark or shore-lark—a very pretty arctic bird, which in winter goes as far south as Georgia, but we have never heard of it in these highlands. On the coast of Long Island it is quite common. It is said also to breed on the Western prairies.

Tuesday, 31st.—Refreshing shower in the morning; gentle rain, no thunder or lightning; it is remarkable how little electricity we have had this summer. We have often, in common seasons, heavy showers, with very sharp lightning, and thunder which echoes grandly among our hills. We have known the lightning to strike seven times in the course of an hour, in the village and the immediate neighborhood, twice in the lake, and five times on the land; but very happily, no serious accident occurred on that occasion, though one or two persons were stunned. This summer we have hardly seen a flash.

First melons to-day.

Wednesday, August 1st.—Pleasant; walked over Mill Bridge in the afternoon. Gathered a fine bunch of the crimson lobelia by the river-side. What an exquisite shade of red lies on the petals of this brilliant plant! It reminds one that the Russian word for beauty and for red is said to be the same—*krasnoi*, as M. de Ségur gives it; most of us would probably consider rose-color or blue as more beautiful, but certainly the inimitable, vivid and yet delicate tint of the lobelia, may claim to be identical with *krasnoi*, or beauty. The blue lobelia, also very handsome in its way, is not found here, though very common on the Mohawk.

Walking through a wood, found hawk-wort and asters in bloom, also a handsome rattlesnake plantain, or Goodyera, with its veined leaves and fragrant spike of white flowers; this is one of the plants formerly thought to cure the bite of the rattlesnake, though little credit is given to the notion now-a-days.

Thursday, 2d.—Long drive down the valley.

There is not a single town of any size within a distance of forty miles, yet already the rural population of this county is quite large. The whole country, within a wide circuit north, south, east and west, partakes of the same general character; mountain ridges, half tilled, half wood, screening cultivated valleys, sprinkled with farms and hamlets, among which some pretty stream generally winds its way. The waters in our immediate neighborhood all flow to the southward, though only a few miles to the north of our village, the brooks are found running in an opposite course, this valley lying just within the borders of the dividing ridge. The river itself, though farther south it becomes one of the great streams of the country, cannot boast of much breadth so near its source, and running quietly among the meadows, half screened by the groves and thickets, scarcely shows in the general view.

The whole surface of the country is arable; very little marsh or bog is found in the lower lands, and there are no barren tracts upon the hills. Rocks rarely break through the surface, except here and there where a low cliff runs along the hill-sides, and these are usually shaded by the forest. This general fertility, this blending of the fields of man and his tillage with the woods, the great husbandry of Providence, gives a fine character to the country, which it could not claim when the lonely savage roamed through wooded valleys, and which it must lose if ever cupidity, and the haste to grow rich, shall destroy the forest entirely, and leave these hills to posterity, bald and bare, as those of many older lands. No perfection of tillage, no luxuriance of produce can make up to a country for the loss of its forests; you may turn the soil into a very garden crowded with the richest crops, if shorn of wood, like Sampson shorn of his locks, it may wear a florid aspect, but the noblest fruit of the earth, that which is the greatest proof of her strength, will be wanting.

Cross-roads occur frequently, and many more are seen in the distance, winding over the hills toward other valleys and other villages. Indeed, the number of roads by which the country is cut up in every direction, crossing each other at short intervals, hither and thither, might alone lead a foreigner to suppose it much older in civilization; and when the great extent of the country and the date of its settlement are remembered, these roads bear very striking testimony to the spirit and activity of the people. It is true that many of them are very imperfectly worked, yet in summer and winter they are all in respectable condition, and many of them as good as need be; these new plank roads, which are just beginning, promise, indeed, to be admirable, and the workmanship, filling up hollows and grading hills, is often quite imposing. It must also be remembered that the climate is much against us in this respect, owing to the deep frosts of winter and sudden thaws of spring, which are enough to injure greatly the best-made roads in the world.

The soil, without being so rich as that farther west, is very good, and the school of agriculture respectable, though scarcely very scientific. A portion of the farmers are graziers and dairymen, and large herds are seen feeding in some pastures. Wool is also a staple of the county, and one cannot go very far without coming upon a flock of sheep, nibbling quietly by themselves, unwatched by dog or shepherd. During the summer months, the cattle of these valleys have generally good cause to be satisfied with their lot; the grass seldom fails, and those excessive heats, accompanied by long parching droughts— almost a matter of course in the lower counties—are seldom felt here; the continued warm weather of this last summer has been something uncommon. But though dryer than usual, our meadows are still greener than those in other parts of the State; we have just heard that two hundred head of cattle, and two thousand head of sheep, have been driven into our county from St. Lawrence, to be pastured here during the drought. Generally, our grass and foliage are refreshed by passing showers, during the warmest weather, and the beauty of the verdure is a source of great pleasure to those who come from the *brown* fields about New York and Philadelphia.

The crops are those which belong naturally to a temperate, hilly country. Wheat, oats, buckwheat, maize, potatoes, and barley are the most common, with some turnips and carrots for fodder. Rye is rather rare. Hop-grounds are frequent, for although this is not much of a beer-drinking community, yet a large amount of hops is carried hence to the sea-ports for European markets. These fields are said to be very profitable for the owners, but they are by no means so pleasing in a landscape as grain or pasture lands. Those two vines, the hop and the grape, so luxuriant and beautiful in their natural state, alike lose much of their peculiar grace, when cultivated in the common way; at a distance, a hop-ground and a vineyard very much resemble each other, though the hop is trained much higher than the grape; the poles and stakes in each case go far toward destroying the beauty of the plants. Both these vines, by-the-by, the grape and the hop, are natives of this part of the country.

The new disease among the potatoes, which has already done so much mischief in past years, has only shown itself this season in some few fields. Generally, the crop looks quite well in our neighborhood. This disease seems to be one of the most singular on record in the vegetable world, unaccountable in its origin, and so very general in both hemispheres; is it not the only instance of such a general and prolonged blight? Probably in time the evil will mercifully be removed, for it scarcely belongs to the nature of vegetable productions to perish entirely and become extinct like tribes of animals.

About a couple of miles from the village there is a very pretty pool in a field near the road, covering, perhaps, an acre or more of ground; marvellous tales were formerly told of its depth, and for a long time people tried to believe it unfathomable; but unfortunately, actual measurement has destroyed the illusion, and it is found to be only five or six feet in depth! All agree, however, that it has become much more shallow since the country has been opened and the woods cut away:

> "Before these fields were shorn and tilled,
>   Full to the brim our rivers flowed;
> The melody of waters filled
>   The fresh and boundless wood.
> And torrents dashed, and rivulets played,
> And fountains spouted in the shade."

But now, as the old Indian sings, these things are changed:

"The springs are silent in the sun,
The rivers by the blackened shore
With lessening current run."

This little lake, Pappoose Pool, as it is called, looks very prettily as one comes and goes along the highway, with its border of evergreens of various kinds sweeping half round it, and making a fine background to the water, which they color with their dark branches.

Presently, after passing this little pool, one comes to a factory on the bank of a pretty stream of some size, which received its name from the number of oaks standing on its banks in former times; most of these have been felled years ago, and the river now runs among open fields, just beyond the factory, however, a few hoary old trunks are seen rising far above the younger trees and shrubs; but these are sycamores, and with their white bark and scanty branches, they look like lingering ghosts of the fallen forest. The banks of this stream are the only ground in the neighborhood, I believe, where sycamores are found, and there are but a few, scattered here and there, along its track.

The factory, a stone building of some size, with its usual neighbors, a mill and a store, make up a little hamlet, with a cluster of red wooden cottages, and a yellow house for the agent. A couple of thriving maples, good-sized trees, have been left standing in the open space crossed by the road, much to the credit of those who have spared them—"may their shadows never be less!" It is a pity that a few more were not scattered about with a bench or two in the shade; the spot would then make a neat hamlet green.

Some people think that public seats would not answer in our part of the world; it is said that if made of stone they would be cracked and broken; if made of wood chipped and defaced by the knives of the thoughtless men and boys of a country neighborhood. But surely it is time we began to learn a lesson of civilization in this respect; to put things to their

313

proper uses is one of the first precepts of good sense and good manners. Benches were not made to be chipped, nor knives to mutilate and deface with. One would like an experiment of this kind to be fairly tried; if it failed, then it would be time enough to complain; and wherever it succeeds, it must be very creditable to the rural community who carries it out. Travellers in Switzerland remember with pleasure the seats placed at intervals along the road-side in that country for the weary and wayfaring; near Berne these seats are very common indeed, and although they are often found in quiet, secluded spots, the fear of their being injured by the people seems never to have been suggested. Cannot we in this country, where schools, and books, and churches are so common, follow, in this respect, the pleasant, simple custom offered by the example of our fellow-republicans of Berne? These public benches form, indeed, only a part of a general system, the first step toward the open green of the village, the public walks of the larger towns, and the noble gardens of great cities, so happily provided in most countries of Europe, for the health and innocent recreation of the people. Surely it would be very desirable to introduce all these into our own country, and here, where land is cheaper, they ought to be more easily carried out than in the Old World. A bench or two of this description beneath a cluster of trees on a little green in any hamlet, would have a good effect in bringing many a mother out into the open air, with her baby, at odd moments, when it would be good for both to be there, such a play-ground would be better than the dusty street for the children; and if fathers and husbands were content to talk politics under the trees rather than in the smoky, drinking bar-room, it would certainly do them no harm.

Besides this cotton factory at the Twin-Maples, there is another on the opposite side of the valley, upon the main stream; several others are found in different parts of the county, but they are all on a moderate scale.

Another large stone building is seen across the valley, on

the brow of an abrupt bank, looking in the distance like an old French *auberge*. It is the county poor-house, and rising in the midst of a prosperous country, tells us that even under the most favorable circumstances, within a young and vigorous society, there must be poor among us, some the victims of their own follies or vices, some the victims of those of others.

The valley becomes broader and more level about four or five miles from the village; a hamlet has grown up here about an Academy, founded early in the history of the county, by a Lutheran clergyman, who has left his name to the spot. Farmhouses and cottages are springing up here along the highway in close neighborhood, for a mile or more. Many of these, painted white, with green blinds, and pleasant door-yards, and a garden adjoining, look very neat and cheerful. Green-house plants, geraniums, callas, cactuses, &c., &c., are seen on these cottage porches at this season; they are much prized during the long winter, and something of the kind is found in many houses. A very broad field, remarkably level for this part of the world, lies on one side of the highway; sugar-maples line the road here, and they bear marks of having been tapped for the sap, thus serving the double purpose of a pleasant, shady avenue, and a sugar-bush where the trees are close at hand. A burying-ground lies at one corner of the broad field, and a little meeting-house at the farther point. But the great edifice of the hamlet is of course the Academy, a brick building, colored gray, flanked by wings, with a green before its doors, and a double row of maples, planted in a semicircle, forming its academic shades. The institution was endowed by the Lutheran clergyman, a German by birth, who was the original owner of a small patent covering this spot; the worthy man is said to have been an eccentric character, but he was one of the first preachers of the Holy Gosple, perhaps the very first, in this valley, and his preaching from a cart is one of the local traditions. A little parsonage close at hand is occupied by the principal of the Academy; with its garden, flowers, arbor, and bee-hives, it looks pleasantly from the road-side. Some years since it was a Swedish clergyman who officiated here.

From the summit of a hill on the left, crossed by a country road, there is a fine view over the valley, and the lake in the distance; there are also several little sheets of water, limpid, mountain tarns, among those hills; the stream flowing from one of these forms a modest little cascade. It is rather remarkable that we have so few cascades in this county, abounding as it does with brooks and streams, and lesser lakes lying at different levels; but the waters generally work their way gradually down the hills without taking any bold leaps.

On the opposite side of the valley, a mile or two farther down the stream, there is a singular fissure in the rocks, a sort of ravine, called "The Jambs," where a geologist might perhaps find something to interest him, if one ever found his way here. A low barrow is also observed on that side of the valley, which some persons believe to be artificial; it has very much the character of the Indian mounds in other parts of the country, very regular in its outline, and not larger than many which are known to be the work of the red man; occasionally it is proposed to open it, but no step of the kind has yet been taken. There are, however, very many low knolls about our valley, near the banks of the river, and it is sometimes difficult to decide, from a partial examination, whether they were raised by man, or shaped by floods.

Friday, 3d.—Walked in the woods. Our sweet-fern is a pleasant plant; there is always something very agreeable in a shrub or tree with fragrant foliage; the perfume is rarely sickly; as occasionally happens with flowers, it is almost always grateful and refreshing. These aromatic leaves of the sweet-fern are frequently used in rustic practice to stop bleeding; we have never seen the remedy tried, but have often heard it recommended. Some of our good-wives also make a tea of the leaves, which they say is very strengthening, and good for hemorrhage of the lungs. The plant is also used in home-made beer.

Strictly speaking, the botanists do not call this a fern, but it looks very much as if Adam may have called it so. It is the only plant of the kind, in temperate climates, with a woody stem. The botanical name of Comptonia was given it, after a bishop of London, of the last century, who was a great botanist.

In some of the northern counties of New York, Herkimer and Warren, for instance, acres of wild lands, whole mountain-sides, are covered with this plant, even to the exclusion, in many places, of the whortleberry; in that part of the country it also grows as a weed by the road-side, like the thistles and mulleins. In our own neighborhood it is chiefly confined to the woods.

Saturday, 4th.—Pleasant day. At nine o'clock in the evening set out for a moonlight walk on Mount —. Beautiful night; the rising moon shone through the branches, filling the woods, as it were, with wild fantastic forms never seen by day; one seems at such moments to be moving in a new world, among trees and plants of another creation. The brake had a very peculiar aspect, a faint silvery light lay upon its fronds, even in the shade, giving the idea that in the sunshine they must be much paler in color than their neighbors, which is not the case; the same sort of pale, phosphorescent light gleamed about other plants, and upon the chips and stones in the path.

The views, after leaving the woods, were beautifully clear and distinct. The reflections in the lake below were strangely perfect for a night scene; village, woods, and hills lay softly repeated on the bosom of the flood, as though it were dreaming by night of objects dear and familiar by day. One might have counted the trees and the fields; even the yellow coloring of the grain-fields beside the green meadows was distinctly given.

As the night winds rose and fell with a gentle murmuring sough, the deep bass of the frogs, and the higher notes of the insect throng, continued in one unbroken chaunt. What myriads of those little creatures must be awake and stirring of a fine summer night! But there is a larger portion of the great family on earth in movement at night, than we are apt to remember; because we sleep ourselves, we fancy that other creatures are inactive also. A number of birds fly at night besides the owls, and night hawks, and whip-poor-wills; very many of those who come and go between our cooler climate and the tropics, make their long journeys lighted by the moon or the stars. The beasts of prey, as is well known, generally move at night. Of the larger quadrupeds belonging to this continent, the bears, and wolves, and foxes, are often in motion by starlight; the moose and the deer frequently feed under a dark sky; the panther is almost wholly nocturnal; the wary and industrious beaver also works at night; that singular creature, the opossum, sleeps in his tree by day and comes down at night. The pretty little flying-squirrel wakes up as twilight draws on; our American rabbit also shuns the day; that pest of the farm-yard, the skunk, with the weasels, rove about on their mischievous errands at night. Some of those animals whose furs are most valued, as the ermine and sable, are nocturnal; so is the black-cat, and the rare wolverine also. Even our domestic cattle, the cows and horses, may frequently be seen grazing in the pleasant summer nights.

Monday, 6th.—Bright, warm day. Thermometer 84.

Heard an oriole among some elms on the skirts of the village this morning; it is rather late for them. We generally see little of them after July; when they have reared their family, and the young have come to days of discretion, these brilliant birds seem to become more shy; they are very apt to leave the villages about that time for the woods. Some few, however, occasionally remain later. But toward the last of this month they already take their flight southward.

A change has come over the bobolinks also—in July they lose those cheerful, pleasant notes with which they enliven the fields earlier in the season; it is true they are still seen fluttering over the meadows from time to time, with a peculiar cry of their own, and the young males acquire a pretty note of their own, which they sing in the morning, but they are already thinking of moving. They are very cheerful birds, and one misses them when they disappear. We seldom see them here in those large flocks common elsewhere; those about us are probably all natives of our own meadows. They travel southward very gradually, visiting first, in large parties, the wild rice-grounds of Pennsylvania and Maryland, where they remain some weeks; in October, they abound in the cultivated rice plantations of Carolina, where they also linger a while, but finally they retreat to the tropical islands. Altogether, few birds are so long on their progress southward.

Tuesday, 7th.—Walked in the Great Meadow. The old trees which bordered this fine field in past years are fast falling before the axe. A few summers back, this was one of the most beautiful meadows in the valley: a broad, grassy lawn of some twenty acres, shut out from the world by a belt of wood sweeping round it in a wide circle; it was favorite ground with some of us, one of those spots where the sweet quiet of the fields, and the deeper calm of the forest, are brought together. On one hand, the trees were of a younger growth, luxuriant and grove-like in aspect, but beyond, the wood rose from the bank of the river in tall, grand columns, of lighter and darker shades of gray. Nothing can be more different than the leafy, bowery border of a common wood, where one scarcely sees the trunks, and the bounds which mark a breach in the ancient forest. The branchless shafts of those aged oaks, pines, chestnuts, hemlocks and ashes, are very impressive objects, forming in such positions a noble forest portal. We have frequently stood upon the highway, perhaps half a mile off, to admire those great trunks lighted up by the sunshine, with which they had so lately made acquaintance; there are few such forest colonnades left in our neighborhood, and this is now falling rapidly before the axeman.

The hoary trunks of the ashes are particularly fine in such situations; they are the lightest in coloring among our larger trees, as the shaft of the hemlocks is the darkest. The ashes of this country very frequently grow in low grounds on the banks of rivers. We have many varieties of this fine tree in the United States: the white, the red, the green or yellow, the blue, and the black, besides the small and very rare flowering ash, only twenty feet high. Of these different kinds, only the white and the black are understood to belong to our highland county; both these are common here, and both are handsome and valuable trees, used for very many mechanical purposes. The white ash, indeed, is said to be as desirable as the hickory—our American tree being considered superior for timber to that of Europe, which it much resembles. When used for fuel, it has the peculiarity of burning nearly as well in a green state as when dry, and the timber also scarcely requires any seasoning. The black ash, more especially a northern tree, is abundant here; it is smaller than the white, and is much used by the Indian basket-makers, being thought rather preferable to the white for their purposes. It is amusing to remember that the small bows and arrows made to-day by the roving Indians as playthings for our boys, are manufactured out of the same wood used for the arms of heroes in the ancient world; many a great warrior besides Achilles has received his death-wound from an ashen spear; ashen lances were shivered in the tournaments of chivalrous days, by the stout knights of the middle ages, the Richards and Bertrands, Oliviers and Edwards. At the present day the ash is still used, with the beech, to arm the regiments of modern lancers. Bows, also, were made of the ash, as well as of the yew, in ancient times. For all we know, the bow of William Tell may have been an ashen one. There is one very remarkable association connected with the European ash, which is a hardy tree, clinging to the rocky mountains of Northern Europe. It figures largely in Scandinavian mythology. The ash-tree, Yggdrassil, was their tree of life, or an emblem of the world. It is singular that a sacred tree should be found in the mythology of several different nations of the East; India, Persia, Egypt, and Assyria. We are not told that any particular kind of tree is specified in Eastern mythology; the Scandinavian Sagas, however, are very particular in pointing out the ash as their sacred tree, Yggdrassil. Major Frye, in his translations of Œhlenschlœger, quotes the following passage from the Edda, describing this great ash:

"This ash is the first and greatest of all trees, which spreads its branches over the whole earth. It springs from three roots. Near one of these roots, which pushes the trunk and branches toward Asagard,[10] flows the fountain of Urda, which contains the water of wisdom, and of which Mimer[11] is the guardian. The gods often descend to this spot to sit in judgment on the actions of mankind, and of one another. They interrogate Urda. [12] The second root of Yggdrassil stretches toward the region of the Hrimthusser[13] frost-giants of Utgard.[14] The third root extends below, as far as Niffelheim,[15] and is continually gnawed by the dragon Nidhòg.[16]

"On the branches of this ash dwells an eagle; he knoweth much, and between his eyes sits a Hawk, called Vaderfalner. A squirrel, called Ratatosk, runs up and down the trunk of the ash-tree, and endeavors to excite discord between the eagle and the dragon Nidhòg, who dwells at its root. Four stags spring round the ash-tree and bite its branches: their names are, Dainn,

10　Asagard, the country of the gods.

11　Mimer, the god of eloquence and wisdom.

12　Urda, the Norna, or destiny of the past.

13　Hrimthusser, frost-demons; hrim, or frost, is the origin of our English word rime, for hoar frost; and thuss, or demon, is supposed by Major Frye to be the origin of the English word deuce, though the dictionaries give another derivation.

14　Utgard, land of giants.

15　Niffelheim, land of fog.

16　Nidhog, a monster dragon.—(See Major Frye's Translations of the "Gods of the North.")

Dvalen, Dunneyr, and Durathzor."

Many versions of this allegory have been given by different Northern writers, and any one who pleases may try his ingenuity on it, as he sits in the shade of the ash-tree. They are all connected with the good and evil in man; with the good and evil above, and about him,—faint gleams of great truths.

Wednesday, 8th.—Very warm; thermometer 86. It is sad to see how many of our springs are wasting away from the drought; in some places where we are accustomed to meet the limpid waters flowing cheerfully through the fields and woods, we now find a parched and thirsty track; at other points, not entirely dry, an ample fountain has dwindled away to a meagre, dropping rill. Rain is much needed.

Thursday, 9th.—Very warm; thermometer 90. Passed the afternoon and evening on the lake. Land and water were both in great beauty; the lake was in that sweet mood when it seems to take pleasure in reflecting every beautiful object; all the different fields, and buildings, and trees, were repeated with fidelity, while the few white clouds floating above were also clearly given below. The waters of our narrow lake are more frequently seen reflecting the village, the hills, and the woods, than the clouds; in still weather they receive much of their coloring from the shores. But this afternoon we noticed several of these visionary islands lying on its bosom, and whenever seen here, they are the more pleasing from our having nothing more substantial in this way; our islands are all of this shadowy character.

On the larger lakes further westward, and in still weather, these cloud islands are often very beautiful; in that more level region the broad expanse of Cayuga and Seneca is very much colored by the skies. Some people find fault with the great size of those islandless lakes; but assuredly, living water is never to be quarrelled with in a landscape; smaller basins with higher banks are no doubt more picturesque, but those ample, limpid lakes are very fine in their way. There is a noble simplicity in their every-day aspect which, on so great a scale, is in itself imposing.

The high winds so frequent in that part of the country having full scope over their broad bosoms, often work out fine storm views, while on the other hand the beautiful sunsets of that level region color the waters exquisitely.

Landed at Signal-Oak Point; the noble spring here was quite full, though so many others have failed; while standing near the little fountain, one of our party had the good luck to discover an Indian relic in the gravel, a flint arrow-head. It was very neatly cut, though not of the largest size. One would like to know its little history; it may have been dropped by some hunter who had come to the spring, or been shot from the wood at some wild creature drinking there at the moment. Another of these arrow-heads was found a while since in the gravel of our own walks; they are occasionally turned up in the village, but are already more rare than one would suppose.

Gathered several August flowers on the banks of the brook; the yellow knot-root, or Collinsonia, with its horned blossom; yellow speckled-jewels, more rare with us than the orange kind; purple asters, and a handsome bunch of red berries of the cranberry-tree. We have frequently found the blue gentian growing here, but it is not yet in flower, and the plants have been so much gathered that comparatively few are left.

There is the skeleton of an old oak lying on the gravelly beach of this point, which was well known in the early years of the little colony. Deer were very common here at that time, and of course they were much hunted; these poor creatures, when pursued, always take refuge in the water, if there be a lake or river at hand; and when a party was out hunting in the hills it was a common practice to station some one in the old oak at this spot, which overhung the water, and commanded a view of the lake in its whole length; a set of signals having been agreed on beforehand, the scout in the tree pointed out to the hunters, by this means, the direction taken by the game. Some few years since this signal-oak fell to the ground, and a fragment of it now lies on the shore. This whole grove was formerly very beautiful, composed chiefly of noble oaks of primeval growth, many of them hung with grape-vines, while a pretty clump of wild roses grew at their feet; some of the vines and many of the rose-bushes are still left, but the trees are falling rapidly. They have been recklessly abused by kindling fires against their trunks, using them as chimney shafts, which of course must destroy them. In this way, oaks that might have stood yet for centuries, with increasing beauty, have been wantonly destroyed. Not a season passes that one does not fall, and within the last few years their number has very sensibly diminished. The spot is but a wreck of what it was.

It is a long time since the signal-oak was needed by the hunters, the deer having disappeared from these woods with wonderful rapidity. Within twenty years from the foundation of the village, they had already become rare, and in a brief period later they had fled from the country. One of the last of these beautiful creatures seen in the waters of our lake occasioned a chase of much interest, though under very different circumstances from those of a regular hunt. A pretty little fawn had been brought in very young from the woods, and nursed and petted by a lady in the village until it had become as tame as possible. It was graceful, as those little creatures always are, and so gentle and playful that it became a great favorite, following the different members of the family about, caressed by the neighbors, and welcome everywhere. One morning, after gambolling about as usual until weary, it threw itself down in the sunshine, at the feet of one of its friends, upon the steps of a store. There came along a countryman, who for several years had been a hunter by pursuit, and who still kept several dogs; one of his hounds came to the village with him on this occasion. The dog, as it approached the spot where the fawn lay, suddenly stopped; the little animal saw him, and started to its feet. It had lived more than half its life among the dogs of the village, and had apparently lost all fear of them; but it seemed now to know instinctively that an enemy was at hand. In an instant a change came over it, and the gentleman who related the incident, and who was standing by at the moment, observed that he had never in his life seen a finer sight than the sudden arousing of instinct in that beautiful creature. In a second its whole character and appearance seemed changed, all its past habits were forgotten, every wild impulse was awake; its head erect, its nostrils dilated, its eye flashing. In another instant, before the spectators had thought of the danger, before its friends could secure it, the fawn was leaping wildly through the street, and the hound in full pursuit. The bystanders were eager to save it; several persons instantly followed its track, the friends who had long fed and fondled it, calling the name it had hitherto known, but in vain. The hunter endeavored to whistle back his dog, but with no better success. In half a minute the fawn had turned the first corner, dashed onward toward the lake, and thrown itself into the water. But if for a moment the startled creature believed itself safe in the cool bosom of the lake, it was soon undeceived; the hound followed in hot and eager chase, while a dozen of the village dogs joined blindly in the pursuit. Quite a crowd collected on the bank, men, women, and children, anxious for the fate of the little animal known to them all; some threw themselves into boats, hoping to intercept the hound before he reached his prey; but the plashing of the oars, the eager voices of the men and boys, and the barking of the dogs, must have filled the beating heart of the poor fawn with terror and anguish, as though every creature on the spot where it had once been caressed and fondled had suddenly turned into a deadly foe. It was soon seen that the little animal was directing its course across a bay toward the nearest borders of the forest, and immediately the owner of the hound crossed the bridge, running at full speed in the same direction, hoping to stop his dog as he landed. On the fawn swam, as it never swam before, its delicate head scarcely seen above the water, but leaving a disturbed track, which betrayed its course alike to anxious friends and fierce enemies. As it approached the land, the exciting interest became intense. The hunter was already on the same line of shore, calling loudly and angrily to his dog, but the animal seemed to have quite forgotten his master's voice in the pitiless pursuit. The fawn touched the land—in one leap it had crossed the narrow line of beach, and in another in- stant it would reach the cover of the woods. The hound followed, true to the scent, aiming at the same spot on the shore; his master, anxious to meet him, had run at full speed, and was now coming up at the most critical moment; would the dog hearken to his voice, or could the hunter reach him in time to seize and control him? A shout from the village bank proclaimed that the fawn had passed out of sight into the forest; at the same instant, the hound, as he touched the land, felt the hunter's strong arm clutching his neck. The worst was believed to be over; the fawn was leaping up the moimtainside, and its enemy under restraint. The other dogs, seeing their leader cowed, were easily managed. A number of persons, men and boys, dispersed themselves through the woods in search of the little creature, but without success; they all returned to the village, reporting that the animal had not been seen by them. Some persons thought that after its fright had passed over it would return of its own accord. It had worn a pretty collar, with its owner's name engraved upon it, so that it could easily be known from any other fawn that might be straying about the woods. Before many hours had passed a hunter presented himself to the lady whose pet the little creature had been, and showing a collar with her name on it, said that he had been out in the woods, and saw a fawn in the distance; the little animal, instead of bounding away as he had expected, moved toward him; he took aim, fired, and shot it to the heart. When he found the collar about its neck he was very sorry that he had killed it. And so the poor little thing died; one would have thought that terrible chase would have made it afraid of man; but no, it forgot the evil and remembered the kindness only, and came to meet as a friend the hunter who shot it. It was long mourned by its best friend.

This, if not the last chase in our waters, was certainly one of the very latest. The bay crossed by the frightened creature has been called "Fawn Bay," and the fine spring in the field above also bears the name of "Fawn Spring."

Friday, 11th.—Very warm; thermometer 89. The village has not been so dusty for years; of course, walking and driving are less agreeable than usual; and yet the country looks so beautifully that one is unwilling to remain long within doors.

This afternoon, by striking into a narrow cross-road which carried us over the hills, we had a very pleasant drive; the track was quite grassy in places, the shady boughs of an unfenced wood overhung the carriage, and pretty glimpses of the lake and hillsides opened as we slowly ascended. It may be well at times to come suddenly upon a beautiful view; the excitement of surprise adds in many instances to the enjoyment. Where the country is level and commonplace, the surprise becomes an important element from being less easily attained; after driving through a tame, uninteresting country, if we come suddenly upon a wild nook, with its groves, and brook, and rocks, we no doubt enjoy it the more from the charm of contrast. Where the landscape depends for its merit upon one principal object, as a cascade, a small lake, a ruin, &c., &c., the effect is the same, and it is generally desirable that the best view be seen at once. But as regards hills and mountains, the case is very different, for the gradual ascent is in itself a full source of enjoyment; every turn we reach in the climbing path, every rood we gain in elevation, opens some fresh object of admiration, or throws what we have already seen into a new light; the woods, the farms, the hamlets, ay, whole valleys, great hills, broad rivers, objects with which we are already familiar perhaps, are ceaselessly assuming novel aspects. Even the minute beauties which we note one by one along the ascending pathway, the mountain flower, the solitary bird, the rare plant, all contribute their share of pleasure; the very obstacles in the track, the ravine, the precipice, the torrent, produce their own impression, and add to the exultation with which we reach at length the mountain-top, bringing with us a harvest of glowing sensations gathered by the way, all forming delightful accessories, to the greater and more exalted prospect awaiting us at the goal. Between an isolated view, though fine in its way, and the gradual ascent of a commanding height, there lies all the difference we find in the enjoyment of a single ode and that which we derive from a great poem; it is the Lycidas of Milton beside the Othello or Lear of Shakspeare; a sonnet of Petrarch compared with the Jerusalem of Torquato. So at least we thought this afternoon, as we slowly ascended our own modest hills, and remembered the noble mountains of other lands.

The country is looking very rich; the flowery character of summer has not yet faded. Buckwheat crops, in white and fragrant bloom, are lying on half the farms; the long leaves of the maize are still brilliantly green, and its yellow flowers unblighted; late oat-fields here and there show their own pallid green beside recently-cut stubble, which still preserves the golden color of the ripe wheat. In several meadows of the valley mowers were busy, hay-cocks stood about the fields, and loaded carts were moving about, carrying one back to the labors of midsummer, but these were doubtless crops of seed grass, timothy and clover, and not hay for fodder. The glowing August sunshine was just the light for such a scene, gilding the hanging wood, and filling the valleys with warmth, while a soft haze gave distance and importance to every height.

From the most elevated point crossed by the road we looked over two different valleys, with their several groups of broad hills, and many a swelling knoll. Looking down from a commanding position upon a mountainous country, or looking upward at the same objects, leave very different impressions on the mind. From below we see a group of mountains as pictures in one aspect only, but looking abroad over their massive forms from an adjoining height, we comprehend them much more justly; we feel more readily how much they add to the grandeur of the earth we live on, how much they increase her extent, how greatly they vary her character, climates, and productions. Perhaps the noble calm of these mountain piles will be more impressive from below; but when we behold them from a higher point, blended with this majestic quiet, traces of past action and movement are observed, and what we now behold seems the repose of power and strength after a great conflict. The most lifeless and sterile mountain on earth, with the unbroken sleep of ages brooding over its solitudes, still bears on its silent head the emotion of a mighty passion. It is upon the brow of man that are stamped the lines worn by the care and sorrow of a lifetime; and we behold upon the ancient mountains, with a feeling of awe, the record of earth's stormy history. There are scars and furrows upon the giant Alps unsoftened by the beaming sunlight of five thousand summers, over which the heavens have wept in vain for ages, which are uneffaced by all the influences at the command of Time. This character of former action adds inconceivably to the grandeur of the mountains, connecting them as it does with the mystery of the past; upon a plain we are more apt to see the present only, the mental vision seems confined to the level uniformity about it, we need some ancient work of man, some dim old history, to lead the mind backward; and this is one reason why a monument always strikes us more forcibly upon a plain, or on level ground; in such a position it fills the mind more with itself and its own associations. But without a history, without a monument, there is that upon the face of the mountains which, from the earliest ages, has led man to hail them as the "everlasting hills."

In ancient times, this expression of individual action in the mountains was acknowledged by seer and poet. The fabled wars of the Titans, with the uptorn hills they hurled in their strife with the gods, may probably be traced back to this source, and similar fables in the form given them, by Scandinavian Sagas, are but a repetition of the same idea. We who have the most Holy Bible in our hands, may reverently read there also imagery of the like character. We are told by those familiar with the ancient tongues of the East, that in the early ages of the world the great mountains were all called the "mountains of the Lord." The expression occurs repeatedly in the Pentateuch. But after the supernatural terrors which accompanied the proclamation of the Law in the wilderness, the same idea of mountains paying especial homage to the power of the Creator, seems to have become blended among the Hebrews with recollections of the quaking of Sinai. In the 68th Psalm, written by King David, when the ark was transported to Mount Zion, there are two different passages in which this grand image occurs:

"The earth shook, the heavens also dropped, at the presence of God; even Sinai itself was moved at the presence of God, at the presence of the God of Israel."

"Why leap ye, ye high hills? This is the hill which God desireth to dwell in; yea, the Lord will dwell in it forever."

The 114th Psalm, supposed to have been composed by a different prophetic writer, is a sublime ode, expressive throughout, in brief and noble language, of the power of God, as shown in the deliverance of the Israelites, and in the miraculous ministry of the earth herself, her floods and her hills, in their behalf:

"The sea saw it, and fled; Jordan was driven back.

"The mountains skipped like rams, and the little hills like lambs.

"What ailed thee, O thou sea, that thou fleddest? Thou Jordan, that thou wast driven back?

"Ye mountains, that ye skipped like rams, and ye little hills like lambs?

"Tremble, thou earth, at the presence of God; at the presence of the God of Sinai!"

The lowly hills about us are but the last surges of a billowy sea of ridges stretching hundreds of miles to the southward, where they rise to a much more commanding elevation, and attain to the dignity of mountains. But even standing upon the humble hills of our own county—all less than a thousand feet in height—we see some of the sights, we hear some of the sounds, we breathe the air, we feel the spirit of a mountain land; we have left the low country; the plains lie beneath us; we touch at least upon the borders of the "everlasting hills."

Saturday, 12th.—Thermometer 87. The birds seem to mind the heat but little. True, the full gush of summer song is over, and the change is decided from May and June; but many of the little creatures sing very sweetly yet. A wren gave us this morning as fine a song as one could wish for, and all his family sing yet. The song-sparrows also are in voice, and so are the greenlets. The goldfinches also sing; we heard one this afternoon as musical as in May; generally, however, their note differs at present from what it was earlier in the season. Their families are now mostly at large, and one sees the birds moving idly about, as if no longer thinking of the nest. At this moment their flight is more irregular than at first; they rise and they drop carelessly with closed wings, moving hither and thither, often changing their course capriciously, and while in motion, they repeat over and over again a series of four notes, with the emphasis on the first. In short, many of our little friends are seen about the fields and gardens yet, and the country is by no means silent, though the most musical season is over. Perhaps one enjoys these occasional songs all the more from their being heard singly, having become more of a favor than in June. But certainly August is not the voiceless month some people seem to fancy it.

Monday, 14th.—Very warm. Thermometer 83 in the shade. It is not often that this valley suffers so much from drought; the last month has been unusually dry. This morning a few light clouds were seen about sunrise, and they were anxiously watched, with the hope of a shower; but as the sun rose, they melted away.

There is no walking out of the woods, and even in the shade of the trees it is close and sultry. Many of the forest trees are getting a parched look, and even the little wood-plants, screened from the direct influence of the sun, looked thirsty and feeble this afternoon.

But if vegetation suffer, the insect world rejoices in this dry, warm weather. Day and night, in the hot noontide sun, and in the brilliant moonlight, there is an unceasing hum about the fields and woods, much fuller in tone than usual. This is very pleasant in its way;—all the more so from being, like the songs of birds, a proof that the little creatures are happy in the passing hours. We are told that insects have, in truth, no voices, and that the sounds we hear from them are produced generally by friction, or by striking together hard substances of different parts of their bodies. But the character of the sound remains the same, however it be produced. No doubt the fly enjoys the idle buzzing of its own wings, the bee the hum which accompanies its thrifty flight, and the loud chirrup of the locust is probably as much an expression of ease and pleasure, as the full gush of song from the breast of his neighbor, the merry wren.

There are said to be very many varieties of locusts in this country. We have but few in our own neighborhood compared with the great numbers found in other counties of this State. The large tree-locusts are only heard with us in the warmest weather.

The Katy-did also, a very common insect elsewhere, is rare here. We have only a few, and their pleasant cry is seldom heard excepting in very warm evenings. During this last week, however, we have been greeted by the locust[17] and the Katy-did also.

Tuesday, 15th.—Very sultry; thermometer 95 in the shade. [18] The sun rose clear and bright; but soon after a few clouds gathered on the hills, and hopes of rain were again awakened. Many anxious eyes were cast upward, but the clouds dispersed, and the heat continued unrelenting.

The geometric spiders are weaving their neat and regular

17   The Cicada, or great harvest-fly.

18   We have known it 97 in the village; 103 is said to be the highest it has ever reached in the State, and that was in Orange County.

webs about the gardens and out-buildings. The pea-brush and beanpoles are well garnished with them. The earth also is covered with webs, as usual at this season. In France the peasants call these, as they lie spread on the grass, *fils de Marie*— Mary's threads—from some half-religious fancy of olden times.

Sitting in the shade this afternoon, we watched a fierce skirmish between a black wasp and a large spider, who had spun its web among the tendrils of a Virginia creeper. The wasp chanced to alight on the outskirts of the spider's domain, where his legs became partially entangled; he had scarcely touched the leaf when the watchful creature made a rapid dash at him. The antagonists were placed face to face; whether the wasp wounded his enemy one could not say, but after the first touch, the spider instantly retreated several inches, still keeping, however, a bold, undisguised position, her great fixed eyes staring fiercely at the intruder. The wasp was getting more and more entangled in the web; he grew angry, moved his wings and legs rapidly, but to no purpose. Seeing his situation as clearly as the spectator, or probably more so, the spider made another attack, and the adversaries closed in a fierce struggle. The wasp seemed anxious to bring his sting to bear upon the enemy; the spider equally determined to wound her long-legged foe on the head, probably by a bite with her poisonous fangs; now the wasp seemed the sufferer; now again the spider relaxed her hold a little. A fresh assault of the spider was followed by a violent struggle of the wasp, when, suddenly, whether by good luck or good management one could not see, the web broke, the wasp's wings were free; he rose from the leaf, and he carried the spider with him, whether as a captive or a pertinacious enemy, one could not determine; they were soon out of sight. Perhaps the wasp found, before he alighted, that he had "caught a Tartar." About five minutes after the disappearance of the combatants, a wasp alighted on the very same spot where the joust had taken place, and he had a sort of agitated, eager flutter about him. It was either the same individual who had been engaged in the fray, or else a stranger, who, by scent or otherwise, discovered traces of the contest. If it was the hero of the fight, possession of the field of battle and the enemy's country, established his claim as victor; but if only an ally, the fortune of the day still remains in the dark, and, like many other great battles, may be claimed by both parties.

Some of our American wasps are said to hunt spiders, and then enclose them in the cell with their young, who feed upon them. But in the battle this afternoon the spider was clearly the aggressor. These battles between the two races are frequent; but the bees and spiders seem to keep the peace.

We have but few wasps here; our most common kind is this black variety; the large, brown wasps, so abundant elsewhere, are unknown about the village. A smaller variety, called hornets here, are not uncommon. But fortunately for us, the pleasant, thrifty bees far outnumber the other members of their family about our lake.

Wednesday, 16th.—Thermometer 92. The whole country pining for rain; not a drop has fallen here since the last of July.

During these prolonged heats the cattle suffer more, probably, than man. In summer they love the cool shade and refreshing waters, but now the sweet pastures, to which they are accustomed, are blighted and parched, while many a little pool and spring about the fields, well known to them, and where they go of their own accord to drink, they now find entirely wasted away. It is touching to see their patience; and yet, poor creatures, unlike man, they know nothing of hope and their Maker's mercy.

Thursday, 17th.—Rain at last, to our great joy. This morning the sun rose clear; but light clouds were soon seen gathering slowly about the hills, then spreading gradually over the whole sky, and veiling the valley in grateful shade. About noon the first drops fell; the hum of insects, so loud during the last fortnight, suddenly ceased, and was succeeded by the refreshing sound of the rain-drops pattering among the leaves. Most persons thought the long drought and great heat would have been followed by a severe gust and thunder-shower, which is usually the case, but the blessing fell gently and mildly upon us this morning. About a quarter of an hour after it had commenced raining, the sunshine broke through the clouds, and it was feared the sky would clear; happily, another and a fuller cloud came slowly down the lake, pouring a plentiful supply upon us, and it has continued raining all day.

Friday, 18th.—Decidedly cooler. Everything much refreshed by the shower. Still raining this morning.

Saturday, 19th.—Decided change in the weather; thermometer 62, with cool, north wind. This sort of atmosphere is very unfavorable to the scenery; it lowers the hills, narrows the lake, and altogether, the familiar objects of the landscape do not look half so well as when a soft haze hangs upon the hills. The natural features of the country are not on a scale sufficiently grand to rise superior above such accidents of light and shade. Most summers, we have a touch of this sort of weather—sometimes in July, sometimes in August—this sort of cool, matter-of-fact atmosphere, when things look unenjoyable without, and people feel cross at having to close their doors and windows, and sometimes light a fire.

Saw a large flock of barn-swallows hanging in clusters upon the mullein-stalks in a waste field. They are thinking of moving.

Monday, 21st.—Very pleasant again. Walked some distance. The grain harvest is now over, very generally, and cattle are seen feeding among the stubble on many farms.

In this part of the world, although we have once seen a woman ploughing, once found a party of girls making hay with the men of the family, and occasionally observed women hoeing potatoes or corn, we have never yet seen a sight very common in the fields of the Old World: we have never yet met a single gleaner. Probably this is not entirely owing to the prosperous state of the country, for there are many poor among us. "The poor ye have with you always, and whensoever ye will, ye may do them good."

In the large towns, who has not seen the wretched creature who pick up the filthy rags from the rubbish and mud of the streets? Where human beings can earn a livelihood in this way in the cities, gleaning in the fields of the country ought not to surprise one. Even about our villages there are not only many persons in want, a number supported by the public, but there are usually others, also, who may be called regular beggars; men, and women, and children, who had rather beg than work. Let not the accusation be thought a harsh one. There are, even in our small rural communities, fathers and mothers who teach their children to beg, alas! who deliberately encourage their children in thieving and lying, and vice of the foulest kinds. Where such things exist, it cannot be the great prosperity of the country which keeps the gleaner from following in the reaper's steps. Probably there are several reasons why gleaning is not practiced here. Food is comparatively cheap; our paupers are well fed, and those who ask for food, are freely supplied by private charity. Wheat bread, and meat, and butter, and sugar, and tea, and coffee, are looked upon as necessaries, openly asked for by the applicant, and freely bestowed by the giver. This comparative abundance of food in the early days of the different colonies, and the full demand for labor, were probably the reasons why the custom of gleaning was broken up on this side the Atlantic; and the fact that it is not customary, is one reason why it is never thought of to-day. Then, again, our people, generally, are not patient and contented with a little; gleaning would not suit their habit. Many of them, probably, had rather beg than glean.

But although the practice is entirely abandoned on this side the ocean—in our part of the continent, at least—it prevails very generally in the Old World. In some countries it has been regulated by law; in others it is governed by long-established usage. In some villages of France and Germany, a certain day is fixed in the *commune*, when the gleaning is to begin; sometimes the church-bell rings, in other villages the beat of the drum calls the gleaners to the fields; peasant mothers, with their little children, boys and girls, old and infirm men and women, are seen in little parties moving toward the unfenced fields, and spreading themselves through the yellow stubble. In Switzerland, parties of the very poor, the old and the little ones who cannot earn much, come down from the mountain villages, where grain is not raised, into the more level farms of the lower country, expressly to glean. One never sees these poor creatures without much interest; mothers, children, and the aged make up the greater number of their bands, and humble as the occupation may be, it is yet thoroughly honest, and, indeed, creditable, so far as it shows a willingness to undertake the lowliest task for a livelihood, rather than stand by wholly idle.

There is no country in Europe, I believe, where gleaning is not a general custom, from the most northern grain-growing valleys, to the luxuriant plains of Sicily. Even in fertile Asia, and in the most ancient times, gleaning was a common practice. The sign of the Zodiac, called the Virgin, is said to represent a gleaner, and that carries one back very far. The Mosaic laws contain minute directions for gleaning. While the children of Israel were yet in the wilderness, before they had conquered one field of the Promised Land, they received the following injunctions:

"And when ye reap the harvest of your land, thou shalt not wholly reap the corners of thy field; neither shalt thou gather the gleanings of thy harvest. And thou shalt not glean thy vineyard, neither shalt thou gather every grape of thy vineyard; thou shalt leave them for the poor and the stranger: I am the Lord your God."—Lev. xix.

"When thou cuttest down thine harvest in thy field, and thou hast forgot a sheaf in the field, thou shalt not turn again to fetch it: it shall be for the stranger, for the fatherless, and for the widow: that the Lord thy God may bless thee in all the work of thine hands."—Deut. xxiv.

Whether a custom of this kind already prevailed in the ancient world before the days of Moses, we cannot determine,

337

since the Pentateuch is the oldest authority extant. The earlier books of the sacred writings, Genesis and Exodus, contain nothing on the subject. Some of the precepts of the Mosaic code, however, are known to be merely a confirmation and repetition of those given still earlier, such as those which enjoin sacrifice and circumcision, &c., &c. Many others doubtless flowed first, at the period of the Exodus, from Almighty wisdom and mercy, like the raising of the tabernacle, the establishment of the Levitical Priesthood, &c., &c. The protection of the gleaner may have belonged to either class of precepts; but its minuteness partakes very much of the character of the Hebrew law, and it is quite possible that it may have been first inculcated from the lips of Moses in the wilderness. Whatever be the origin of the custom, it has since spread far and wide; it was a simple form of charity, natural to a primitive age, and during thirty-three hundred years at least, it has prevailed in the world. There is, I believe, no part of the Old World where it has not been more or less practiced, whether in Asia, Africa, or Europe; and it is possible there may be some portions of this continent also where it is customary, though we have never seen any allusion to it by travellers, either in North or South America. Within the limits of our own country, it is believed to be entirely unknown.

One never thinks of gleaning without remembering Ruth. How wholly beautiful is the narrative of sacred history in which we meet her! One of the most pleasing pictures of the ancient world preserved to our day, it is at the same time delightful as a composition. Compare it for a moment with the celebrated episode in the "Seasons," and mark how far above the modern poet stands the ancient Hebrew writer. Undoubtedly, Thomson's imitation is an elegant, graceful, polished pastoral, in charmingly flowing verse, but, as Palemon himself expresses it, the tale is rather "romantic." Lavinia, though "beauty's self," and charmingly modest, is yet, alas! rather doll-like; one doubts if she really suffered very much, with that "smiling patience" in her look, and those "polished limbs," "veiled in a simple robe."

And Palemon, "pride of swains," "who led the rural life in all its joy and elegance," "amusing his fancy with autumnal scenes"—we have always had certain misgivings that he was quite a commonplace young squire. It is unwise to be very critical in reading, for one loses much pleasure and instruction by being over-nice and fault-finding in these as in other matters; but really, it was such a bold step in Thomson to remind one of Ruth, that he himself is to blame if the comparison inevitably suggests itself, and as inevitably injures his pretty little English lass. We never look into the Seasons, without wishing that Crabbe had written the gleaning passages.

As for Ruth, the real Ruth, her history is all pure simplicity, nature and truth, in every line. Let us please ourselves by dwelling on it a moment. Let us see Naomi, with her husband and sons, driven by famine into the country of the Moabites; let us hear that the two young men married there, and that, at the end of ten years, the mother and her daughters-in-law were alike widowed. Naomi then determines to return to her own country; both her daughters-in-law set out with her. Orpah and Ruth had alike been faithful to the Jewish family: "The Lord deal kindly with you as ye have dealt with the dead, and with me," says Naomi, as she urges them to leave her and go back to their own friends. Both the young women wept, and both answered, "Surely we will return with thee unto thy people." Naomi again urges their leaving her: "Turn again, my daughters, why will ye go with me?" "And Orpah kissed her mother-in-law, but Ruth clave unto her." This is the first sentence that betrays the difference between the young women; both had been kind and dutiful to their husbands and mother-in-law, but now we see one turning back, and the other cleaving to the poor, and aged, and solitary widow. No positive blame is attached to Orpah, but from that instant we love Ruth. Read over her passionate remonstrance with her mother-in-law: "Thy people shall be my people; thy God my God. Where thou diest will I die, and there will I be buried." We follow the two women to Bethlehem, the native town of the family: "And all the city was moved about them, and they said. Is this Naomi?" "And she said, Call me not Naomi, call me Mara, for the Almighty hath dealt very bitterly with me: I went out full, and the Lord hath brought me home again empty." It was at the beginning of the barley harvest when they came to Bethlehem, and now we find Ruth preparing to glean. Probably gleaning was at this time a custom among the neighboring nations also, for the proposal comes from Ruth herself, and not from her Jewish mother-in-law, who merely signifies her assent: "Go, my daughter." The young widow went, and "her hap was, to light upon a part of the field belonging to Boaz." An obsolete word that, "her hap," for she happened. Presently we see the owner of the field coming from Bethlehem, and we hear his salutation to the reapers: "The Lord be with you; and they answered him, The Lord bless thee."

Doubtless, in those ancient times, the people all lived together in towns and villages for mutual protection, as they did in Europe during the middle ages—as they still do, indeed, to the present hour, in many countries where isolated cottages and farm-houses are rarely seen, the people going out every morning to the fields to work, and returning to the villages at night. While looking over his reapers, Boaz remarks a gleaner, a young woman whom he had not yet seen; the other faces were probably familiar to the benevolent man, the poor of his native town, but this was a stranger. Now, it is nowhere said that Ruth was beautiful; very possibly she was not so; we have always been rather disposed to believe that of the two Orpah may have been the handsome one. The beauty of many women of the Old Testament is mentioned with commendation by the different writers of the sacred books, as that of Sarah, Rebecca, Rachel, and a number more; but we are nowhere told that Ruth was "well favored." We read of her devotion to Naomi; of her gentleness, her humility; of her modesty, for she did not "follow young men," and all the people knew she was "a virtuous woman;" but not a word is uttered as to her being fair to look at. The omission is the more marked, for she is the principal character in a narrative of four chapters. With the exception of Sarah and Esther, no other woman of the Old Testament fills so large a space; and it will be remembered that the beauty of both Sarah and Esther is distinctly mentioned. No; with Ruth the attention is wholly fixed on the moral qualities, and the sacred historian has thus assigned her a place beside the Christian women of the New Testament, where personal appearance is in no instance even alluded to. May we not, then, please ourselves with believing that Ruth was not beautiful; that she had merely one of those faces which come and go without being followed, except by the eyes that know and love them? Boaz no sooner learns who she is than he gives her a most kindly welcome: "Hearest thou not, my daughter? Go not to glean in another field; neither go from hence, but abide here fast by my maidens. Have I not charged the young men that they shall not touch thee? And when thou art athirst, go unto the vessels and drink of that which the young men have drawn." We are not told that Boaz was an old man, but it is implied in several places. He calls Ruth "My daughter," and he is mentioned as a kinsman of Naomi's husband; he commends her for not following "young men, whether rich or poor," and there is a certain calmness and dignity in his manner and conduct throughout the narrative, such as one would naturally connect with the idea of an elderly man. The generous kindness and the upright simplicity of his conduct toward Ruth are very beautiful. When the young widow, "falling on her face," asks humbly, "Why have I found grace in thine eyes, that thou shouldst take knowledge of me, seeing I am a stranger?" He answers, "It hath fully been showed me all that thou hast done unto thy mother-in-law, since the death of thy husband;"—"a full reward be given thee of the Lord God of Israel, under whose wings thou art come to trust." Ruth was poor, and had doubtless met with neglect and harshness. She was generous and warm-hearted herself, and could justly value the kindness of others; she thanks the owner of the field, "for that thou hast comforted me, and for that thou hast spoken friendly unto thine handmaid." The word given here as friendly, is rendered in the margin "to the heart." The phrase may be a common Hebrew expression, but it has a strength of feeling characteristic of the speaker. Blessed, indeed, are the lips that "speak to the heart" of the afflicted; and blessed is the sorrowing soul who hears them! Boaz asks the young widow to eat with his people at meal-time: "Eat of the bread, and dip thy morsel in the vinegar." "And she sat beside the reapers, and he reached her parched corn." The vinegar mentioned here is supposed to mean a kind of acid wine frequently named by ancient writers; and the parched corn was probably half-ripe ears of wheat or barley roasted in this way; a common article of food in the East during all ages. "And when she was risen up to glean, Boaz commanded his young men, saying, Let her glean even among the sheaves, and reproach her not. And let fall some of the handfuls of purpose for her, and leave them that she may glean them, and rebuke her not. So she gleaned in the field until even, and beat out that she had gleaned; and it was about an ephah of barley." An ephah was about a bushel of our measure; and barley was a grain highly valued in Judea, where it was much used for food. A bushel seems a large quantity; but it is surprising what full sheaves some of the gleaners will carry home with them, now-a-days, and in fields where no handfuls are dropped on purpose. It was only when Ruth told her mother of her good success that she learned that Boaz was a near kinsman of her former husband, and, consequently, according to the Jewish law, one upon whom she might have claims. Naomi bids her follow the reapers of Boaz according to his wish; and she did so "through the barley-harvest, and through the wheat-harvest, and she dwelt with her mother-in-law." It was at the close of the harvest that Ruth, following Naomi's directions, laid herself down at night, at the feet of Boaz, as he slept on the threshing-floor; an act by which she reminded him of the law that the nearest of kin should marry the childless widow. This act has been very severely commented on. Upon this ground only, M. de Voltaire has not scrupled to apply to Ruth one of the most justly opprobrious words in human language; and several noted skeptics of the English school have given this as one among their objections against the Holy Scriptures.[19] As though in a state of society wholly simple and primitive, we were to judge of Ruth by the rules of propriety prevailing in the courts of Charles II. and Louis XV. Ruth and Boaz lived, indeed, among a race, and in an age, when not only the daily speech, but the daily life also, was highly figurative; when it was the great object of language and of action to give force and expression to the intention of the mind, instead of applying, as in a later, and a degenerate society, all the powers of speech and action to concealing the real object in view. The simplicity with which this peculiarly Jewish part of the narrative is given, will rather appear to the impartial judge a merit. But the Christian has double grounds for receiving this fact in the same spirit as it is recorded, and upon those grounds we may feel confident that, had Ruth been a guilty woman, or had Boaz acted otherwise than uprightly toward the young widow, neither would have been spared the open shame of such misconduct. The Book of Ruth has always been received by the Church, both Jewish and Christian, as a part of the inspired Scriptures; it must, therefore, be essentially true, and no evil word or deed finds a place in the narrative. Then, again, the impartiality of the sacred biographers, from the first to the last books of the Holy Scriptures, is so very striking, so very peculiar to themselves, so widely different from the eulogies or apologies of uninspired men under similar circumstances, that reason alone requires us to receive each narrative simply as it is given. We read with a feeling of awe of the occasional failings and sins of such men as Noah, Abraham, Aaron, and David; the whole nature of man stands humbled before us, while the mercy of our God rises, indeed, exalted above the heavens! We feel that these

19   See Letters of the Jews to Voltaire.

passages are laid open to us by the same Omniscient Spirit which searches our own hearts by the same just hand which weighs our own words, and thoughts, and deeds in the balance. And if such men as Abraham, and Aaron, and David were not spared by the inspired pen, why should it screen the Moabitish widow, and the comparatively unimportant Boaz? The writer of the narrative has not, by one word, imputed sin to either. How dare the mind of the reader do so? One may add a word for the skeptic, since this passage has been made a pointed subject of objection by men of that school. There are but three positions which the infidel can take upon the subject: he may, with the Christian, believe the Book of Ruth to be true, in which case he is bound to receive the facts as they are given; he may hold the narrative to be a compound of fiction and truth, and then plain justice requires that those points upon which the Scriptural writers have always shown such marked impartiality be charged to the side of truth, and he is at liberty to doubt any other passage of the book rather than this particular one; he may, lastly, declare the book to be, in his opinion, wholly fictitious; in this case he is bound, by common sense, to receive the narrative precisely as it is written, since it is a broad absurdity to judge fictitious characters otherwise than as they are represented. If he suppose one act or one view beyond what the writer presents or implies, he may as well sit down and compose an entire fabric of his own, and then the world will have one Book of Ruth in the Holy Bible, and another among the works of Mr. A., B., or C.

When Boaz found Ruth lying at his feet, he immediately understood the action as figurative. "And it came to pass at midnight that the man was afraid, and turned himself, and behold a woman lay at his feet."—"And he said, Who art thou? And she answered, I am Ruth, thine handmaid; spread therefore thy skirt," or wing, "over thy handmaid, for thou art a near kinsman." Her whole answer is figurative, like the act. Spreading the skirt, or wing, was a common Hebrew phrase, implying protection, and it is said to be, to this day, a part of the Jewish marriage ceremony. Boaz well knew that the action and the words were intended to remind him of the law, that the "near kinsman" should marry the widow. "And now, my daughter, fear not; I will do thee all that thou requirest: for all the city of my people doth know that thou art a virtuous woman. And now it is true that I am thy near kinsman, howbeit there is a kinsman nearer than I. Tarry this night, and it shall be in the morning, that if he will perform unto thee the part of a kinsman, well; let him do the kinsman's part: but if he will not do the part of a kinsman to thee, then will I do the part of a kinsman unto thee, as the Lord liveth: lie down until the morning." And she lay at his feet until the morning." When, at dawn, she is going, he bids her bring her veil, and measures six measures of barley in it, saying, "Go not empty unto thy mother-in-law." The occurrences in the concluding chapter, at the gate of the town, are strikingly ancient, oriental, and Jewish. The nearer kinsman declines to fulfill the duties enjoined by the law, he does not wish to buy the "parcel of land," or to marry Ruth, "lest he mar his own inheritance;" he makes over the duty to Boaz, giving him his shoe as a token, a singular and very primitive custom; but we are reading now of times before the date of the Trojan war, chronology having placed these incidents in the fourteenth century before Christ. Boaz then calls upon all present to be witnesses to the contract by which he engaged to buy the land, and to marry the widow. "And all the people that were in the gate, and the elders, said, We are witnesses. The Lord make the woman that is come into thine house like Rachel, and like Leah, which two did build the house of Israel: and do thou worthily in Ephratah, and be famous in Bethlehem." Probably before the six measures of barley were eaten, Ruth entered the house of Boaz as his wife. Naomi went with her; and in time Ruth gave a grandson to the aged widow: "And Naomi took the child, and laid it in her bosom, and became nurse unto it." "And the women said unto her, He shall be unto thee the restorer of thy life, and a nourisher of thine old age, for thy daughter-in-law *which loveth thee, which is better to thee than seven sons,* hath borne him." This child became in the course of years the grandfather of David; Ruth received the honor coveted by every Jewish woman—she was one in the line between Sarah and the Blessed Virgin, the mother of our Lord. It was undoubtedly to record her place in the sacred genealogy, or rather for the sake of that genealogy, that the book was written, and has received a place in the Holy Scriptures.

We have meanwhile strayed a wide way from our own ungleaned fields; but the history of Ruth is in itself so very beautiful, and it is so full of interest, as connected with a very remote antiquity, beyond the reach of the oldest Greek literature, that one never turns to it without pleasure. While plodding on our daily round of duties, if the eye fall by chance upon a picture of some great old master, we gladly linger a moment to enjoy its beauty and excellence; and thus the noble devotion of Ruth, seen amid the ancient frame-work of the sacred historian, never fails to delight the imagination, to refresh the mind, to strengthen the heart, whenever we turn to it from the cares of our own path through life.

Tuesday, 22d.—Pleasant; walked in the woods. Gathered a fine bunch of ferns. All the plants of this kind growing in our neighborhood belong, I believe, to the common sorts. We have none of the handsome climbing-fern here, with its palmate leaves; it is found nearly as far north as this, but nearer the coast, and on lower ground. The walking-fern, also, another singular variety, rooting itself like the banyan, from the ends of its long entire leaves, is a stranger here, though found within the State. The maiden-hair, with its very delicate foliage, and polished brown stem, is the prettiest variety we have near us.

Wednesday, 23d.—The swallows have left the chimneys. This evening they were flying over the grounds in parties, as though preparing to take leave. There was something peculiar in their movement; they were flying quite low, through the foliage of the trees, and over the roof of the house, returning again and again, upon their former track. We watched them for more than an hour, while they kept up the same evolutions with much more regularity than usual; perhaps they were trying their wings for the journey southward.

It is amusing to look back to the discussions of naturalists during the last century, upon the subject of the migration of swallows: a number of them maintained that these active birds lay torpid during the cold weather in caves and hollow trees; while others, still more wild in their theories, supposed that swallows went under water and passed the winter in the mud, at the bottom of rivers and pools! Grave and learned were the men who took sides in this question, for and against the torpid theory. One might suppose that it would have required a great amount of the clearest evidence to support a notion so opposed to the general habits of those active birds; but the facts that among the myriads of swallows flitting about Europe, one was occasionally found chilled and torpid, that swallows were frequently seen near the water, and that during the mild days of autumn a few stragglers appeared again, when they were supposed to revive, made up the chief part of what was urged in favor of these notions. It would be difficult to understand how sensible people could be led to maintain such opinions, were it not that men, both learned and unlearned, often show a sort of antipathy to simple truths.

Thomson, in the Seasons, alludes to this strange notion; speaking of the swallows, he says:

"Warn'd of approaching winter, gathered, play
The swallow people; and toss'd wide around
O'er the calm sky, in convolution swift,
The feather'd eddy floats; rejoicing once
    Ere to their wintry slumbers they retire;
In clusters clung, beneath the mould'ring bank,
And where, unpierc'd by frost, the cavern sweats.
Or rather into warmer climes convey'd

With other kindred birds of season,
There they twitter cheerful."

He seems rather to have inclined himself to the better opinion.[20]

In ancient times the swallows were very naturally included among other migratory birds; there is said to be an old Greek ode in which the return of the swallow is mentioned. The Prophet Jeremiah has an allusion to the wandering of the swallow, which he includes among other migratory birds: "Yea, the stork in the heavens knoweth her appointed times, and the turtle, and the crane, and the *swallow*, observe the time of their coming; but my people know not the judgment of the Lord."— Jer., viii. 7. Indeed, it is but just to the common sense of man to say that the obvious fact of the migration of those swift-winged birds seems only to have been doubted during a century or so; and among the achievements of our own age may be numbered that of a return to the simple truth on this point of ornithology. We hear nothing now-a-days of the mud or cave theories.

Thursday, 24th.—Brilliant day. Passed the afternoon on the lake. The views were very beautiful. Downy seeds of various kinds, thistle, dandelion, &c., &c., were thickly strewed over the bosom of the lake; we had never before observed such numbers of them lying on the water.

Saw a crane of the largest size flying over the lake, a mile or two to the northward of our boat. A pair of them have been about the lake all summer; they are said to be the large brown crane. We found one of their young this afternoon lying dead upon the bank of a brook, to which we gave the name of Crane Brook on this occasion. It was a good-sized bird, and seemed to

---

20   It is said that Linnæus firmly believed that the swallows went under water during the winter; and even M. Cuvier declared that the bank swallows had this habit. At present the idea is quite abandoned for want of proof.

have been killed in a fight with some winged enemy, for it had not been shot. As for the boldness of calling the brook after it, the pretty little stream had no name before; why not give it one?

Last summer a pair of eagles built their nest on one of the western hills, which we ventured to call Eagle Hill, on the same principle. These noble birds are occasionally seen hovering over the valley, though not often.

Measured an old grape-vine in the glen, near Crane Brook; it proved to be seven inches in circumference.

Friday, 25th.—Observed the chimney swallows again this evening wheeling in a low flight over the roof, and through the foliage of the trees. It looked as though they were taking leave of us. They have deserted the chimneys, but we have not discovered where they pass the night. Perhaps in the hollow trees in the woods, for there are many such at hand. Mr. Wilson says, it frequently happens that these birds make their general rendezvous when they first come, and just before they leave, in the chimneys of the Court-House, if there be one in the place; they seem to find out that such chimneys are little used. But we have never heard of the swallows honoring our own Court-House in this way.

Saturday, 26th.—Again we observed the chimney swallows, flying over the house and through the trees, just as they have done these four or five evenings. Perhaps there is some particular insect among the leaves which attracts them just now.

Saw a few barn-swallows also, this afternoon; but most of these seem to have left us already.

Monday, 28th.—About sunset this evening observed many night-hawks flying over the village.

We happened once to see a large flight of these birds. We were travelling a short distance north of the Mohawk, at this very date, the 28th of August, when, about an hour before sunset, a number of large birds were seen rising from a wood to the eastward, all moving slowly in a loose, straggling flock, toward the south-west. They proved to be night-hawks; and they continued passing at intervals until an hour after sunset. They seemed to heed each other very little, being seldom near together, but all were aiming in the same direction. We must have seen several hundreds of them, in the course of the two hours they were in sight.

Tuesday, 29th.—The swallows have moved their parade-ground this evening. We missed them about the house, but found them wheeling over the highway, near the bridge, the very spot where we first saw them in the spring.

Wednesday, 30th.—Walked in the woods. Observing an old branchless trunk of the largest size, in a striking position, where it looked like a broken column, we walked up to examine it. The shaft rose, without a curve or a branch, to the height of perhaps forty feet, where it had been abruptly shivered, probably in some storm. The tree was a chestnut, and the bark of a clear, unsullied gray; walking round it, we saw an opening near the ground, and to our surprise found the trunk hollow, and entirely charred within, black as a chimney, from the root to the point where it was broken off. It frequently happens that fire steals into the heart of an old tree, in this way, by some opening near the roots, and burns away the inside, leaving merely a gray outer shell. One would not expect the bark to be left in such cases, but the wood at the heart seems more inflammable than the outer growth. Whatever be the cause, such shafts are not uncommon about our hills, gray without, charred within.

There is, indeed, much charred wood in our forests; fires which sweep over the hills are of frequent occurrence here, and at times they do much mischief. If the flames are once fairly kindled in dry weather, they will spread in all directions as the wind varies, burning sometimes for weeks together, until they have swept over miles of woodland, withering the verdure, destroying the wood already cut, and greatly injuring many trees which they do not consume. Several years since, in the month of June, there was quite an extensive fire on the eastern range of hills; it lasted for ten days or a fortnight, spreading several miles in different directions. It was the first important fire of the kind we had ever seen, and of course we watched its progress with much interest; but the spectacle was a very different one from what we had supposed. It was much less terrible than the conflagration of buildings in a town; there was less of power and fierce grandeur, and more of treacherous beauty about the flames as they ran hither and thither along the mountain-side. The first night after it broke out we looked on with admiration; one might have thought it a general illumination of the forest, as the flames spread in long winding lines, gaining upon the dark wood every moment, up and down, and across the hill, collecting here and there with greater brilliancy about some tall old tree, which they hung with fire like a giant lustre. But the next day the sight was a sad one indeed: the deceitful brilliancy of the flames no longer pleased the eye; wreaths of dull smoke and hot vapors hung over the blighted trees, and wherever the fire had wandered there the fresh June foliage was utterly blasted. That night we could no longer take pleasure in the spectacle; we could no longer fancy a joyous illumination. We seemed rather to behold the winding coils of some fiery serpent gliding farther and farther on its path of evil; a rattling, hissing sound accompanying its movement, the young trees trembling and quivering with agitation in the heated current which proclaimed its approach. The fresh flowers were all blighted by its scorching breath, and with its forked tongue it fed upon the pride of the forest, drying up the life of great trees, and without waiting to consume them, hurrying onward to blight other groves, leaving a blackened track of ruin wherever it passed.

Some fifty years since a fire of this kind is said to have spread until it enclosed within its lines the lake and the valley, as far as one could see, surrounding the village with a network of flame, which at night was quite appalling in its aspect. The danger, however, was not so great as it appeared, as there was everywhere a cleared space between the burning forest and the little town. At times, however, very serious accidents result from these fires; within a few days we have heard of a small village, in the northern part of the State, in St. Lawrence county, entirely destroyed in this way, the flames gaining so rapidly upon the poor people that they were obliged to collect their families and cattle in boats and upon rafts, in the nearest pools and streams.

Of course, more or less mischief is always done; the wood and timber already cut are destroyed, fences are burnt, many trees are killed, others are much injured, the foliage is more or less blighted for the season; the young plants are killed, and the earth looks black and gloomy. Upon the whole, however, it is surprising that no more harm is done. On the occasion of the fire referred to in these woods, we found the traces of the flames to disappear much sooner than we had supposed possible. The next season the smaller plants were all replaced by others; many of the younger trees seemed to revive, and a stranger passing over the ground to-day would scarcely believe that fire had been feeding on those woods for a fortnight only a few seasons back. A group of tall, blasted hemlocks, on the verge of the wood, is the most striking monument of the event. The evergreens generally suffer more than other trees, and for some cause or other the fire continued busy at that point for several days. We repeatedly passed along the highway at the time, with the flames at work on either side. Of course, there was no danger, but it looked oddly to be driving quietly along through the fire. The crackling of the flames was heard in the village, and the smell of smoke was occasionally quite unpleasant.

A timely rain generally puts a stop to the mischief; but parties of men are also sent out into the woods to "fight the fire." They tread out the flames among the dry leaves by trampling them down, and they rake away the combustible materials, to confine the enemy to its old grounds, when it soon exhausts itself. The flames spread more frequently along the earth, than from tree to tree.

Thursday, 31st.—The water-lilies are still in blossom; opening quite early in the season, they continue to flower until the frost cuts them off. We found numbers of them in Black-bird Bay this evening.

Our water-lilies in this lake are all of the yellow kind. The fragrant white lily is not known to grow either in the lake, or in any of the little pools and marshy spots very near. It is, however, to be found a short distance to the northward of our own waters.[21] The yellow variety is common enough about the neighborhood.

The roots of this yellow lily were a favorite repast with the moose, and no doubt those great, unwieldy animals have often stood in the shallow water of the little bay we now call after the black-birds, feeding on the lilies, which must have always grown there.[22] The beaver, also, was very partial to these plants, and as he was no stranger here in Indian times, probably he may often have been at this spot taking his share of the lilies. But it is now more than fifty years since these plants have bloomed only for man, and the bees, and the black-birds. The last, probably, heed them very little, although they are near neighbors, generally haunting the low point which forms the bay, whenever they visit our neighborhood.

One of the noblest plants of our country belong to this tribe of the water-lilies: the Nelumbo, or sacred bean, or water-chinquapin, as it is sometimes called. Its great leaves are from one to two feet broad, and its pale yellow blossom about half a foot in diameter. It is chiefly in our western waters that the Nelumbo is found; in this part of the country it is much more rare. There is, however, one locality in our own State where it grows, and that is on the northern frontier, Sodus Bay, Lake Ontario. It is also found at one point in the Connecticut, and in

---

21 We have recently heard of a white lily gathered from the lake about two years since, but have never seen one ourselves. Formerly, they are said to have been more common here.

22 The deer are also very fond of the water-lilies.

the Delaware, below Philadelphia. Wherever it is seen, it attracts attention, from the great size of the leaves and the blossom.

This noble flower belongs to a very celebrated family; it calls cousin with the famous Hindoo and Egyptian Lotus, being one of the varieties of that tribe. In Hindoo and Egyptian fable, these plants were held very sacred, as emblems of the creation. In Hindostan, the lotus was an attribute of Ganga, the goddess of the Ganges, and was supposed to have been produced by Vishnu, before the earth was created, and when its first petals unfolded, they discovered the deity Brama lying within. In Egypt, the flower was sacred to Isis, believed to have been given her by Osiris, and was associated with their own sacred river, the Nile; it was also the emblem of Upper Egypt, as the papyrus was of Lower Egypt. Very many traces of these ancient superstitions are still seen blended with the architecture, bas-reliefs, paintings, &c., &c., and whatever remains to us of those nations. There appear to have been several kinds of lotus represented on the ancient Egyptian monuments. One was white, with a fruit like that of the poppy; another bore blue flowers, with the same fruit; the third, and the most celebrated, is mentioned by Herodotus as the lily-rose, and was also called the flower of Antinous; the blossom was of a beautiful red, and the fruit like the rose of a watering-pot, with large seeds like filberts. These are all said to be found at present in India, but what is singular, the finest, the lily-rose, has now disappeared from Egypt, where it was formerly in such high consideration. The blue variety is still found there.

At the present day, the lotus is more honored in Asia than in Egypt. The Hindoos still consider it a sacred flower. In Ceylon, they have a variety which they call Nelumbo, whence our own name. A number of varieties are said to be found in China, where it is also sacred; this does not prevent the Chinese from eating it, however, and it is much cultivated by them as an article of food. The seeds of the Lien Wha, as they call it, are of the form and size of an acorn, and are considered more delicate than almonds; the root, also, is boiled; or sliced raw, and served with ice in summer; or laid up in salt and vinegar for winter use.

These fine plants seem to have an aversion to the soil or climate of Europe; it is said that the ancient Romans attempted to cultivate them in Italy, without success, and that modern European horticulturists have also failed in their efforts to cultivate them in hot-houses. And yet, in this part of the world, the Nelumbo grows in the icy waters of Lake Ontario. Both the large seeds, and the root of our American variety, are said to be very pleasant to the taste—the latter is not unlike the sweet potato.

A CHAPTER FROM
Rural Hours, 1851

Printed in Great Britain
by Amazon

75118746R00210